Praise for Stanton Friedman and

"The most explosive book yet on UFOs."

—*Star Magazine*

"Friedman operates mostly as a scientist, carefully weighing all evidence before coming to a conclusion."

—*Library Journal*

"This book will delight those who can't get enough of crashed saucers and government cover-ups."

—*Booklist*

"Can they get here from there? If so, have they already arrived? And what is the evidence? Nuclear physicist Stanton T. Friedman, a 50-year veteran scientific ufologist known for his impeccable research, shares his findings with us. A must-have for anyone who wants to know the truth with the documented evidence to back it up."

—Kathleen Marden, coauthor of *Captured! The Betty and Barney Hill UFO Experience*

"Friedman has been involved in UFO research for more than a quarter century. During that time, he has struggled tirelessly against a vast amount of resistance on almost every level. He has uncovered hoaxes, discovered hidden truths, and has fought arrogant bureaucrats and fallacy-happy UFO debunkers, not to mention other researchers eager to discredit him for their own ends. He is one of the few truly professional UFO researchers."

—Whitley Strieber, *New York Times* best-selling author of *Communion and 2012: The War for Souls*

FLYING SAUCERS
AND
SCIENCE

A SCIENTIST INVESTIGATES THE
MYSTERIES OF UFOS:
INTERSTELLAR TRAVEL, CRASHES,
AND
GOVERNMENT COVER-UPS

By

Stanton T. Friedman, MSc.

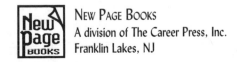

NEW PAGE BOOKS
A division of The Career Press, Inc.
Franklin Lakes, NJ

Quoted material from "Whatever Happened to Flying Saucers?" by Arthur C. Clarke, reprinted with permssion from *The Saturday Evening Post* magazine. Copyright 1971 Saturday Evening Post Society.

"Brass Tacks" section of *ANALOG* from December 1975, page 172, used with permission from Ben Bova.

Park, Robert L., "Welcome to Planet Earth," used with permission from the New York Academy of Sciences, *www.nyas.org*.

Images from the Fort Worth Star-Telegram used with permission from the Photograph Collection, Special Collections at the University of Texas at Arlington Library.

FLYING SAUCERS AND SCIENCE
EDITED BY KARA REYNOLDS
TYPESET BY EILEEN DOW MUNSON
Cover design by Lu Rossman / Digi Dog Design NY
Printed in the U.S.A. by Book-mart Press

To order this title, please call toll-free 1-800-CAREER-1 (NJ and Canada: 201-848-0310) to order using VISA or MasterCard, or for further information on books from Career Press.

The Career Press, Inc., 3 Tice Road, PO Box 687,
Franklin Lakes, NJ 07417
www.careerpress.com
www.newpagebooks.com

Library of Congress Cataloging-in-Publication Data

Friedman, Stanton T.
    Flying saucers and science : a scientist investigates the mysteries of UFOs : interstellar travel, crashes, and government cover-ups / by Stanton T. Friedman.
        p. cm.
    Includes index.
    ISBN 978-1-60163-011-7
        1. Unidentified flying objects. 2. Interstellar travel. I. Title.

TL789.F6793 2008
001.942--dc22

                                                                2008006291

*This book is dedicated to
my loving wife,
Marilyn,*

*who has so patiently—for decades—tolerated my
fixation on getting to the truth about flying saucers.*

*She has put up with late-night radio programs and
phone calls, my long trips away from home, visits from
a wide variety of media people, and a huge accumulation
of (hopefully) relevant papers, books, and videos.*

I only hope it has been worth the effort.

Acknowledgments

I wish to gratefully acknowledge the Mutual UFO Network for sponsoring my numerous appearances at its annual symposia, forcing me to prepare papers for inclusion in the symposia proceedings.

Thanks also to The Fund for UFO Research, which provided some research grants to assist in my field investigations related to Roswell and my visits to a number of document archives.

To Robert Bigelow for a generous research grant for Roswell and MJ-12-related research.

To the producers of a large number of radio and TV programs who have given me a platform.

To the hundreds of colleges who have allowed me to stimulate campus communities with lectures and class visits.

To my literary agent, John White, who has successfully pursued publishers.

To all those brave witnesses who have been willing to speak out despite the antipathy from nasty, noisy negativists.

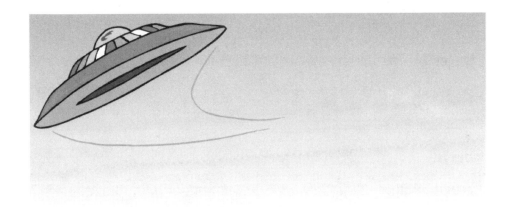

Contents

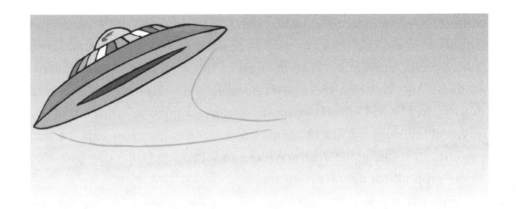

Forewords by Dr. Edgar Mitchell, ScD, and Dr. Bruce Maccabee, PhD

The fact of an extraterrestrial presence on and around Earth for at least half of the 20th century has been increasingly accepted in the United States and much of the Western world in recent times, albeit slowly. This has happened in spite of continuous efforts of political, military, and cultural authorities in the United States and other nations to obscure and even deny that fact through the release of distorted and false information pertaining to sightings and other reports.

Discovery that we are not alone in the universe must rank, for us humans, as one of the most portentous events in our entire history. Only in the time of generations now living has our own technology progressed to the point that we can venture off our planet, and also create the means necessary to view the vastness of the cosmos as no generations before us have done.

Debate about the propriety, morality, and even legality of such official denial and cover-up of these events in a free and open society will likely continue for some decades. Justifications involving national security, potential use of the knowledge by military opponents, public unrest, and even fear of public uprisings may be invoked by those seeking to defend these policies. The fact that the now-famous Roswell UFO crash occurred shortly after World War II, the most widespread and disastrous war in history, and following the first use of nuclear weaponry in war—weaponry that was initially tested at the nearby White Sands Proving Grounds—provided ample grounds for military concerns.

Whether these were valid concerns has yet to be determined. However, in the context of the cold war era, it is understandable that the military and intelligence communities might have been concerned that the aliens were hostile, yet were unable to do anything about their presence, and thus would not want the public to know. (The famous radio program *War of the Worlds* had been broadcast on the East Coast of the United States only a few years earlier, causing widespread panic.) Additionally, in light of the recovery of an alien craft at Roswell, the military and intelligence communities would not want America's Cold War enemies to know we had gained access to an advanced technology that might be used by the United States to deliver weapons. So there may have been sound reasons for enforcing a cloak of secrecy, denial, and misdirection about UFOs.

But if so, one must wonder why the policy continues today, when the public is well informed and largely accepting of the subject.

Irrespective of how one views the pros and cons of 60 years of official denial of alien presence on and around our planet, the truth has slowly seeped out into public awareness and acceptance, due in part to many of the inane stories and contradictions offered by official sources. Mostly, however, discovery of the truth has been due to the dedication, thoroughness, and capabilities of a handful of investigators such as Stanton Friedman.

A 40-year veteran in the pursuit of truth about UFOs, Stan Friedman has used his knowledge of science, his training as a nuclear physicist, and his penchant for digging persistently to discover the facts, sifted from an excess of fantasy and misinformation, to become a major figure in the effort to disclose the presence and activities of our alien visitors. His work and his writing in this field deserve the very highest acclaim.

—Edgar Mitchell, ScD, Captain USN (ret.)
Lunar Module Pilot, *Apollo 14*
Sixth man on the moon

"UFO believers are 99 44/100% kooks."

The editor of the technical journal *Applied Optics* wrote that opinion in a letter to me about publishing my short article on the then-internationally famous New Zealand sightings of December 1978. Despite his reservations about "UFO believers," he did allow publication, even though my article claimed that the light that had been seen was unidentified. He also allowed publication of a second article by scientists who disputed my claim, and then a third article—by me—that rebutted the second article. There are some more details of this following, but the complete story and the published articles are available at *http://brumac.8k.com/NEW_ZEALAND/NZSB.html*.

The publication of three short articles discussing one of the New Zealand sightings is one of the few times—or perhaps the only time—that a specific UFO case has been discussed in a point-counterpoint manner in the refereed scientific literature. The reluctance to publish discussions of UFO reports and the previously stated opinion of the editor of *Applied Optics* illustrate the low opinion that the general scientific community (but not all scientists) has of UFO sightings and "ufology" (the study and analysis of UFO sightings and associated phenomena) in general.

The tendency of scientists to reject UFO reports as being spurious sightings by untrained observers, [claiming that sightings are] all explainable as misidentifications, hoaxes, or delusions, goes way back to the beginning, in late June of 1947, when experienced pilot Kenneth Arnold, who had about 4,000 hours of flying time, reported seeing many unidentified semicircular-shaped objects fly past Mt. Rainier and Mt. Adams in the state of Washington. They had no recognizable aircraft features (no wings, no vertical stabilizers, no engines). He said they flew with a wobbling or skipping motion, comparable to that of a spinning disc skipping over the water. (A newspaperman converted the description of the flight dynamics to a description of the objects themselves and called them "flying saucers." The name stuck, even though Arnold didn't say they looked like saucers.) Within a few weeks of Arnold's report, which was published throughout the United States, there were hundreds of other reports of strange objects flying through the sky. The U.S. Army Air Force began collecting reports and publicly stated that "they aren't ours." Air Force spokesmen admitted that they didn't know what was causing the sightings. Over the next few years the Air Force claimed that most of the sightings could be explained as prosaic phenomena (weather phenomena, birds, misidentified airplanes, stars or planets, hoaxes, and so on), and the ones that couldn't be explained simply didn't have enough information to allow identification of the phenomena. The Air Force also said to the general public (and to the scientific community), "Don't worry, we are working on it, and we haven't found anything yet." They added that there seemed to be no evidence of a threat from flying saucers.

The scientific community considered the sightings from two points of view: theoretical and experimental. There was no theory that could explain the generally reported characteristics of saucers: typically circular or semicircular in shape, ability to alternately fly at high speed or hover, little or no evidence of propulsion mechanisms, and silent or nearly silent when hovering or traveling. (Note: all high-speed flight we humans have achieved depends upon the rapid combustion of fuel. Combustion makes noise, as in the cylinders of a piston engine, in the turbine of a jet, or in the combustor of a rocket. Balloon-borne craft can be very quiet, but they also don't move very fast.) Some of the Air Force scientists and engineers working on the newest propulsion devices initially considered the possibility that the unexplainable saucers might be atomic-powered Soviet flying machines that were based on advanced designs developed by the Germans in WWII. They soon dropped this idea because they were certain that the Soviets would not allow secret, advanced devices to fly over the United States, where they might crash and their secrets could be discovered. With "advanced Soviet devices" ruled out, that meant that the saucer reports resulted from misidentifications, hoaxes, or delusions. There was no theoretical reason to allow for a fourth possibility: flying craft made "elsewhere" (in other words, not from Earth). The chief theoretical reason against this possibility was essentially that the distances between Earth and other hypothetical planets are so great that "they can't get here from there." The theory was that it would take too much time and energy to build a fleet of flying saucers (or "motherships" analogous to aircraft carriers) to travel from some other star system to ours. (In more recent years, Stanton Friedman has disputed this theoretical objection to extraterrestrial saucers in his lectures, and now he does it in this book.)

In the early years of UFO sightings (1947 to 1952 and beyond) the scientific community also relied upon the opinions or claims of those few scientists who actually studied and proposed explanations for individual sightings. These scientists took the experimental/theoretical approach: Imagine each sighting to be a non-repeatable experiment resulting in observational data, and try to find a phenomenon theoretically capable of explaining the data. This approach would have turned up unexplainable sightings, except for one factor: anti-saucer bias by the mainstream scientists. This bias arose from the theory discussed previously ("they can't get here from there"). Hence these mainstream scientists often "force-fit" an explanation onto a sighting. They would claim that they had explained a sighting, without actually proving the explanation was valid. For example, one "theory" of the Kenneth Arnold sighting is that he saw a "mountaintop mirage." It is fine and "scientific" to consider theory such as this to explain a sighting, but once the theory has been generated it is necessary to determine exactly what part or parts of a sighting the theory might explain. In this case, mountaintop mirages are associated with mountains. Because Arnold reported seeing the saucers near Mt. Rainier, this could be considered a (weak) point of agreement between the theory and the observation. However, further study of this theory shows no agreement with other aspects of the observation: mountaintop mirages are above the mountaintops, but Arnold claimed the saucers were *below* the top of Mt. Rainier (he saw them silhouetted against the side of the mountain); mirages have no lateral motion—they stay above the tops of the mountains— but Arnold saw the saucers traveling from north to south at a high speed (he even measured the speed at about 1,700 mph!); mirages are typically dim (inverted) images of the mountaintops, but Arnold said he saw bright sunlight reflections from the objects. So the mountaintop mirage theory has one point of weak agreement and three points of strong disagreement. It must be rejected. Failure to agree with the observation did not, however, prevent this explanation from being published. Some people probably read the explanation and decided that Arnold saw a mirage.

One scientist who claimed to have explained the Arnold sighting, Dr. Donald Menzel (who is discussed in this book), proposed that Arnold saw "blasts of billowing snow" from the sides of Mt. Rainier. The wind would carry the snow southward from Mt. Rainier, thus explaining the lateral motion. However, it would look white, like snow, not like shiny semicircular metal objects. Furthermore, the winds blowing the snow would have been detected by Arnold as he flew past (south of) Mt. Rainier while heading east. Yet Arnold reported calm conditions—no wind. Reject the blasts of snow. Menzel also proposed "wave clouds" and "water drops on the windshield," two more explanations that failed. These theoretical explanations, and others, were offered for Arnold's sighting without careful checks against the sighting details. Not one of the proposed explanations provided a satisfactory fit to the observational data.

Because Menzel and others suggested so many potential explanations, the general scientific community seemed to conclude that Arnold's sighting had been explained. But this conclusion was arrived at without independent analysis of the data by other scientists. Apparently scientists felt that, because there was no theoretical reason to believe saucers could be anything other than ordinary phenomena, there was also no reason to question the explanations proposed by Menzel and others throughout the years since 1947. The scientific community has also failed to question the explanations offered for other sightings by other scientists (and non-scientists).

Another factor during the early years (1947–1960) that has led the scientific community to avoid the study of UFO sightings is that the Air Force kept control of the best sighting data by military observers that involved multiple witnesses, radar, and so on. Civilian scientists were generally not sufficiently interested in the sightings to travel to Wright-Patterson Air Force Base to view the sighting data, so few outside the military were aware of the best sightings. At the same time the Air Force was effectively covering up the data, it was also publicly claiming that, despite their "best efforts," the investigations [Projects Sign (1948), Grudge (1949–1951), and Blue Book (1952–1969)] were finding no evidence of unknown technology. Thus, in the early years, a "tradition" was established that saucer sightings are not a result of unknown science or technology, and can all be explained. It is this tradition that explains why there have been few UFO sightings (or perhaps only one—New Zealand), discussed in the refereed literature. It is this tradition that led the editor of *Applied Optics* to make the "99 44/100 %" comment. And it is within this tradition that the editor of *Science Magazine* was acting when, in 1974, he rejected my first attempt at publishing a scientific article about a UFO sighting.

In 1967 it was "legitimate" to openly discuss UFOs because there had been many publicly reported sightings in the middle 1960s, which caused Congress to order the Air Force to support an investigation independent of Project Blue Book. (This turned out to be the two-year-long "Condon Study" at the University of Colorado.) During that year, in its September 15 issue, *Science Magazine* published an article by William Markowitz with the title "The Physics and Metaphysics of Unidentified Flying Objects." This article was entirely consistent with the tradition. Markowitz argued that, because the reported objects do things that seem to violate some laws of physics and engineering as we know them, and because he was unaware of any convincing evidence in the form of sightings or hardware, no flying saucer was an extraterrestrial craft. Three years later (November 6, 1970), *Science* published another article consistent with the tradition, entitled "Status Inconsistency Theory and Flying Saucer Sightings." In this article Donald Warren argued that people who have inconsistencies in their lives (such as a person with a sixth-grade education being the chief executive officer of a large corporation, or a former bank executive who is now a janitor), may feel excessive stress, leading to alienation from society, and so may be more likely to report seeing a flying saucer. Science has also published letters to the editor responding to the Markowitz article, many of them critical of Markowitz, so I felt that it might be possible to get a "pro"-UFO article into *Science*.

After the flap of UFO sightings in the fall of 1973 I decided to make my move. I submitted an article with the title, "Why Might a Scientist Decide to Investigate UFOs?" This article pointed out that some sightings seemed unexplainable, and then offered as an example the details of a multiple-witness, long-duration sighting of a strange rocket-shaped object that hovered above a mountain near the Shenandoah Valley in Virginia. Two weeks later I received a letter from the editor advising me that he already had enough articles to last for six months, so if I wanted to get the article published I should try some other journal. Of course, I would have been willing to wait a year to get an article published in *Science*, so I took this as an immediate and final rejection. The tradition had won out.

Five years later, when I submitted my first letter to the editor of *Applied Optics*, the tradition was still in force. This first letter had nothing to do with the New Zealand sightings—they had not yet occurred. Instead, this letter was in response to a tradition-based article published in the November 1 issue of *Applied Optics*, in which the authors suggested that some unexplainable UFO sightings were actually flying swarms of glowing insects. They were supposedly glowing because of electrical discharges from their pointed body parts (legs, antennae) as the swarm flew through a strong electrical field that can occur under some calm atmospheric conditions (not just during thunderstorms). My letter disputed this "Buggy UFO Hypothesis (BUFOH)." Several months later the editor said he would publish my letter if I shortened it. However, during that time the New Zealand sightings occurred, and I had carried out an on-site investigation, had performed an optical analysis of the color movie film of the lights, and had managed to obtain a quantitative estimate of the power that was radiated by one of the lights. I had also tried to get my estimate published in *Nature Magazine*, because *Nature* had carried a report on the sightings soon after they occurred. However, *Nature* had rejected it—not because there was something wrong with the analysis, but because the editor of *Nature* had expected a more comprehensive study. Because my power estimate was, therefore, both timely and unpublished, I proposed to the editor of *Applied Optics* that, instead of publishing my rebuttal of the BUFOH, he might consider publishing my optical analysis and power estimate as an indirect rebuttal of the BUFOH (certainly the light recorded on the New Zealand movie film was not a swarm of glowing insects!). He agreed, but I believe it was not because he was taking an unbiased, scientific attitude toward UFO sightings, but rather that he felt he "owed me one" because he had delayed so long in publishing my letter about the BUFOH. Subsequently, he published a rebuttal to my letter, and then, very reluctantly, my response to the rebuttal.

The point here is that, even under the "best" of conditions, mainstream scientists accept the tradition. In this book Stanton Friedman shows why scientists should reject the tradition. Instead, they should look for themselves at some of the most puzzling sightings in the last 60-plus years. He shows that the arguments often made to support the tradition, such as "there are no very interesting sightings that aren't explainable, and no unexplainable sightings that are really interesting" (paraphrase of a comment by Carl Sagan), or "all UFO witnesses are poor observers" (paraphrase of Edward Condon), are just plain wrong. In the open literature (as opposed to secret government "closed" literature, about which we can only guess) there are sighting reports that combine multiple witnesses (two or more) with long duration (many seconds to minutes or longer) and relatively large angular size so shape details can be seen (1/3 of the full moon size or larger). There are some that include radar (ground, airborne, or both), some that include physical effects on machines (car stopping, effects on aircraft controls), some that include landing traces, and many that include photos or film or videos. (The New Zealand sighting is the only one known to this author that combines multiple witnesses with air and ground radar, as well as color movie film and audiotape recordings made during the sightings.)

Stan, having given hundreds of lectures, literally throughout the world, is very familiar with the questions people ask, and he has answered many of them in this book. You will find out why he thinks the Search for Extraterrestrial Intelligence (SETI), which attempts to detect radio or light signals from other civilizations, is "silly" and likely to fail even if there are ET civilizations "out there." You will find out why he believes there is a government cover-up or "Cosmic Watergate." You will find out where scientists have gone wrong in predicting physics-based limitations on technological advances (for example, predicting that manned flight in a heavier-than-air vehicle was impossible three months before it was accomplished by the Wright brothers). You will learn about the disconnect between ufology and science fiction writers (who fully accept the "tradition"), and, considering the ufologically negative aspects of the "tradition," you may be surprised to learn what public opinion polls show. You will also find discussions of the most up-to-date information on the Roswell crash, the Betty and Barney Hill abduction, and the infamous MJ-12 documents.

This book should help you break through the tradition barrier, as I did years ago. After studying this subject for more than 40 years I have to agree with Stan: AFCs are real (where AFC = Alien Flying Craft). We are not alone!

—Dr. Bruce Maccabee, PhD

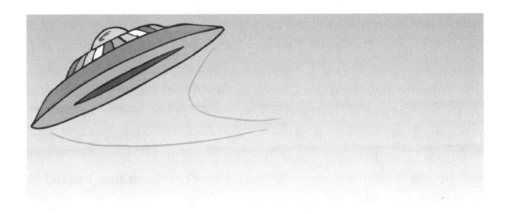

Introduction

It was way back in 1958 that I casually ordered a book called *The Report on Unidentified Flying Objects* by Air Force Captain Edward J. Ruppelt. (I needed one more book for my order from a mail-order discount book supplier to save paying shipping costs.) The book had been marked down from $2.95 to $1, which would have been the cost of shipping anyway, if I hadn't ordered it. Thus, it was free. Ruppelt, the ad said, had been in charge of Project Blue Book. At the time I was working as a young nuclear physicist on nuclear airplanes for General Electric near Cincinnati, and figured Ruppelt ought to know what he was talking about. The United States Air Force (USAF) was cosponsor of our program with the old Atomic Energy Commission. I thought, maybe if UFOs were real, they were using nuclear power for their craft. Might be worth a laugh, anyway. I read a lot back then.

The book intrigued me, and, with hindsight, I can say it was a very lucky first UFO book. (Many I have since discovered aren't worth the paper on which they are printed.) I read a bunch more, and discovered a very important volume called *Project Blue Book Special Report No. 14* at the University of California, Berkeley library. It really caught me up short (as I will describe fully in Chapter 2). I then joined two serious groups: The National Investigations Committee on Aerial Phenomena, and the Aerial Phenomena Research Organization (both long gone), to get their newsletters and read a lot more. I talked with my colleagues as I went from one cancelled government-sponsored classified advanced research and development program to the next, never dreaming that I would be writing my own magnum opus in 2008.

I gave my first lecture about flying saucers in 1967 in the living room of a woman who was a technician at Westinghouse Astronuclear Laboratory near Pittsburgh, Pennsylvania. We were designing, building, and testing nuclear rocket engines for possible use as upper stages in deep-space propulsion systems. Her book review club was covering Frank Edwards's book, *Flying Saucers Serious Business*, which was a best-seller. I had become friends with Edwards when living in Indianapolis working for General Motors on another eventually cancelled nuclear program, and had just recently read the book he had sent me. On his advice, I had called KDKA, a 50,000-watt Clear Channel radio station, to talk to the producer of a talk show called *Contact*. They told me, "Don't call us; we will call you." Within a few weeks they did call me, but only because a guest had cancelled at the last minute, and I lived near the station. My book-club hostess heard the show, and the rest is history. I have since given more than 700 lectures in all 50 states, nine Canadian provinces, and 16 other countries. Some were to audiences as large as 2,000 people. Most were at colleges and universities. Many were to engineering societies, management clubs, sections of the American Institute of Aeronautics and Astronautics, the American Nuclear Society, the Institute of Electrical and Electronic Engineers, and the like. In addition, I have appeared on many hundreds of radio and TV shows. I have been incredibly lucky to have been questioned by so many people.

As a result of those questions, I have felt there really was a need for a comprehensive book that covers, in depth, many details that there was no time to cover in a single lecture or interview or video documentary. Each of my previous books has focused on a relatively narrow area: *Crash at Corona: The Definitive Study of the Roswell Incident*, with Don Berliner, of course focused on Roswell, as I was the initial civilian investigator of that case. My second book, *TOP SECRET/MAJIC*, was concerned with the genuine, controversial, and very important classified Operation Majestic 12 documents, as well as a number of phony MJ-12 documents. My third book, *Captured! The Betty and Barney Hill UFO Experience*, was primarily written by my coauthor, Kathleen Marden (Betty's niece). It provides a great deal of never-before published information about the Hill case, including the attacks on it by noisy negativists, as well as the very important star map seen by Betty onboard the craft. I was the first to write about that very exciting work by Marjorie Fish—and first to deal with the critics.

I finally decided it was long past time to provide an overview and a sort of ufology textbook covering in far more depth the material that I could only touch on in a 60- to 90-minute lecture, or in one of my monthly columns in the Mutual UFO Network (MUFON) journal, *UFO Magazine*, or on my Website, *www.stantonfriedman.com*. After all, at the ripe old age of 73, how many more years of good health (and sound mind) do I have left? Being an optimist and having had both my parents live until they were 89, I do presume I will have some more good years left.

In addition, I had written numerous medium-sized articles for my presentations at a number of annual MUFON symposia. All speakers are required to submit a paper to be included in the symposium proceedings distributed at the conference. Mine had titles such as "Flying Saucers and Physics," "Debunking the Roswell Debunkers," "Roswell and Majestic 12 in the New Millennium," "Star Travel? YES!" and the like. Of course, I didn't read any of the papers out loud at the conferences; I spoke extemporaneously, using slides. Each symposium presentation forced me to think in detail about a particular area of ufology.

This book covers, in depth, my answers to such questions as *Is there really any evidence that some UFOs are alien spacecraft?* and covers the large-scale scientific studies the debunkers seem consistently to avoid. It deals at length with the question of whether interstellar travel within our local galactic neighborhood is feasible—drawing on my own work as a nuclear physicist on far-out nuclear airplanes, fission nuclear rockets, fusion nuclear rockets, and nuclear power plants for space applications. It is also easy to make the case for definite major—and generally effective—efforts on the part of the U.S. government to cover up the facts and misdirect the press and scientific communities with lies and half-truths. There really is a Cosmic Watergate. Naturally, I will take advantage of my 14 years of classified nuclear work (my specialty seemed to be exciting, challenging, and eventually cancelled government-sponsored research and development programs for major corporations), and my visits to 20 document archives.

It seems necessary to confront the mass of false arguments against flying saucer reality by such stalwart science fiction writers as Dr. Isaac Asimov, Ben Bova, Arthur C. Clark, and others. In addition, I seem to be one of the few willing to throw down the gauntlet to the practitioners of SETI (Silly Effort To Investigate, I say) who have provided no scientific data to support their strange assumptions about alien technology, motivations, and actions, and have betrayed total ignorance of actual UFO evidence. The emperors of science fiction and SETI have demonstrated that their attacks are bare of reason and lack a basis in facts and data. Clearly, ignorance is bliss for them and those willing to take whatever they say as the gospel truth.

It is also useful to deal at some length with the results of a number of public opinion polls that clearly debunk the notion that most people—and especially most scientists—don't believe in flying saucers. The acceptance of these false notions has kept many people from reporting their sightings, many scientists from teaching a course or sponsoring a thesis, and many journalists from doing their homework and digging into the topic of the Cosmic Watergate that flying saucers represent.

Because I have spent so much time on the Roswell Incident and on the Majestic 12 documents, I will also deal separately with many of the false attacks on both stories. There seems to be no limit to the baloney being served up by the nasty, noisy, unenlightened group of critics who have consistently been guilty of ignoring the facts in both situations.

Because I have been asked more than 40,000 questions about UFOs—many of the *Why?* variety—I feel comfortable dealing with a host of these, such as:

> *Why the government cover-up?*
>
> *Why would aliens come here, out in the boondocks of the local galactic neighborhood?*
>
> *Why have there been no landings on the White House lawn?*

There is also the provocative question as to from where alien spacecraft might originate. Beneath the ground? From other planets in our solar system? From other solar systems? From other galaxies? My idea for one starting place for alien visitors (as would be obvious to those who have read *Captured!*) is from a planet near either Zeta 1 or Zeta 2 Reticuli. These two sun-like stars in the southern sky constellation of Reticulum (meaning "the net" in Latin) are the closest-to-each-other pair of sun-like stars in our entire local neighborhood. They are only 1/8 of a light-year apart from each other, only about 39.2 light-years from here, and are a mind-boggling *billion* years older than our sun. They are very special. It is no wonder that the SETI cultists tend to ignore them—except for a silly claim that they were listened to with radio telescopes more than a decade ago and nothing was heard. Chapter 6 on SETI details the foolishness of that claim.

I must say, I have had a number of surprises along the way. Working my way through five years of college as a busboy in the Catskills of New York state, a dishwasher in a fraternity at Rutgers, a union waiter at a Southside Chicago hotel, I had been under the naïve impression that scientists and journalists were seekers of truth. It turns out that often, they are not. Doing a weekly science commentary for six years for CBC Radio here in Fredericton, New Brunswick, I frequently ran across bad science published in good journals. Speaking at hundreds of colleges, I frequently hear comments about one or another aspect of the UFO question that was quite unscientific, even though the speaker had a PhD. Ignorance is often bliss for the academics. I also learned to have facts in hand before putting mouth in gear. A good lesson for all.

As with all nonfiction books, *Flying Saucers and Science* is intended to stimulate, enlighten, and entertain. It will also provide some one-stop shopping for those with a serious interest in flying saucers who are bewildered by the mass of information and misinformation in both debunking and "believer" books, on the Internet, in so-called TV documentaries, and on some radio talk shows.

There is no general law against lying. As a physicist, I believe one must ask the right questions, have a large "gray basket" for those questions about which there is too little solid information to reach a scientific conclusion, and dig deeply for answers.

Finally, I am especially interested in those former military personnel who have had direct exposure to aliens and alien spacecraft, and who feel it is about time to tell it like it is, instead of continuing the cover-up. Please contact me. My Website is *www.stantonfriedman.com*, which shows my address and phone number. Witness names will not be used without permission.

It has been a fascinating 50 years.

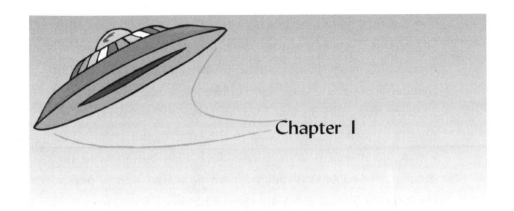

Chapter 1

The Case for the ET Origin of Flying Saucers

One of the standard claims of UFO debunkers is that there is no evidence that any unidentified flying saucers (UFOs) are intelligently controlled extraterrestrial spacecraft. After all, they say, we have only anecdotes, usually from uneducated people looking for publicity. No scientists have seen UFOs; there are no radar cases; there is no physical evidence; governments can't keep secrets; all that crash landed at Roswell was an array of Mogul balloons; so on and so forth. As it happens, all of these claims are false. This chapter will replace these myths with the facts.

I start all of my "Flying Saucers ARE Real" lectures with these four conclusions, which I've reached after more than 50 years of study and investigation:

1. The evidence that planet Earth is being visited by intelligently controlled extraterrestrial spacecraft is overwhelming. In other words, *some* UFOs are ET spacecraft. Most are not—I don't care about them.

2. The subject of flying saucers represents a kind of Cosmic Watergate. That means that some few people in our government have known since at least 1947, when at least two crashed flying saucers and several alien bodies were recovered in New Mexico, that indeed *some* UFOs were alien spacecraft. This does not mean that everybody in the government knows. The way to keep secrets is to restrict their distribution to as few people as possible and stick by a strong need-to-know policy. (In Chapter 5 I will prove that there has been a cover-up.)

3. There are no good arguments against conclusions number 1 and 2, despite the very vocal claims of a small group of noisy negativists such as the late Carl Sagan, a classmate of mine for three years at the University of Chicago. The debunking claims sound great. However, once one examines the data, they collapse, because of an absence of evidence to support them, and the presence of evidence that contradicts them.

4. Flying saucers are the biggest story of the millennium: visits to planet Earth by alien spacecraft and the successful cover-up of the best data, bodies, and wreckage, for more than 60 years.

I will be focusing on evidence. I seldom use the term *proof*. Some people have insisted that if I can't provide a piece of a saucer or an alien body, there is nothing to support my claims. I was quite surprised during my last visit with Carl Sagan in December 1992, when he claimed that the essence of the scientific method was reproducibility. In actuality, as I wrote Sagan later on, there are at least four different kinds of science:

1. Yes, there is a lot of excellent science done by people who set up an experiment in which they can control all the variables and equipment. They make measurements and then publish their results, after peer review, and describe their equipment, instruments, and activity in detail so that others can duplicate

the work and, presumably, come to the same conclusions. Such science can be very satisfying, and certainly can contribute to the advancement of knowledge. However, it is *not* the only kind of science.

2. A second kind of science involves situations in which one cannot control all the variables, but can predict some. For example, I cannot prove that on occasion the moon comes directly between the sun and the Earth and casts a shadow of darkness on the Earth, because I cannot control the positions of the Earth, moon, or sun. What *can* be done is predicting the times when such eclipses will happen and being ready to make observations when they occur. Hopefully the weather where I have my instruments will allow me to make lots of measurements.

3. A third kind of science involves events that can neither be predicted nor controlled, but one can be ready to make measurements if something does happen. For example, an array of seismographs can be established to allow measurements to be made at several locations in the event of an earthquake. When I was at the University of Chicago, a block of nuclear emulsion was attached to a large balloon that would be released when a radiation detector indicated that a solar storm had occurred (something we could neither produce nor predict). Somebody would rush to Stagg Field and release the balloon. When the balloon was retrieved, the emulsion would be carefully examined to measure the number, direction, velocity, and mass characteristics of particles unleashed by the sun.

4. Finally, there is a fourth kind of science, still using the rules to attack difficult problems. These are the events that involve intelligence, such as airplane crashes, murders, rapes, and

automobile accidents. We do not know when or where they will occur, but we do know they will. In a typical year more than 40,000 Americans will be killed in automobile accidents. We don't know where or when, so rarely are TV cameras whirling when these events take place. But we can, after the fact, collect and evaluate evidence. We can determine if the driver had high levels of alcohol in his or her blood, whether the brakes failed, whether the visibility was poor, where a skid started, and so on. Observations of strange phenomena in the sky come under this last category.

In all the category-4 events, we must obtain as much testimony from witnesses as possible. Some testimony is worth more than other testimony, perhaps because of the duration of observation, the nearness of the witnesses to the event, the specialized training of the observer, the availability of corroborative evidence such as videos and still photos, or the consistency of evidence when there is testimony from more than one witness. Our entire legal system is based on testimony—rarely is there conclusive proof such as DNA matching. Judges and juries must decide, with appropriate cross-examination, who is telling the truth. In some states, testimony from one witness can lead to the death penalty for the accused.

We should take note of the fact that even instrument data is dependent on testimony from the observer of the instruments, and on appropriate calibration and validation under standardized circumstances. Also, our courts place limits on requirements for testimony, such as that against one spouse by the other. Furthermore, there are rules about hearsay testimony, and rules regarding legal evidence are complex and detailed.

When it comes to flying saucers, we must remember that the reason most sightings can be determined to be relatively conventional phenomena, often seen under unusual circumstances, is that most people are relatively good observers. The problem comes with the interpretation of what was observed. People watching the sky late at night may get excited about a very bright light that moved very slowly. Checking on the position of the planets at that time may reveal that that light was Venus, because we have good information as to the angle of observation, the direction of the light from the observer, the relatively slow rate of motion, the location of Venus at that time, and so on. On three occasions, when living in Southern California, I was called by people who described an unusual object moving rapidly. I tried to make sure that I analyzed their observations, such as, what time was it? In what direction were you looking? In what direction did it seem to be moving? Was there any sound? What was its apparent size, say, as compared to the moon (just covered by an aspirin held at arm's length)?

Two of the people wanted to tell me that the object was just over the next hill. I stressed that this was an interpretation, because even huge objects far away can seem to be small objects nearby. In all three cases, I felt that what was being described sounded similar to a rocket launched down the California Coast when the sun had gone down, but while the object was high enough to still be in sunlight. I had seen such a spectacular case once myself. I checked, in all three cases, with Vandenberg Air Force Base, which launches many rockets down the U.S. West Coast. Indeed, there had been a launch at the right time in each case. One case was especially intriguing, because several witnesses were looking out across the ocean from a beach area and described the thing they saw as similar to a string of popcorn. It turned out to be the launch of a special weather satellite with extra solid boosters being dropped off multiple times.

The people were good observers. To say the least, it would be irrational to say that people are good observers when their input allows us to identify the object being observed, and yet poor observers if we can't identify the UFO as something conventional.

Categories

Every UFO sighting can be placed in one of three groups:

A. Those reports of UFOs that eventually, after careful investigation, turn out to be identified flying objects (IFOs). This is by far the largest category. Subcategories include astronomical phenomena, aircraft, balloons, advertising planes, experimental aircraft, unmanned aerial vehicles, flocks of birds, and hoaxes.

B. Those reports of UFOs that provide insufficient data on which to base a conclusion. Sometimes for old reports, people aren't sure of the exact date and time, for example, or can't recall the direction of motion, or the color, and so on. Not much one can do with these.

C. The UNKNOWNS. These are reports by competent observers of strange objects in the sky or on the ground, which cannot be identified by the witness, and which remain unidentified after investigation by competent investigators, and whose appearance indicates that they were manufactured (this rules out most lights), and whose flight behavior indicates that they were made somewhere other than Earth. We Earthlings can't build things that look and act that way. If we could, we would, because of the military applications of such craft.

Remember that the question is not *Are all UFOs alien spacecraft?* The question is, *Are any?* As shall be seen, my answer is definitely yes. If you were to ask me, "Are any UFOs secret, government-sponsored research-and-development vehicles?" my answer would again be yes.

There are some logical traps awaiting the unwary here. Some people want to claim: "Isn't it reasonable to say that, if most UFOs can eventually be identified, all can be?" Think about that for a minute. Would it be reasonable to say that because most people are not 7 feet tall, no one is?

Because most isotopes aren't fissionable, none are; because most people don't have AIDS, no one does; because most chemicals will not cure any diseases, none do? Obviously we learn, early on, to focus on the data relevant to the question at hand. The basketball coach is well aware that there are far more people shorter than 7 feet than those taller than 7 feet. But he knows there are some of the latter. When I was at Rutgers University in New Brunswick, New Jersey, Dr. Selman Waksman of the microbiology department collected soil samples from all around the world seeking chemicals with anti-disease properties. One of his major discoveries, after checking on many thousands of soil cultures, was streptomycin, the first cure for tuberculosis.

He won the Nobel Prize in 1952 for that work. Other antibiotics were later found; most of the cultures were worthless. Gold miners know that ore is worth mining if there is a half-ounce of gold per ton of ore; that's less than .001 percent of the ore.

I learned early on, when working on designing and testing radiation shielding for aircraft nuclear propulsion systems and other compact nuclear reactors, that by far the majority of gamma rays and neutrons produced in the reactor get absorbed in the surrounding shielding material. But it is the tiny percentage that penetrates the shield that had to be my focus, if I wanted to protect crewmembers. It is the category-C cases that matter: The UNKNOWNS.

The problem then becomes finding the UNKNOWNS. Many books talk about individual cases; how can a reader evaluate them? There are tens of thousands of newspaper articles and videos about UFO cases, YouTube has loads of videos—the Internet is chock full of UFO-related material—much of which is worthless. But how can one evaluate this mass of uneven and usually uninvestigated cases? I think that, in general, the best place to search involves the several large-scale scientific studies...almost never mentioned by the UFO debunkers.

Project Blue Book Special Report Number 14

The largest official scientific study of UFOs performed for the United States government was reported in *Project Blue Book Special Report No. 14*. The work was done by professional engineers and scientists at the Battelle Memorial Institute in Columbus, Ohio. BMI is a highly respected research and development organization that does contract research for private and government groups. This study was the result of a contract with Project Blue Book, a USAF group at the Foreign Technology Division at Wright-Patterson Air Force Base in Dayton, Ohio.

The contracting agency has had many names throughout the years, including Air Technical Intelligence Center and Aerospace Technical Intelligence Center, and is now known as the National Air Intelligence Center (NAIC). Blue Book, in turn, was the continuation of Projects Sign and Grudge that had preceded it. At that time (mid-1950s) Project Blue Book was the only publicly acknowledged government group concerned with UFOs. We now know that there were others.

It was BMI's job to review all the UFO sightings in the Blue Book files for the period 1948 through 1953. Exactly 3,201 sighting reports were eventually categorized as something such as *Astronomical, Balloon, Aircraft*...and UNKNOWN. Every report was also evaluated for quality: *Excellent, Good, Doubtful,* or *Poor*. Presumably, a sighting by a priest, a physicist, and a pilot, of something observed for 10 minutes from 50 feet away in daylight would have been considered a higher quality observation than a 4-second observation by the town drunk at 4 a.m. of a light zipping by in the sky. Obviously these are subjective judgments, but they are certainly meaningful. All sorts of data about each case (duration, speed, color, shape, and the like) was stored on punch cards so it could be sorted with the primitive computer systems then available.

The professionals who worked on the project established a number of sensible ground rules and definitions. For example, no sighting could be listed as an UNKNOWN unless all four Final Report evaluators agreed it was an UNKNOWN. Any two could label it as anything else.

The BBSR 14 definition for UNKNOWN (My category C) is: "This designation in the identification code was assigned to those reports of sightings wherein the description of the object and its maneuvers could not be fitted to the pattern of any known object or phenomenon."

Their definition of Insufficient Information (My category B) is: "This identification category was assigned to a report when, upon final consideration, there was some essential item of information missing, or there was enough doubt about what data were available to disallow identification as a common object or some natural phenomenon. It is emphasized that this category of identification was not used as a convenient way to dispose of what might be called 'poor unknowns,' but as a category for reports that, perhaps, could have been one of several known objects or natural phenomenon."

Psychological Manifestations: "This identification category was assigned to a report when, although it was well established that the observer had seen something, it was also obvious that the description of the sighting had been overdrawn. Religious fanaticism, a desire for publicity, or an overactive imagination were the most common mental aberrations causing this type of report." This includes the crackpot reports that so fascinate debunkers.

It is worthwhile to note that, before tabulating their findings, UFO debunkers have often made negative statements about UFO evidence, such as the following:

"The reliable cases are uninteresting and the interesting
cases are unreliable. Unfortunately there are no cases
that are both reliable and interesting."

—Dr. Carl Sagan, astronomer,
Cornell University, *Other Worlds*

"Almost every sighting is either a mistake or a hoax. These reports are so riddled with hoaxes, and the flying saucer enthusiasts have so many cranks, freaks, and nuts among them that Hynek is constantly running the risk of innocently damaging his reputation by being confused with them."

—Dr. Isaac Asimov, author, "The Rocketing Dutchman," *Fantasy and Science Fiction*

"All non-explained sightings are from poor observers."

—Dr. Donald Menzel, astronomer, Harvard University, *Physics Today*

"The Unexplained sightings are simply those for which there is too little information to provide a solid factual basis for an explanation."

—Ben Bova, writer, editor, *Analog*

"The number of people believing in flying saucers remains at about 6 percent of the adult population, according to Gallup Polls."

—*Science*

"A two-year-old Gallup Poll reported that more than 3 million Americans believe flying saucers are real. But that still leaves 98 percent of the country somewhat doubtful."

—*Los Angeles Times*

"...[L]ike most scientists, he puts little credence in UFO reports."

—*Science News* (speaking of Carl Sagan)

"On the basis of this study we believe that no objects such as those popularly described as flying saucers have overflown the United States. I feel certain that even the unknown 3 percent could have been explained as conventional phenomena or illusions if more complete observational data had been obtained."

—Donald A. Quarles,
secretary of the U.S. Air Force

These statements have several things in common:

1. None includes any accurate references to data or sources.

2. All are demonstrably false.

3. All are proclamations, rather than the result of evidence based investigations.

4. All are many years old, but my 40 years of lecturing and hundreds of media appearances have indicated that many people still share these views, despite their inaccuracy.

Together they certainly illustrate the four basic rules of the true UFO nonbelievers:

1. Don't bother me with the facts; my mind is made up.

2. What the public doesn't know, I am not going to tell them.

3. If one can't attack the data, attack the people. It is much easier.

4. Do your research by proclamation rather than investigation. No one will know the difference.

A major reason for these false claims can be seen in the comments in the press release issued on October 23, 1955, by the U.S. Air Force, in conjunction with the supposed release of *Project Blue Book Special Report No. 14.* Surprisingly, there is no mention of the organization that did the study: the Battelle Memorial Institute. There is no mention of the names of the authors of the report. There is no mention of the actual title of the report, though it was not classified. If it had been noted, surely some journalist would have asked what happened to reports 1 through 13? The answer, if it had been honest, would have been that they were all still classified at the time. Although a large summary was provided in the press release, amazingly it includes no data from the more than 240 charts, tables, graphs, and maps that are in the report. How could it be called a summary?

The key quote is given from Donald B. Quarles, then the secretary of the United States Air Force: "Even the Unknown 3 percent could have been identified as conventional phenomena or illusions if more observational data had been available."

There would appear to be two factual statements here:

1. The percentage of the sightings listed as UNKNOWN was only 3 percent.

2. These UNKNOWNS were simply reports for which there wasn't enough data (my category 2).

In that case, "there is nothing to flying saucers" would be a reasonable conclusion.

However, these statements are both flat-out lies. Table 1 on page 41 shows the tabulation of the categorization of the 3,201 cases investigated. This table, somehow, is not actually compiled in the report.

Notice that the percentage of UNKNOWNS was actually 21.5 percent of the cases studied—*seven times* as many as stated by the secretary of the USAF. Note especially the category listed as "Insufficient Information": 9.3 percent. No sightings for which there was insufficient data, by definition, could be listed as UNKNOWNS. Clearly, both "factual" statements by Secretary Quarles were bunk. More accurately, he lied big time.

Table 1: Project Blue Book Special Report 14 Data (work by Battelle Memorial Institute)

Categorization	Designation Number	Percentage
Balloon	450	14.0
Astronomical	817	25.5
Aircraft	642	20.1
Miscellaneous	257	8.0
Psychological Manifestations	48	1.5
Insufficient Information	298	9.3
UNKNOWN	689	21.5
TOTAL	3,201	100.0

Table 2: Quality Evaluation

	Sightings		Unknowns		Insufficient Information	
	#	%	#	%	#	%
Excellent	308	9.6	108	35.1	12	3.9
Good	1,070	33.4	282	26.4	33	3.1
Doubtful	1,298	40.5	203	15.6	150	11.6
Poor	525	16.4	96	18.3	103	19.6
TOTAL	3,201	100.0	689	21.5	298	9.3

It is tempting to think that perhaps it was only the poor-quality reports, those 4-a.m., 4-second observations by the town drunk, that were listed as UNKNOWNS. This proclamation is clearly destroyed by the data in Table 2. It shows that the better the quality of the sighting, the more likely it was to be an UNKNOWN, and the less likely it was to be listed as "Insufficient Information." This is not surprising at all, though it is exactly the opposite of the unsubstantiated and false claims of the "true non-UFO believers," as I call them. It is exactly what one would expect, if the UNKNOWNS were really different from the knowns. This tabulation is also not shown explicitly in *PBBSR 14*.

Notice that 35.1 percent of the excellent cases were listed as UNKNOWN, but only 18.6 percent of the poor cases were. In other words, the better the quality of the report, the more likely to be unexplainable. Another proclamation often made by the debunkers is that the unexplained sightings were of short duration—certainly not long enough to make a scientific determination as to what was observed. Table 3 on page 43 provides information on the duration of observation.

The average UNKNOWN was observed for longer than the average known: 63.5 percent of the UNKNOWNS were observed for longer than 1 minute; 36.1 percent were observed for longer than 5 minutes, and 12.9 percent for longer than 30 minutes. So much for the nonsense that unexplainable UFOs are only observed for a few seconds. Some debunkers like to claim that only nutty people report seeing UFOs. Notice that only 1.5 percent of the sightings were listed as "Psychological Manifestations." The American Physical Society, to which I (and most other professional physicists) belong, has said that 2 percent of the papers submitted to it for publication by physicists are crackpot papers. This suggests that there are more crackpots associated with physics than with flying saucers. Fortunately, I am not the only physicist with a foot in each camp. Finally, comments are often made by the true nonbelievers that there is really no difference between the UNKNOWNS and the knowns. That being the case, why pay

Table 3: Duration of Observation for All Sightings and Unknowns

Duration	All Sightings		Unknowns		
			U	U/S	U/512
	#	%	#	%	%
Under 5 Seconds	437	18.6	39	8.9	7.6
5–10 Seconds	167	7.1	31	18.6	6.1
11–30 Seconds	265	11.3	56	21.0	10.9
31–60 Seconds	196	8.3	61	31.1	11.9
1–5 Minutes	508	21.6	140	27.6	27.3
6–30 Minutes	527	22.5	119	22.6	23.2
Over 30 Minutes	249	10.6	66	26.5	12.9
Total (Time Specified)	2,349	100.9	512	21.8	100.0
Time Not Specified	852		177	20.8	
Grand Total	3,201		689	21.5	

attention to the knowns? The UNKNOWNS must simply be missed knowns. The professional engineers and scientists doing the work presented in the *PBBSR 14* were clearly concerned about this possibility, so they sought answers to the question, "Is there any difference between the characteristics of the knowns and the UNKNOWNS?"

To be technical about it, they did a Chi-square statistical analysis based on six different characteristics of the UFOs: apparent size, shape, speed, color, duration of observation, and number of objects seen. They found that the probability that the UNKNOWNS were just missed knowns was less than 1 percent! UNKNOWNS were *not* missed knowns.

Obviously this doesn't prove that the UNKNOWNS are alien spaceships. It does show that no matter how much they manipulated the data, they couldn't get a match between the UNKNOWNS and the knowns. It is important that one of the crucial characteristics of the UNKNOWNS—maneuverability—wasn't considered in this part of the BMI effort.

My reason for saying that some UNKNOWNS are intelligently controlled extraterrestrial spaceships is very simple: Witness reports clearly indicate that the observed objects are manufactured, and behave in ways we can't duplicate. Generally they are small, 10-foot to 40-foot disc-shaped vehicles without wings, tails, or visible external engines. Frequently they demonstrate high maneuverability—right-angle turns at high speed (as observed on radar), the ability to fly straight up and hover, and to go forward and then backward without making a big turn. Usually there is no sound, no exhaust, and often there is a glow around the object (not the observer). A much smaller number of observations are of huge "mother" ships, perhaps 1/2 to 1 mile long. In recent years there have been a number of triangular objects observed as well. If we Earthlings could make things that look and act as described, we would, because they would make wonderful military vehicles. There have been several wars in which we haven't used such craft. So if they weren't built on Earth, they were built somewhere else. This doesn't tell us where they are from, why they are here, or why they don't behave the way some Earthlings would want them to.

Despite all the data available in the Blue Book report, its summary contains none. The press release was given very wide distribution, whereas the report itself was available for review in only a few places. It is perhaps no wonder that quotes from the totally misleading press release appeared in newspapers across the United States and in other parts of the world. The deception was clear and effective. No newspaper that I have seen noted any of the actual report, and the false comments have been repeated over and over again by the news media and so-called scientists as if they were facts instead of lies.

The reader should not get the impression that I look upon *PBBSR 14* as a perfect study. There were some serious problems, besides the totally misleading press release, such as the failure to note relevant data, and the title itself. For example, there was a shameful effort made to put together a composite picture of a UFO based on 12 cases—that is, frankly, ludicrous, with drawings that would make any sensible artist ashamed. There is no section of recommendations as to how to get more and better data with all the available resources of the Army, Navy, and Air Force. There is no discussion of the military and security implications of alien spacecraft violating U.S. airspace with impunity. There is not even an indication of the many highly classified military reports that must have existed. After all, a January 31, 1949 FBI memo stated that the Army and USAF considered the subject of flying saucers TOP SECRET. Where is all the data obtained by the Air Defense Command? These data are all born classified. Newspapers do not receive listings of military aircraft being scrambled to go after "uncorrelated targets"—a much less intriguing term than *flying saucers* or *UNKNOWNS*.

USAF General Carroll Bolender, in a memo dated October 20, 1969, stated that "Reports of UFOs which could affect national security are made in accordance with JANAP 146 and Air Force Manual 55-11, and are NOT part of the Blue Book system." In a later paragraph, discussing the impact of closing Blue Book (it was closed because of his memo) and denying the public a place within the government to which sightings could be reported, he stated, "As noted above, reports which could affect National Security would continue to be handled through the standard Air Force procedures designed for this purpose." The public has never been officially told that the important cases didn't go to Project Blue Book—it wasn't even on the distribution list for the cases reported through JANAP 146 or AF Manual 55-11. I managed to locate and speak with retired General Bolender, who certainly understood the implications of having a separate channel for the most important cases. Then, when I showed a copy of the Bolender memo to the former Project Blue Book scientific consultant, Dr. J. Allen Hynek, in 1979, he was very upset, and felt that he had been badly used by the USAF: The best cases didn't go to Blue Book!

Blue Book, throughout its existence, did not comprise a high-level technical group. Typically there was a major and a sergeant, some secretaries, and a monthly visit from Dr. Hynek, a professor of astronomy, by nature not a boat-rocker. Neither did Blue Book have sophisticated instrumentation or communication systems. And it did not have a need-to-know for classified data collected by the Air Defense Command.

We know of only two fully classified TOP SECRET documents connected with UFOs: One was a report of a fascinating observation in the Soviet Union by U.S. Senator Richard Russell and associates in 1955. This was finally declassified in 1985. The other is AIR (Air Intelligence Report) No. 100-203-79, dated December 10, 1948. The objective of this joint USAF and U.S. Navy report was to evaluate the possibility of UFOs being from the Soviet Union, and the implications for national security if that were the case. A history of sightings is given in these documents, but clearly, the authors did not have a need-to-know for TOP SECRET information about such events as the recovery of a crashed flying saucer and alien bodies outside Roswell, New Mexico, in July 1947, or of the destruction of U.S. aircraft as they tried to attack flying saucers. I have quietly heard of several examples of such disastrous events, and the cover-up that followed. (As an aside, it took many years for Americans to finally find out that 166 aircraft crew members had been lost in U.S. planes shot down doing reconnaissance missions too close to the USSR, China, or North Korea, as described in *By Any Means Necessary* by William E. Burrows.)

From the larger viewpoint of a scientist interested in obtaining measurements of UFO characteristics, it is the most classified observations by our most sophisticated monitoring systems (such as the several radar networks, the spy satellites, and the web of observing systems operated by the National Security Agency and the National Reconnaissance Office) that are of most interest. The latter, of course, didn't come into being until after *Project Blue Book Special Report Number 14*. But where are the TOP SECRET cases? Is there any precedent of BMI being involved in highly classified work that could not be revealed in an unclassified report?

I suspect that there are many examples, but I can certainly provide one from my own professional experience. In the early 1960s I was employed by Aerojet General Nucleonics in the walnut orchards of San Ramon, California, south of Walnut Creek. The area is now wall-to-wall housing. I was project engineer on a contracted study with the Foreign Technology Division of the Air Force with the title "Analysis and Evaluation of Fast and Intermediate Reactors for Space Vehicle Applications." One key word was missing in the title: *Soviet*. It was essentially a one-man project. Every month or so I would go back to Dayton, meet with my contract monitor, and usually spend time at BMI over in Columbus. They had a huge collection of Soviet technical literature in translation. I could give them key words and author's names and/or affiliations, and would get abstracts of a slew of relevant papers. I was familiar with American technology related to compact nuclear reactors for space applications, and collected large bibliographies of Soviet publications in each area of interest, such as reactor physics, radiation shielding, liquid metal heat transfer, and such. It was an educational project for me, not only about advanced Soviet technology, but it also demonstrated that Soviet scientists and engineers and their American counterparts both wanted to publish, even when the basic reason for their often difficult research was related to an unnamed far-out technology.

I put together two final reports. One was a large, unclassified bibliography of Soviet papers in all technical areas of interest. The other, of course not mentioned in the first report, was a highly classified report giving my bottom-line judgment as to what their work meant. I was probably the only scientist in North America who was pleased to hear of the reentry in the

Northwest Territories of Canada of the Cosmos 954 spacecraft on January 24, 1978. It had contained what was touted as the 13th Soviet nuclear reactor to operate in space.

My analysis had correctly concluded that all the right kind of technical work was going on for the Soviet development of such systems. The United States has operated only one such reactor, and not a very good system at that. It was also of interest that, despite all the press coverage of the crash of the radioactive material, none of the many articles noted that the most significant aspect was that the Soviets had much more power available to them in space than we had. The power could be used for sideband radar to monitor ships at sea, particle beam and/or laser weapons, and more. Instead, the coverage focused on the possible radioactive contamination of the caribou in the desolate area. (As a side note, the U.S. Air Force later bought one of the Russian systems.) The last number I heard was that the Russians had launched more than three dozen advanced space nuclear reactors. The recovery of the debris, as reported by Operation Morning Light, also, not surprisingly, established that the U.S. government had access to recovery teams that could immediately go into action to recover items deemed of interest—including a crashed saucer, if such an event takes place. In fact, during World War II, military intelligence had made a substantial effort to acquire crashed enemy aircraft for technical evaluation.

My point here is that my experience indicated that the Battelle Memorial Institute and the Foreign Technology Division of the Air Force could together produce an unmentioned highly classified technical report, *and* an unclassified technical companion report that didn't mention the classified report. I believe that such a report was Blue Book Report 13, produced by the same two groups. Two people have each quietly told me of seeing a copy of it in classified files. The Air Force has variously said there was no Report 13, or that it was contained in *PBBSR 14*. The old National Investigations Committee on Aerial Phenomena (NICAP) actually published Reports 1 through 12. Nobody I have spoken with has a copy of 13. Based on my 14 years of professional scientific work on classified projects, I am absolutely convinced that secrets can be kept. Chapter 5 goes into much more detail about the Cosmic Watergate, which, unlike the political Watergate, has been very successful.

One more important fact about *Project Blue Book Special Report Number 14* is that when I check my lecture audiences after talking about it, I find that fewer than 2 percent have read it, even though presumably an audience coming to hear me speak is biased in the direction of believing in flying saucers. I should also note that I once compiled a list of 13 anti-UFO books by such debunkers as Donald Menzel and Philip Klass. None of the books mentioned the report, though I can prove they were all aware of it. The rule is: *What the public doesn't know, I won't tell them.* Even the University of Colorado study, despite having a long chapter on government involvement in UFO studies, doesn't mention it. I had personally written to Dr. Condon about it and even received a letter acknowledging mine.

The UFO Evidence

Richard Hall, who is still an active ufologist, compiled another outstanding report on UFOs for the Washington, D.C.–based NICAP in May 1964. The 184-page large-format report, *The UFO Evidence*, has information on 746 UNKNOWNS—or 16 percent of the 4,500 cases investigated by the (mostly) professional members of NICAP. There are entire chapters on sightings by military and civilian pilots, by police officers, and by scientists and engineers, and not as evidence for intelligent control. There are special sections on the major UFO wave of 1952, and on official UFO investigations. It is truly an outstanding volume; copies were given to all members of Congress. Again, fewer than 2 percent of my lecture attendees are aware of it. Hall put out a huge update, volume 2, *The UFO Evidence: A Thirty Year Report* in 2000. It has 681 fact-filled pages.

There is an 87-page comprehensive section on UFO abductions, and a 10-page overview of the Roswell Incident. The book has very extensive bibliographies, and really should be in all libraries, but isn't.

Congressional Hearings

Thanks primarily to the efforts of Dr. James E. McDonald, an atmospheric physicist at the University of Arizona, the U.S. House Committee on Science and Astronautics held a Symposium on Unidentified Flying Objects in Washington, D.C., on July 29, 1968. McDonald had become interested in UFOs in the mid-1960s, and was shocked when visiting Project Blue Book in Dayton, Ohio, to find a host of sighting reports of very interesting cases. He noted that the explanations often made little sense. He became upset that Dr. Hynek had not called the attention of the scientific community to the wealth of data in the files. (Their battle is discussed in detail in the excellent book by Ann Druffel: *Firestorm: James E. McDonald's Fight for UFO Science*.) Six scientists testified in person. They were Dr. J. Allen Hynek, chairman of the astronomy department a Northwestern University in Evanston, Illinois (and Project Blue Book consultant for almost 20 years); Dr. Carl Sagan, professor of astronomy at Cornell University; Dr. James E. McDonald, professor of physics at the University of Arizona; Dr. James Harder, professor of civil engineering at the University of California, Berkeley; Dr. Robert L. Hall, head of the department of sociology at the University of Illinois, Chicago (and Richard Hall's brother); and Dr. Robert M.L. Baker, senior scientist for System Sciences Corp. in El Segundo, California.

In addition, the printed 247-page proceedings (available on the Internet at *www.project1947.com/shg/symposium/index.html*) included written submissions from six more scientists. They were Dr. Donald Menzel, astronomer at Harvard University in Cambridge, Massachusetts; Dr. R. Leo Sprinkle, psychologist at the University of Wyoming in Laramie; Dr. Garry C. Henderson, senior research scientist for Space Sciences at General

Dynamics in Fort Worth, Texas; Dr. Roger N. Shepard, department of psychology at Stanford University in Palo Alto, California; Dr. Frank Salisbury, head of the plant science department at Utah State University in Logan; and myself, then a nuclear physicist at Westinghouse Astronuclear Laboratory in Large, Pennsylvania. I have taken pride that I was the only one of the 12 without a PhD. In my opinion, the best paper by far was that from Jim McDonald. He presented information on 41 separate cases, including multiple-witness radar-visual cases, sightings over big cities, sightings by scientists and astronomers, and clear indication of intelligent control of some UFOs. His paper alone is 71 pages long, and should be read by anyone who thinks there are no good UFO cases. John Fuller, who earlier had written *The Interrupted Journey*, the story of the abduction of Betty and Barney Hill, and *Incident at Exeter*, also wrote *Aliens in the Skies*, which includes most of the papers, but without the references.

Quite frankly, I have found throughout the years that very few people have read this very valuable volume, the *Symposium on UFOs*. The reward for Indiana Congressman J. Edward Roush, who presided over the session, was that in the next election he was Gerrymandered out of his district. Another member of the Committee on Science and Astronautics was Donald Rumsfeld of Illinois, who later became Secretary of Defense under George W. Bush. Hynek, also from Illinois, once told me of approaching Rumsfeld much later, saying he thought he had a need-to-know for what was happening. Rumsfeld told him in no uncertain terms that he did not. There is a substantial difference between the factual content of most of the papers by people who had really dug into the facts, and those of Menzel and Sagan, whose papers revealed a lack of concern with facts and data, instead full of proclamations and little investigation. If Jim McDonald had lived many more years, instead of dying in 1971, I believe the situation today would be very different. He spoke to many sections of the American Institute of Aeronautics and Astronautics, and many other professional organizations, and used hard-nosed science to destroy the often foolish explanations of Menzel (who often proclaimed "temperature inversions" without doing the required computations that Jim did) and Philip Klass (who often proclaimed "plasma explanations"—again without doing the scientific calculations that Jim did, which destroyed those proclaimed explanations).

The Condon Report

There is no doubt that the largest and most publicized study of UFOs is the 965-page, 1968 *Scientific Study of Unidentified Flying Objects*. Its editor was Daniel S. Gillmor, and the study was done under the direction of Dr. Edward U. Condon, a professor of physics at the University of Colorado in Boulder, with funding from the Air Force Office of Scientific Research. Many universities had been approached by AFOSR in response to recommendations from the O'Brian Panel (established after the big fuss about Hynek's swamp-gas explanation for sightings in Michigan in 1966). Condon was known as a tough cookie, and much earlier had taken on the House Un-American Activities Committee.

Problems with the Condon study have been described in many places, well after its publication. At the time, early 1969, it was lauded by the press primarily because of the introduction by Walter Sullivan, science editor of the *New York Times*, and the complimentary comments by a special panel of the National Academy of Sciences (NAS)—who did not investigate any cases to evaluate Condon's work. Of course, *he* hadn't investigated any cases either, and had made a number of negative comments along the way. Not enough attention was paid to the fact that Condon was himself a member of the NAS, a self-electing body. What might be described as a minority report was later published by Dr. David Saunders (*UFOs? YES! Where the Condon Committee Went Wrong*), who had been fired by Condon. John G. Fuller had written a *Look Magazine* article entitled "Flying Saucer Fiasco" on May 14, 1968, pointing out, among other important aspects of the unscientific study, a letter from Robert J. Low, an assistant dean at the

University of Colorado, describing how the project would be *made to look* scientific, but of course would not be. In the August 9, 1966 memo he said:

> Our study would be conducted almost entirely by nonbelievers, who, although they couldn't possibly *prove* a negative result, could and probably would add an impressive body of thick evidence that there is no reality to the observations. The trick would be, I think, to describe the project so that to the public, it would appear a totally objective study, but to the scientific community would present the image of a group of nonbelievers trying their best to be objective, but having an almost zero expectation of finding a saucer....

There is much more, and the article is on the Internet (at *www.project1947.com/shg/articles/fiasco.html*). The public wound up paying more than half a million dollars for this so-called study. As a young scientist, I was angry about the whole business, and the praise given the study by the press and the National Academy. I have often wondered in how many other controversial areas the public has been so betrayed by what passes for an objective scientific community and an objective press.

As was the case with *Project Blue Book Special Report 14*, the press coverage was generally based on the press release and on the first chapter—Condon's summary and conclusions—and not on the facts in the report. Frankly, I got the impression that Condon hadn't even read the rest of the volume. It comes as a great surprise to many that, according to a UFO subcommittee of the world's largest group of space scientists—the American Institute of Aeronautics and Astronautics—one could come to the opposite conclusions as Dr. Condon based on the data in the report. Any phenomena with 30 percent unidentified classifications is certainly worth further investigation, as the AIAA noted. I am a member of the AIAA, but they wouldn't allow me on the committee (I must be biased because I had reached a conclusion! One would think that after 11 years of effort I would be expected to have a bias, and that ignorance is the worst bias.) Indeed, 30 percent of the 117 cases studied in detail could not be identified.

There are some good sections in the report, and I have talked to some old-timers who say they were turned on to the subject of UFOs by some very interesting unexplainable cases. One can only wonder in how many fields the exceptional was rejected because only 30 percent of the cases examined could not be explained away—think cures for cancer, and great musicians and athletes. My son-in-law works at the Diavik Diamond Mine in the Northwest Territories of Canada. It is a rich diamond mine, producing 3.5 karats of diamonds (less than a handful) per ton of ore—another case of having a small percentage, but high value.

Both Hynek and McDonald (and several others) have written factual negative reviews of the Condon report. Condon later made public statements that the files of the study had not been preserved, yet I found them at the American Philosophical Society library in Philadelphia. Why lie? Fear of a critical review?

The UFO Experience

Dr. J. Allen Hynek had been a consultant to Project Blue Book for about 20 years, starting at the Ohio State University in Columbus, Ohio (close to Blue Book in Dayton), and then continuing later when he became chairman of the astronomy department at Northwestern University in Evanston, Illinois. He had a PhD from my alma mater, the University of Chicago (1935), as did Carl Sagan (1960). Jim McDonald was a research physicist at the University of Chicago in 1953 and 1954 when Sagan and I were there. As far as I know, Sagan didn't know him then, and neither did I. In order to meet with Hynek I had to pass muster with an associate of his, also at the University of Chicago, who attended my lecture at the University of Illinois, Chicago campus, in 1968. I passed, and was taken up to Evanston. Hynek was 58 years old at the time, the same age as my father. I was 33. His first question was, "Why haven't you received a PhD?" I noted that I had worked my way through college as a union waiter at a Chicago hotel my last three years and was anxious to get out in the real world of industry to work on exciting and challenging programs. We saw each other at conferences and when I was going through Chicago, or in Southern California when I lived there. We existed in very different worlds and had very different personalities. I did arrange a press conference and media appearances for him in L.A. when he published *The UFO Experience*. It was like pulling teeth to get background info for the press release. He suggested I look in *Who's Who*, which contained a very small bio. When I finally got something from Northwestern, UFOs were barely mentioned in it.

Allen's book has information about roughly 70 good sightings that couldn't be explained. It contains the definitions for Close Encounters of the first, second, and third kinds. He was a consultant on the very successful movie *Close Encounters of the Third Kind*, and had a cameo role himself. He also made some fairly strong comments about the inadequacy of the Condon Report and some recommendations as to what should be done. He established the Center for UFO Studies, which still exists, to try to accomplish some of those goals. He had a good sense of humor and even collected some of the cartoons that were published about his swamp-gas explanation. The book is well written and serves as a good introduction to the subject, but I do wish he had done more looking at interstellar travel and atmospheric propulsion technology, among other topics.

The COMETA Report

I decided to include this report even though it is not book length because it is much more recent than any of the other volumes, was done in France, and comes at the subject from a less academic viewpoint, which gets closer to many of my views. The actual title in English is "UFOs and Defense: What Should We Prepare For?" It is 90 pages long, and originally appeared in a special issue of the magazine *VSD* in France in July 1999. It is an independent report on UFOs written by the French association COMETA, presenting the results of a study by the Institute of Higher Studies for National Defense. The foreword is by Professor Andre Lebeau, the former chairman of the French National Center for Space Studies. This is the French equivalent of NASA, but it is hard to imagine NASA leadership having the courage to speak out about UFOs.

The report covers a number of excellent cases from France as well as from the United States, and gives a good overview of various non-ET explanations—but is quite willing to seriously consider the extraterrestrial hypothesis. It discusses Roswell, and, also, in a sensible fashion, the reasons why the United States would keep things secret and not share with its allies what scientists have learned from the examination of Roswell wreckage. The authors of the report seem to definitely understand why it could not be shared with America's enemies.

The Fund for UFO Research paid to have the report translated. Unfortunately, the French group leaders, for reasons still unknown, were very upset when I offered copies of the translation for purchase. They also rejected the notion of letting the Fund distribute it or collecting royalties. This came about only because, when the report became a topic of conversation on the Jeff Rense radio program, I mentioned I had a copy of it. Rense said, "Of course you are going to make it available, right Stan?" I hesitated, and then said yes. As someone who has been complaining about the Cosmic Watergate for decades, I could hardly say no and become part of the cover-up myself. Later, my Website people were threatened, so it isn't listed there. Perhaps the French are sensitive because the report is critical of the United States for not revealing more information to their supposed allies. I have distributed copies of *Project Blue Book Special Report Number 14* for the same reason. It is a government document, so it cannot be copyrighted. I could hardly say, "It is a very important report, but you can't see the data...just trust me."

Fortunately, one of the best investigative journalists about UFOs in the United States, Leslie Kean, managed to prepare a comprehensive article about the COMETA report, which appeared in the *Boston Globe* and a number of other newspapers. She has continued her efforts, taking on NASA about their attempt to hide information about the Kecksburg, Pennsylvania, UFO crash and retrieval of December 9, 1965. She also helped set up the very important National Press Club press conference on November 12, 2007, in Washington, D.C. She and James Fox, a documentary film producer, arranged for pilots and military people from many countries to spill the beans about their own experiences at the conference, and are preparing a documentary.

A statement worth repeating about the U.S. UFO cover-up appears near the end of the 1999 COMETA Report: "Only increasing pressure from public opinion, possibly supported by the results of independent researchers, by more or less calculated disclosures, or by a sudden rise in UFO manifestations, might perhaps induce U.S. leaders and persons of authority to change their stance."

Other Sources

A truly enormous amount of material has been written about flying saucers. Some people don't even want me to use the term, but I use it to make an important distinction: Flying saucers are, by definition, unidentified flying objects, but very few unidentified flying objects are flying saucers. I am interested in the latter, not the former. As an example, all great-grandfathers are men; only a small percentage of men are great-grandfathers.

I can't possibly take note of all the relevant literature here. However, the studies I have listed make an excellent starter kit. I would add the dozen or so PhD theses that have been done on UFOs, and the many excellent books done on UFO abductions (though there are some that are very unscientific, such as Dr. Susan Clancy's *Abducted: How People Come to Believe They Were Kidnapped by Aliens*). I have a detailed review on my Website, at *www.stantonfriedman.com*. I do recommend books by Budd Hopkins and Dr. David Jacobs. An excellent overview with 11 essays is the book *UFOS & Abductions: Challenging the Borders of Knowledge*, edited by Dr. David Jacobs. I would also point to the outstanding work done by Ted Phillips concerning physical trace cases. Phillips was a protégé of Allen Hynek, and has for more than 40 years collected information about more than 4,000 such cases from more than 70 countries. These are cases in which a flying saucer is observed on or near the ground, and where, after the saucer has left, one finds physical traces in the dirt or vegetation. In about 1/6 of these cases humanoids are observed. Phillips still hasn't written a book about his work, but he has been doing a monthly column for the MUFON journal for some time. The next time debunkers claim that there is no physical evidence, refer them to Phillips's work.

Two other topics I am not covering here are crop circles and animal mutilations. These are in my "gray basket"—they are interesting, but it is not easy to find a direct connection to the flying saucer phenomena.

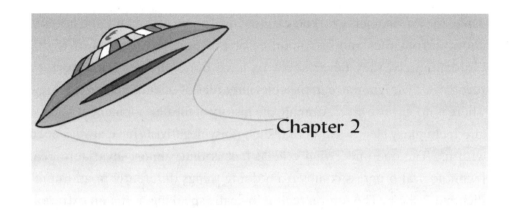

Chapter 2

You *Can* Get Here From There

As noted in Chapter 1, the most common argument against the idea that some UFOs are intelligently controlled extraterrestrial spacecraft is that there is no evidence to support such a "crazy" conclusion. This argument is false. There is an enormous amount of good, solid data indicating that indeed some UFOs are "flying saucers," or ET spacecraft. That conclusion cannot, by itself, answer other key questions, such as the source of the visitors, their purpose in coming here, why the governments of planet Earth have been unwilling to tell Earthlings the facts about visitations, how the alien spacecraft work, and so on.

The second most frequent anti-ET argument is that one can't get here from there. The distances are much too great, they say; it would take too much energy; humankind is forever isolated on planet Earth; and so on, ad nauseum.

As with the not-enough-evidence arguments, these claims are often made by well-educated, sometimes well-intended scholars, such as academic astronomers who know a great deal about astronomy and nothing about aeronautics and astronautics or the practical aspects of flight. Unfortunately, they never seem to have done enough homework to recognize their ignorance in the relevant areas of science and technology. There is no surprise here. After all, the history of the development of science and technology clearly shows that such noisy negativists have always been with us. The one underlying crucial fact is that, almost invariably, real technological progress comes from doing things differently in an unpredictable fashion. The future, technologically speaking, is *not* an extrapolation of the past. One has to change how one does things. Lasers are not just better light bulbs; very different physics is involved.

In 1903, Dr. Simon Newcomb, one of the top American astronomers of the 19th century, published a paper in which he showed that flight by man using anything other than a balloon (a lighter-than-air vehicle) was impossible. His paper clearly showed that he knew much less about flight than did two bicycle mechanics named Wilbur and Orville Wright, who first flew a heavier-than-air vehicle at Kitty Hawk, North Carolina, on December 17, 1903, less than three months after Newcomb's article was published. When notified about this historic event, he, similar to many others, had trouble believing that such a flight had occurred—there were no TV or radio reporters back then. He also claimed that, although perhaps a pilot had flown a heavier-than-air vehicle, it would certainly never carry any passengers. He knew nothing about the lift over a wing, about relatively lightweight engines driving a propeller, and all the other engineering aspects of flight that the Wright brothers had investigated in a systematic fashion.

Progress in flight was quite slow. The first flight was only 120 feet long and lasted for all of 12 seconds. The entire flight and plane would have fit inside a modern 747 aircraft. By 1908, the U.S. Army Signal Corps had awarded the Wrights a contract calling for a bonus for every mile per hour faster than 40 mph that their newest airplane could fly. They collected a $5,000 bonus. The First World War brought aviation into much greater view as airplanes were built that could fly higher, farther, and faster than pre-war planes. Creative military personnel could see then that an airplane could drop bombs on (or supplies for) troops, could observe battlefields much easier and farther from the air than from the ground, and could be used to attack other aircraft.

In 1925, General Billy Mitchell (1879–1936) was court-martialed for claiming (and demonstrating) that an aircraft could sink a large naval vessel. In the 1940s, it was commonly claimed that an airplane had an absolute speed limit of the speed of sound: a bit higher than 700 miles per hour at sea level. The sonic barrier would shake airplanes to pieces, it was thought. An underlying assumption was that a high-speed aircraft would have to use an engine driving a propeller. Dr. Frank Whittle, a British aeronautics expert, was pushing the jet engine in the late 1930s. He had almost no support from government "experts," even after it was reported that German engineers were supposedly working on jet engines.

Many arrogant British military experts knew that, because England had defeated the Germans in WWI (with a lot of help from others), of course British technology would be superior to German technology. This line of thinking totally ignored the progress made by German engineers in the 1930s in the development of better, stronger, and lighter materials. Because of the same arrogance, British tanks were slower and not as well armored as German tanks. "They couldn't possibly be ahead of us," the Brits thought. The rout of the British by the German military machines across Europe in 1939 to flee from Dunkirk clearly showed how out of touch with reality the British military experts were.

The first American jet engines were actually copies of the British Whittle engines, made in the United States, away from the bombings. On October 14, 1947, Colonel Chuck Yeager flew the first official supersonic flight using neither a propeller-driven plane nor a jet, but the X-1 rocket plane. The shape of the aircraft and the shape of the wings were designed for high-speed performance. Progress comes from doing things differently.

In 1926, Dr. Alexander William Bickerton (1842–1929), a professor at Canterbury College in New Zealand, presented a paper at the meeting of the British Association for the Advancement of Science in which he claimed that it would be impossible to give anything sufficient energy to put it into orbit around the Earth! In typical academic fashion, he assumed that the details didn't matter and he could demonstrate the impossibility of launching a satellite from basic principles of physics. He said that at orbital velocity, a body would have to have a kinetic energy (energy of motion) of X ergs per pound, which is certainly true. But he also showed that our best explosive (nitroglycerine), indeed a concentrated source of energy, could only provide 1/10 that amount of energy per pound of explosive, which is also true. Therefore, he claimed, such orbital flight could never be achieved, which is definitely false. Unfortunately, Dr. Bickerton had asked the wrong question and made two stupid assumptions. One was that one had to get the *explosives* into orbit rather than the payload. What he actually had shown is that it would take the energy of 10 pounds of explosive to get one pound of payload into orbit, which is a very different conclusion. Secondly, he falsely assumed that explosives, such as nitro or dynamite, could provide the most energy per pound of any known substance. In fact, reacting two different propellants together, such as oxygen and hydrogen, or oxygen and kerosene, could provide more energy per pound of propellant exhausted through a nozzle in a much more useful fashion than using an explosive. Progress comes from doing things differently.

Another very well-educated academic astronomer, Dr. John William Campbell, once again demonstrated that ignorance is bliss when it comes to flight. Dr. Campbell was an astronomy professor at the University of Western Ontario in London, Ontario, Canada, and head of the Royal Canadian Astronomical Society. He was sick and tired of all the noise being made in science fiction circles about using a rocket to get a man to the moon. So he published his paper, "Rocket to the Moon" in *Philosophical Magazine* in January 1941. He set out to determine the required initial launch weight of a chemical rocket able to get a man to the moon and back. (He, unlike Dr. Bickerton, knew that one could indeed build rockets that could leave Earth.) He included a lot of equations in his paper, and concluded in a strictly "scientific fashion" that the required initial launch weight of a chemical rocket able to get a man to the moon would be an incredibly huge million, million tons! In 1969 the very large (365-foot high) *Saturn Five* rocket, which got three men to the moon and back, weighed only 3,000 tons at liftoff. Dr. Campbell was not just a little off in his "scientific" weight calculations; he was off by an astronomically high factor of 300 million!

We can learn a lot from reviewing some of Dr. Campbell's totally inappropriate assumptions—there were many. First of all, he assumed a single-stage rocket. Other real rocket scientists (Goddard, Tsiolkovsky, and so on) had discussed the staging of rockets decades earlier. Dr. Campbell hadn't done his homework. All of our flights to the moon and other deep-space targets involve multi-staged rockets. The advantage is that after the first stage has burned all its propellant at the most difficult portion of the trip, starting from standing still at the surface of the Earth, one throws away the big tank that held the propellant. This means one need not expend further energy accelerating (increasing the speed of) that dead weight. It's the same with the second stage: Get rid of it once it has done its job, especially because now one faces reduced drag in the atmosphere, because the higher one goes, the thinner the atmosphere and the less the drag (air friction).

Dr. Campbell assumed much too low an exhaust velocity for the gas emitted from the nozzle of the rocket. It requires a great effort to get the forward velocity of the rocket to exceed the rearward velocity of the exhaust. But it was already well known that various combinations of rocket fuel could produce much higher exhaust velocities than that assumed by Dr. Campbell. Furthermore, each stage, of course, starts not at zero velocity, as does the first stage, but at the final velocity of the previous stage—the third stage starts at the final velocity of the second stage. Dr. Campbell made a bad assumption when he assumed that the maximum acceleration (rate of change of velocity) of the rocket would be only 1 G.

One G is the acceleration of gravity produced by the Earth's mass if one drops something from a height. I have often asked a classroom of college students, usually science majors, "What is the numerical value of 1 G?" They all seem to know that 1 G equals 9.8 meters per second, per second, or, in British units, 32.2 feet per second, per second. Then I ask how this acceleration relates to a high-performance car such as a Corvette or a Ferrari. All I get is a blank stare.

Unfortunately, we physicists often use units of measurement that mean absolutely nothing in the real world. In fact, 1 G is about 21 miles per hour, per second. So a car able to provide a uniform acceleration of 1 G would be moving at 21 mph after one second, at 42 mph after 2 seconds, and at the end of 10 seconds, would be going 210 miles per hour, well beyond the capability of most cars, though some dragsters really can get moving. A high-powered car can usually get to a speed of 60 miles per hour in less than 6 seconds: an average acceleration of only about 10 mph, per second, or less than 1/2 G.

When it comes to getting off the Earth, the acceleration should be as high as the passengers can stand. The reason is straightforward. In a simple description, there are only three forces acting on a rocket trying to lift off. The first is the thrust of the rocket, moving the rocket upward. The second is the drag produced by the atmosphere (air friction), tending to slow it down. The third is the gravitational force exerted on the rocket by the Earth. This latter force creates, in effect, a downward force deceleration of 1 G or 21 miles per hour, per second, or, at 60 seconds per minute, 1,260 miles per hour, per minute, of flight. If the upward acceleration produced by rocket thrust was only 1 G, the rocket would barely get off the ground. The faster one gets to orbital velocity, the less the overall impact of gravity. Obviously the longer the rocket fires, the less propellant is left in the tank, and, for a constant-thrust rocket, the more it will accelerate because the net force pushing the rocket upward is the difference between the weight being pulled down and the thrust pushing up. Remember all those comic-book blackboard notations of $F=ma$ (force equals mass times acceleration)? Right on. If the force F (rocket thrust) is constant and the mass m is decreasing, then the acceleration a increases. Obviously, then, the question becomes, how much acceleration can the rocket or its passengers safely withstand? It has been clear for a long time that most mechanical devices can withstand far higher accelerations than can people. A myriad of experiments have been run to answer the seemingly simple question of what is the maximum acceptable acceleration for people. The best answer is that it depends on a number of variables; there is no one answer that fits all:

A. Human resistance to forces on the body depends on the direction of the force with regard to the orientation of the body. Most people have probably noted that astronauts going into space are normally launched on their backs, rather than standing up as in an elevator. It turns out that one can stand far more force back to front than foot to head, or front to back.

B. The duration of the accelerating force acting on the body is very important. This is intuitively obvious: The longer the duration, the less acceleration one can stand without damage. The shorter the duration, the more acceleration one can stand.

C. The magnitude of the force acting on the body is important as well. The higher the force, the shorter the time it can be handled without damage.

NASA and others have run many tests to determine the acceleration to which pilots can safely be subjected. Notice that acceleration is rate of change of velocity. Velocity is a combination of direction and speed. Making a sharp turn, even at a constant velocity, subjects the body to an acceleration.

We hear about pilots blacking out because their blood rushes away from their heads. Tests have shown that a trained pilot can, for example, perform a tracking task while being accelerated at 14 Gs for two minutes. That is an acceleration of 14 × 21, or 294 miles per hour, per second. Starting from rest, at the end of one second, the pilot would be moving at 294 mph. At the end of 10 seconds, he would be going 2,940 miles per hour. At the end of the two minutes, he would be going more than 30,000 miles per hour. The pilot would have to be properly constrained with a contour couch, appropriate seat belts, and so on; he cannot be walking around drinking a beer. He must be reasonably healthy as well.

It further turns out that a trained pilot can actually withstand 30 Gs for one second, or from zero to more than 600 miles per hour in one second. There have been many reports of rapid right-angle turns at high speeds by flying saucers. There is even a suggestion in the data on maximum Gs versus duration that one might stand much higher accelerations for much shorter periods of time. As a far-removed example, a laser can be used to both attach a detached retina, and drill a hole in steel—the attachment is done in a very brief instant, as opposed to the steady drilling. Some companies create large, intricate shapes in sheets of flat metal by zapping the sheets into a mold (a die) with a strong, brief magnetic field (called magneto forming). The metal would be smashed if the pulse was too long. The example I like to use is the removal of a hot potato from an oven. Does one get burned or not? Obviously it depends on the length of time one holds on to the potato, even though the temperature of the potato is high enough to burn the skin. No burning will take place if one gets rid of the potato quickly; there is a reaction time necessary to cause a burn. Similarly, if the acceleration time is shorter than the time it takes a sound wave to move from one end of the object being accelerated to the other, it might be that no damage is done to it at very high acceleration for a very brief time.

Some remarkably courageous people have worked on this problem of people and high acceleration, some of whom are featured in the Clyde Tombaugh Space Museum in Alamogordo, New Mexico. I visited it once, and I enjoyed the exhibits inside. Then I went outside and saw the rocket sled that Dr. John Paul Stapp (1910–1999) used to check on the human body's tolerance to acceleration. The sled runs on rails and is powered by several small JATO (Jet Assisted Take Off) bottles at the back. It is not a sophisticated-looking device. During one test that went awry, the sled reached a peak velocity of 620 miles per hour, and was suddenly slowed down very rapidly. The maximum deceleration on Dr. Stapp reached 43 Gs in the 3/4-second time it took to slow down to a stop. Dr. Stapp walked away, though he was not very comfortable and had problems with his eyeballs.

I noted another quite different example while I was filming the video *Flying Saucers ARE Real* at the Kennedy Space Center in Florida. I pointed out that the escape rocket at the top of the *Apollo* Space Capsule was expected to provide a 13-G acceleration to get the capsule quickly away from the rocket, if there was a fire at the bottom of the rocket more than 300 feet below. (I was able to point to an actual escape rocket at the top of the *Saturn* rocket sitting there—much more effective than just talking about it.) Nobody expected the astronauts to be smashed against the walls. (In a book called *Physics for People Who Think They Don't Like Physics*, by Jerry Faughn and Karl Kuhn, the silly claim is made that when one gets to 9 Gs, one dies. True...if one slams into a wall.)

Dr. Campbell's failure to understand acceleration and its role in flight to the moon wasn't his final mistake; two more are worthy of note. Dr. Campbell correctly noted that a vehicle coming back to Earth from the moon would be moving at about 25,000 miles per hour, and should really be slowed down before trying to land. Unfortunately, he assumed that the only way to slow that "bullet" down would be to fire a rocket pushing the vehicle backward: a retrorocket. Of course, every pound of propellant used at the end would have to be launched from the Earth, slowed down to land at the moon, launched from the moon, and then slowed down near Earth. In the initial stage alone, that would cost 10 pounds of propellant per pound of retrorocket fuel. Thus a huge penalty is paid. What did the *Apollo* spacecraft do to slow down? The designers might have said, "Thank you, God, for providing an atmosphere on planet Earth. Not only does it give us air to breathe and protect us against ultraviolet rays, but we can use it to slow down a rocket entering into the atmosphere from outer space." The big difficulty then becomes being smart enough to be able to get exactly the proper angle of entry. Those who saw the movie *Apollo 13* know that achieving the proper angle is crucial for successful reentry. How much propellant is required? Almost none. Brainpower often triumphs over brute force.

This leads naturally to yet another false assumption made by Dr. Campbell. He assumed that the rocket would have to provide all the energy for the flight. But smart engineers realized that "cosmic freeloading" can be a great assist. We launch to the east from near the equator because the Earth's surface there is moving at about 1,000 miles per hour. The Earth, with a circumference of about 25,000 miles, rotates in 24 hours, hence the roughly 1,000 miles-per-hour freebie. We also need not provide all the energy to get to the moon: Just enough is provided so that when the moon come along on its predictable flight schedule, its gravity pulls the rocket in the rest of the way. This increases the available payload. Similarly, just about all of our deep-space flights have involved cosmic freeloading. For example, the early *Pioneer* and *Voyager* spacecraft have flown past Saturn, Uranus, and Neptune using gravitational assists at no cost except being in the right place at the right time to get a free boost from Jupiter. The *Cassini* spacecraft, now orbiting Saturn, was cleverly sent past Venus, which is closer to the sun than is Earth, then past Earth, and then past Jupiter, getting free kicks at each flyby. The *Cassini* orbiter derives its electrical power from radioisotope thermoelectric generators, because solar energy is much weaker at Saturn than it is at Earth. These have no moving parts, but take advantage of the fact that an electrical current can be generated when there is a difference in temperature between the ends of certain wires. Freeloading on Mother Nature.

Dr. Neil de Grasse Tyson, director of the Hayden Planetarium in New York City, demonstrated bias against interstellar travel when he pointed out, on the Peter Jennings ABC-TV mockumentary *Seeing is Believing* on February 24, 2005, that our fastest spacecraft, the *Voyager* spacecraft, would take 70,000 years to get to the nearest star, and that scientists like to be alive when their experiments are completed. He somehow neglected to mention that *Voyager* hasn't had a real propulsion system on it since it left the Earth. His comment was the equivalent of suggesting that throwing a bottle in the ocean tells you how long it would take to cross the ocean. In fact, large liners do it in six days, the *Concorde* did it in a few hours, and the space station covers the distance across the Atlantic in less than 12 minutes.

I have found that many people seem to think that space probes are powered by rockets all during their flights. Not so; they are coasting almost all the way, with gravitational assists changing both directions and speeds. On our journeys to the moon, powered flight consisted of about 17 minutes of the 69-hour journey. The coasting upper stage gradually slowed down under the influence of the Earth's gravitational field. If the moon hadn't come along at the right time, the rocket would have come back to Earth instead of being attracted to the moon, similar to an arrow shot upward. Once again, being clever is more important than being powerful.

Although Dr. Campbell was guilty of false reasoning and ignorance about the engineering aspects of spaceflight, he can't really be blamed for making yet another false assumption. He, as with so many other debunkers of spaceflight, assumed that chemical rockets were the only way to travel in space. Is there another candidate? Of course! Nuclear energy. The technological development of nuclear energy was achieved in secret under the Manhattan Project to develop nuclear weapons. The first atomic bomb (or, more properly, "nuclear weapon," because it is the energy of the nucleus that is being tapped, rather than the energy of the atom) was secretly exploded at Trinity Site at White Sands Missile Range near Alamogordo, New Mexico, on July 16, 1945. The first nuclear chain reaction was accomplished under the direction of Nobel Prize–winning physicist Enrico Fermi, in secret, under the squash court of Stagg Field at the University of Chicago on December 2, 1942. The bombs dropped on Hiroshima on August 6, 1945, and Nagasaki on August 9, 1945, swiftly brought an end to the horrors of World War II on August 15, 1945. The allies alone dropped 3.4 million tons of chemical explosives on Germany and Japan during World War II.

The single bomb dropped on Hiroshima released the energy equivalent to exploding 12,000 tons or 24 million pounds of TNT. Normally, the most powerful conventional bombs dropped during the war had been 10-ton "blockbusters." So, an early nuclear-fission bomb released 1,200 times the energy of our most advanced conventional bomb. How could this be?

Normal chemical reactions, including combustion, involve energies of a few electron volts per event. An electron volt is a measure of energy. In contrast, one nuclear fission event, when a heavy Uranium-235 or Plutonium-239 nucleus absorbs a neutron and fissions (splits), releases about 200 million electron volts of energy because it converts a small amount of mass to a huge amount of energy. $E=mc^2$, as predicted by Albert Einstein. The mass is m, c is a big number (the speed of light), and E is energy. By this equation, a small fuel bundle in the Canadian CANDU nuclear power reactor weighing less than 50 pounds and using natural uranium fuel rather than the fully enriched uranium (or Plutonium) used in weapons, and about 20 inches long, produces as much energy as burning 400 tons of coal (or four railroad coal cars). Much more powerful fission weapons have been built since Hiroshima. Even more impressive (or depressive, from humankind's viewpoint) has been the development of nuclear fusion weapons, or hydrogen bombs. Fission involves the absorption of a neutron and the breaking-up of a big, heavy uranium or plutonium nucleus. In fusion, two very light nuclei of hydrogen and/or helium combine, or fuse, to release millions of electron volts of energy per fusion event. Typically, two positively charged particles would repel each other. However, if a fission weapon is exploded first, it gives hydrogen ions sufficient energy to overcome their normal electrical repulsion and release fusion energy. Now the amount of energy released per large fusion weapon is typically measured in millions of tons of TNT equivalent, or megatons. The Soviet Union has exploded a 50-megaton bomb that released about 4,000 times the energy of the Hiroshima fission weapon. Such a weapon exploded over New Jersey could start fires from Philadelphia to New York, besides all the immediate destruction. The first fusion weapon exploded by the United States in the Pacific in the fall of 1952 produced a fireball 3 miles in diameter. I wonder what the aliens thought of that giant firecracker! This was only 14 years after scientists determined that fusion reactions powered the stars, including our sun.

Scientists recognized in the 1940s that it should be possible, at least theoretically, to use nuclear energy for propulsion for ships, airplanes, and rockets—not just for bombs. In ships, one would use a nuclear reactor to produce steam instead of burning coal or oil. The steam could turn a turbine and a propeller and produce electricity. Theoretically, a ship reactor could run for years without refueling, meaning a ship could move rapidly without any concern for how much fuel was being burned and how near or far fuel replenishment could be. Space otherwise needed for oil or coal could be used for weaponry. In the case of a nuclear submarine, because no air was being burned, it could stay underwater for months or years. WWII submarines were, in reality, surface ships that could operate underwater for a limited time; nuclear submarines have indeed gone completely around the globe under water. The nuclear reactors on a modern aircraft carrier can operate for an incredible 18 years without refueling.

In 1946, the U.S. government established the NEPA (Nuclear Energy for the Propulsion of Aircraft) program, involving the Oak Ridge National Laboratory and Fairchild Aviation Corporation. There were starts and stops in the program. Everyone recognized that if a suitable nuclear fission reactor could be operated on an airplane, it could replace the burning of jet fuel. The range would be unlimited. Refueling of the reactor might only be needed after a thousand or more hours of flight. Any place in the world would be within the range of a nuclear-powered bomber. It was also recognized that there would be very serious engineering problems associated with operating the reactor at a sufficiently high temperature to provide hot air to jet turbines. Providing sufficient radiation shielding around the high-temperature, high-performance reactor to protect the flight crew would also be a real challenge because of the weight limits on airplanes, which are much lower than for ships. In addition, there was the concern about what happens if a highly radioactive system were to crash in a populated area. Further, conventional planes normally land carrying much less weight than when they took off because of the use of the aircraft fuel; a nuclear-powered airplane would weigh as much upon landing as on takeoff.

The program was subject to all kinds of political intervention, feasibility studies, and more. It was in its heyday from about 1956 until it was canceled in 1961. I worked at the General Electric Aircraft Nuclear Propulsion Department in Evendale, Ohio, just north of Cincinnati, from 1956 to 1959, and at full tilt, we employed 3,500 people, of whom 1,100 were engineers and scientists. Our annual budget was running about $100 million, not counting the government-supplied enriched uranium and a multitude of facilities. That was a lot of money for 1958. In my opinion, what the program desperately needed and didn't have was strong leadership, such as provided by Admiral Hyman Rickover to the nuclear submarine program.

Goals were constantly being changed. The plane would be supersonic. No—it would be subsonic. It would be designed to fly very high. No—it would fly very low to avoid radar. We did successfully operate jet engines on nuclear power at the Idaho test station in the late 1950s. Several different relatively primitive systems were tested, with designs being developed for much more sophisticated systems, but were never brought to fruition. An enormous amount of technologically advanced engineering work was done to meet the requirements for materials that could operate at high temperatures in a nuclear environment. For example, for shielding, lead and concrete were out of the question. I did a lot of shielding experiments with such exotic materials as lithium hydride, boron carbide, beryllium, tungsten alloys, depleted uranium, and more. Almost all test data was classified Secret Restricted Data.

Pratt & Whitney Aircraft, which is a major manufacturer of jet engines, had a smaller program going using an indirect cycle: A liquid metal would be heated in the reactor, and then the heat would be transferred to air that was sent through the turbine. The reactor would be smaller than in the air-cooled GE concept, so the shielding would be lighter, but the heat exchanger created serious problems, because materials resistant to corrosion by the liquid metal were not resistant to oxidation in the air at the required high temperatures. Reactor power levels would be about 400 Megawatts. A typical large terrestrial nuclear power plant today operates at 2,000 to 4,000 Megawatts, with an electricity production rate of 600 to 1,300 Megawatts. They are obviously not portable.

The Aircraft Nuclear Propulsion program was canceled in 1961. A few years later, on July 1, 1964, a nuclear ramjet program involving Ling-Temco Vought, Livermore Labs, and the Pluto and Tory projects was also canceled, having begun in 1957. The ramjet, which works most effectively at high speeds, forcing air through the reactor to gain energy, would be carried aloft by a large airplane and then lighted up. It would operate at about 600 Megawatts, would be unmanned, and would carry nuclear weapons almost anywhere because essentially no fuel would be consumed. Ground tests, but no flight tests, were conducted.

Test model GE aircraft nuclear propulsion system, Idaho Test Station. Courtesy of the U.S. government.

General Electric flight type XMA-1A aircraft nuclear propulsion engine, circa 1958. Courtesy of the U.S. government.

All through the 1960s, work was done on a succession of nuclear rocket engines under the KIWI, Rover, Phoebus, XE-1 and NERVA programs sponsored by the Atomic Energy Commission and the NASA Space Nuclear Propulsion Office. Companies involved included Aerojet General, Westinghouse Astronuclear Laboratory, and Los Alamos National Laboratory. A number of different systems were successfully ground tested at the nuclear test site in Nevada, near Jackass Flats and west of Las Vegas, not too far from where nuclear weapons were tested or from the infamous Area 51. They all used cold liquid hydrogen as a propellant. It would be pumped through the reactor to heat it, and exhausted at high temperatures out the nozzle. The fuel elements with their narrow coolant channels were made of various carbon-uranium compounds. The incoming hydrogen was at temperatures close to absolute zero and exited a few feet away at a temperature of around 4,000 degrees. Because hydrogen is the lightest and most abundant of all the elements, it would reach a higher velocity than the heavier exhaust products produced with conventional rocket propellants, such as hydrogen combined with oxygen. It would be available everywhere in the galactic neighborhood, unlike uranium. The most powerful Phoebus 2B system was successfully operated at a power level of about 4,400 Megawatts (twice that of the Grand Coulee Dam), though the reactor was only several feet long and less than 7 feet in diameter.

Almost all of these systems were tested with the nozzle exhausting upward. An XE-1 flight-type system was operated by Aerojet with the nozzle facing down and a huge heavily cooled exhaust duct. This was close to a flight-type system.

One of the most interesting events in my nuclear career in industry involved the successful testing of the NRX-A6 nuclear rocket reactor produced by Westinghouse Astronuclear Laboratory in Pittsburgh, Pennsylvania. The power level was "only" 1,100 Megawatts. We were listening to the Nevada test live in Pittsburgh. I had several radiation-monitoring devices on the system, and had made some earlier measurements to determine nuclear heating rates in the all important reactor control systems. At most, the reactor could be operated for one hour due to a limitation as to how much liquid hydrogen could be stored at the test facility, and the requirement for cooling the reactor after shutdown. No one had any idea how long the system could be operated until the fuel elements gave way because of the high temperatures and pressure in the reactor. Estimates ran from 10 to 40 minutes. Over the public address system we heard the operating time, nominal temperatures, and pressures: 5 minutes, 10 minutes, 20 minutes, 30, 40. Finally, the full 60 minutes. We were one very happy group—that time would cover necessary operations for a flight to Mars for a nuclear upper stage. (It was not intended that they be used as a launch vehicle from Earth.)

FOR OFFICIAL USE ONLY - UNCLASSIFIED
NRX-A6 REACTOR AT TEST CELL 'C' (SIDE VIEW)   612252-1

Westinghouse Astronuclear Lab NRX-A6 nuclear rocket engine (1,100 Megawatts). Courtesy of the U.S. government.

Aerojet General XE-1 flight-type nuclear rocket engine, downward-firing (1,000 Megawatts).Courtesy of the U.S. government.

Los Alamos Phoebus 1-B on nuclear rocket engine (4,400 Megawatts) at test stand.Courtesy of the U.S. government.

Despite numerous successful tests, these programs were also canceled in the early 1970s. Once again, the problem, from my viewpoint, was a total lack of leadership. There were no specific goals for the projects! I sat in on a very sad meeting at Aerojet General in 1968 in Sacramento, California, where the government people were trying to determine what they should do with the nuclear rocket engine! It could be used to set up a lunar base, for Earth orbit–lunar orbit rendezvous, as an upper stage for a trip to Mars, and more. A nuclear fission rocket engine is roughly twice as efficient as a chemical rocket engine, so it could loft roughly twice the payload, for an upper stage, as a chemical rocket. So, of course, the program was canceled. They couldn't decide. I was amused when, 30 years later, as a panel participant at a UFO conference in Cocoa Beach, Florida, I sat next to a NASA representative. He noted that they were thinking about the *possibility* of considering *maybe* starting a nuclear rocket program up again for use on a manned expedition to Mars. Thirty years late.

Although nuclear fission rocket engines have been ground tested, they are certainly not the ultimate in nuclear rocket technology, because they are still limited by the maximum operating temperatures of solid nuclear fuel. One possibility is the use of a gaseous core nuclear rocket engine. The temperature of the fissioning gas in the center could be very high indeed. The Soviets had, many years ago, actually operated a rather low-temperature gaseous core. There are many gaseous compounds of uranium, including uranium hexafluoride, which is passed through huge gaseous diffusion plants to produce enriched uranium having more than the original 0.7 percent U-235. Compact nuclear fission reactors have also been operated in outer space to produce electricity for use onboard a spacecraft. The Soviet Union launched more than three dozen such systems. And the United States only one.

A Megawatt (one million watts of energy) can be generated in a reactor smaller than a waste basket. It would have to operate at very high temperatures to reduce the weight of the radiator (roughly the same function as the radiator on an automobile engine), getting rid of the energy, not producing electricity. A typical plant might be 25 to 50 percent efficient. The reason for the high temperature is the need to radiate energy. A law of physics says that the amount of heat that can be radiated (given off) per unit area is proportional to the fourth power of the temperature. In other words, if one doubles the temperature of the radiating surface, one can get rid of 16 ($2 \times 2 \times 2 \times 2$) times as much energy.

The weight decreases with decreasing size, and weight is the problem for anything launched into space. In a typical example of a very well-educated academic making a pronouncement about a subject about which he knows almost nothing, we have the claim of Dr. Lawrence Maxwell Krauss, professor of physics and astronomy at Case Western Reserve University in Cleveland, Ohio, in his book *The Physics of Star Trek*, noting that perhaps such reactors might be operated in the future. Apparently he was unaware of all those reactors already operated in space by the Soviet Union. I was acutely aware of them because in 1961, I did a study at Aerojet General Nucleonics under contract to the Foreign Technology Division of the United States Air Force at Wright-Patterson Air Force Base in Ohio. (FTD was, by the way, also the organization to which Project Blue Book reported.) The study was entitled "Analysis and Evaluation of Fast and Intermediate Reactors for Space Vehicle Applications." The key word omitted was *Soviet*. I was to review Soviet technical literature (in translation) dealing with all aspects of the design of space nuclear systems, reactor physics, heat transfer, radiation shielding, liquid metal corrosion, and so on. I went back to Columbus, Ohio, every month or two to look at the huge foreign technology files of the Battelle Memorial Institute, which also had done the work on *Project Blue Book Special Report Number 14*, as noted in Chapter 1. I predicted in my classified final report that the Soviets would indeed be launching nuclear reactors for use in space. They were doing all the right research, though often not mentioning the space nuclear power application. I was probably the only scientist in North America pleased to hear about the crash of the *Cosmos 954* satellite in Northern Canada on January 24, 1978. It had on board what was listed as the 13th Soviet space nuclear reactor system. My prediction was right on. Many years later, the U.S. Air Force actually purchased one of the Soviet systems!

None of the many press articles about the crash (in a very remote area) noted that the Soviets had systems producing far more power in space than any U.S. system. This power could be used for particle beam weapons, laser weapons, and side band radar to keep track of the positions of all ships on the ocean. Such reactors could also be used to supply the power for an ion or plasma propulsion system. These would provide low acceleration for a long period of time, and have been demonstrated by keeping a space system from losing altitude because of the slight drag of what little atmosphere is at orbital altitude. Instead of these fascinating points, the focus was on radioactivity that might be ingested by the few caribou in the area!

Of much greater interest than a nuclear electric system is the use of nuclear fusion rockets for deep-space propulsion systems. Fusion is the process that produces almost all of the energy generated in stars. The strong gravitational field and high temperatures make it possible for isotopes of hydrogen and/or helium to react with each other despite the fact that charged particles are normally repelled by other particles of the same charge. There are many different fusion reactions. As noted previously, they produce the huge amount of energy generated by hydrogen bombs, which can be fission-fusion bombs or even fission-fusion-fission bombs. There are two very important design requirements: One is the holding-together of the initial system long enough for the reactions to take place, rather than for the particles to be dispersed. The other is to have a supply of the right kind of isotopes, several of which are not readily available in nature.

Many of the reactions unfortunately deliver most of their energy in the form of energetic neutrons that go out in all directions. To use them for propulsion, one would have to absorb them and heat a material around the reaction chamber to perhaps produce electricity to kick some charged particles out of the rocket. Far more attractive is the use of a reaction, such as hydrogen-2 and helium-3. A normal helium (He-2) nucleus has two protons and two electrons orbiting the outside of the nucleus. Helium-3 has two protons and one neutron. A normal hydrogen atom has one proton in the nucleus and one electron outside. However, heavy hydrogen, or deuterium, has a neutron and a proton in the nucleus and only one electron. Without the electron the positively charged heavy hydrogen isotope is known as a deuteron. Each reaction produces different particles, and different amounts of energy. If a deuteron is reacted with a helium-3 nucleus (two protons and a neutron), a large amount of energy is released. It comes from converting a little of the mass to a lot of energy ($E=mc^2$), and all but 2.5 percent of the energy is in the form of charged particles. These have the enormous advantage of being able to be directed by electric and magnetic fields, so they can be emitted out the back end of the rocket, unlike the situation with the neutrons. The ejected particles typically have about 10 million times as much energy per particle as can be obtained in a chemical rocket. Progress really does come from doing things differently.

Fusion rockets would not generally be used to launch rockets from a dense planet such as Earth with a thick atmosphere, but again, as with fission rockets, for an upper stage. Hydrogen, as noted earlier, is the lightest element known, and makes up more than 90 percent of the universe. No matter where one went, there would be hydrogen around. Helium is the second most abundant and second lightest element. Helium-3 supposedly is in some of the rocks on the moon and also in the atmosphere of Jupiter.

Now, many people may wonder: If fusion is so good for energy production, why are we not producing electricity in fusion power plants? Large central station power plants have to be operated down here on Earth (unless producing electricity from solar energy absorbed in near space). A very good vacuum system is required for the fusion reaction chamber, and the challenge is one of economics, because there are other means long developed for producing electrical power, such as burning coal or oil, or using fission nuclear reactors or hydroelectric plants. Outer space provides an outstanding vacuum chamber at no cost, and allows the achievement of a particular objective—rapid deep-space travel—not otherwise achievable.

Test Cell C, Nuclear Rocket Test Station, Nevada.
Courtesy of the U.S. government.

It seems strange that Dr. Krauss seemed to think there was no way to assure that the products of nuclear fusion reactions could be ejected out the back of a rocket. As one expects, he hadn't done his homework. I can only laugh at the claims of a character named David Adair, who gives lectures and appears on late-night talk shows, that at age 17 he built a fusion rocket and sent it successfully on a flight from White Sands, New

Mexico, to Area 51 in Nevada—the reactions won't work in the atmosphere. And he wouldn't have had access to the right isotopes or the resources to build such a rocket.

Many papers have been published about fusion propulsion, including the Daedalus study published in the *Journal of the British Interplanetary Society*. When I worked for Aerojet General Nucleonics in the walnut orchards (now wall-to-wall housing) of San Ramon in Northern California in 1962, we had an Air Force contract to look at fusion propulsion for deep-space travel. What made it seem feasible was the discovery of new superconducting magnet materials that would allow the fabrication of relatively light-weight, powerful magnets having no resistance to the flow of an electric current, being able to remain superconducting even in high magnetic fields, and requiring little power in contrast with normal heavy magnets used to contain a fusioning plasma. Hospital MRI systems use such magnets. The study was done under the direction of world-famous plasma physicist John Luce, who had headed the DCX Fusion Program at Oak Ridge National Laboratory in Oak Ridge, Tennessee.

Luce was one of the brightest men I ever knew, though he only had a high school diploma (and an honorary PhD in physics). He also had 40 patents on sophisticated plasma physics devices. He had a real understanding of how the plasma world works, and was always doing things that the PhD physicists working under him said couldn't be done. He was a true leader of men as well, and inspired all those working for him mostly by his own example. I worked on designing the radiation shielding needed to protect the crew against those few neutrons emitted. Of course, so far as we know, the government has not decided on any mission to the stars, or to spend the huge amounts of money needed to build and launch such a system. It probably shouldn't be done unless sponsored by planet Earth, rather than by one nation. Incidentally, there are small commercial devices (accelerators) available that use fusion reactions from hydrogen and helium to produce neutrons. These devices are put down oil well bore holes to determine the amount of oil present, because some of the neutrons produced interact with hydrogen atoms in any oil surrounding the bore hole.

This is not science fiction.

Something close to science fiction was studied for several years under the Orion program, involving pulsed fusion propulsion systems. A rocket would carry a large supply of H-bombs and eject them out the back end, one at a time. They would be exploded to give substantial push to a pusher plate at the back of the rocket, eventually producing high velocity for it. The Orion program, using nuclear fusion weapons dropped out of the back of the rocket to accelerate the rocket, involved two well-known scientists, Ted Taylor and Freeman Dyson. The nuclear test ban treaty prohibited testing the weapons in outer space; most of the fusion energy would be wasted and not impinge on the pusher plate.

Is fusion the ultimate means of deep space propulsion? Of course not, because technological progress comes from doing things differently in an unpredictable way. We have had sophisticated technology for less than 200 years, yet, as noted in Chapter 3, there are stars less than 40 light-years away that are a billion years older than our sun. Many different approaches to exploring space have already been suggested: Fourth-dimensional space-time warping using wormholes is a good science fiction technique alluded to in Carl Sagan's *Contact*. Dr. Eric Davis, a physicist working for the National Institute of Discovery Sciences in Las Vegas, Nevada, discussed more scientifically appealing approaches. People have talked about developing antigravity or somehow changing the attraction of gravity to repulsion. As far as I know, this has never been done. There is serious discussion about somehow shielding against gravity by rapidly spinning a superconducting material and supposedly measuring reduced gravity above it. The NASA Marshall Space Flight Center in Huntsville, Alabama, was investigating such an approach based on controversial research by Russian scientist Eugene Podkletnov. There is also considerable interest in tapping the supposedly vast energy of the vacuum: so-called zero-point energy. Several abstruse papers have been published in reputable physics journals by Dr. Harold Puthoff of Austin, Texas, and Dr. Bernard Haisch of California. Both were coauthors of an outstanding refereed scientific paper, "Inflation-Theory Implications for Extraterrestrial Visitation," published by them, Dr. Bruce Maccabee, and Dr. James Deardorff in the *Journal of the British Interplanetary Society*. They conclude that new developments in theoretical physics indicate that interstellar travel is indeed feasible. Not surprisingly, the nasty, noisy negativists somehow manage to avoid referencing this paper, just as UFO debunkers try to avoid mentioning the seminal *Project Blue Book Special Report No. 14* discussed in Chapter 1.

As a nuclear physicist, I have often been fascinated by the simple fact that when one goes from the "huge" atom to the 10,000-times smaller nucleus, one goes up in energy per particle by millions of times. So what will happen when we are able to dig into the quarks that make up neutrons and protons? Will a huge new source of energy be found? What new sources have already been found by civilizations only thousands of years ahead of us, rather than the much more likely millions or billions of years ahead of us that some places in the local neighborhood must be? We know that matter-antimatter annihilation is an efficient process, even if we don't know how to store antimatter.

Some readers may wonder whether it is only new sources of energy that will make star travel feasible. Of course not. It is using our minds in creative ways. And of course there are those who can only think about how *not* to travel. Dr. Edward M. Purcell (1912–1997) was a Nobel Prize–winning physicist at Harvard University, who decided he would settle the question of interstellar travel using just basic physics, and, as with Dr. Campbell many years earlier, ignoring the specifics of how one would do it. He suggested that if one wanted to journey to a star 10 light-years away using a 100-percent efficient process such as matter-antimatter annihilation, one would accelerate at 1 G for a distance of five light-years, decelerate at 1 G for five light-years, and reverse the process coming home. The mass ratio naturally turns out to be absurd; that is, the weight of the rocket would be truly enormous compared to the mass of the payload. Fortunately, no sensible engineer would design such a mission profile. In the first place, at 1 G acceleration, it only takes one year to get close to the speed of light. (I have had mature scientists suggest it would take 100 or 1,000 years.)

Accelerating past that point just wastes huge amounts of energy for no real benefit. Boeing 747s stop accelerating when they get to cruise velocity and throttle down to coast at a convenient speed, as do sports cars, aircraft carriers, and so on. Secondly, as has been proven many times, Albert Einstein was right. Weird as it sounds, at speeds close to the speed of light (670 million miles per hour), time slows down for things moving that fast. Please don't ask me why the universe is created that way, but experiments clearly vindicate this aspect of Einstein's relativity. To give specific examples, let us assume one is going 99.9 percent of c (c is usually used to indicate the speed of light). It would only take 20 months pilot time to go 39 light-years to Zeta Reticuli (as will be detailed in Chapter 3). At 99.99 percent c, it would only take six months pilot time. Yes, one comes back much younger than those left behind. Kind of the gift of immortality. Go out, come back, marry one's grandchild's friend...

Some critics have objected that at velocities close to c, one's mass increases as well, so it would take much more energy to keep accelerating. Well, in the first place, one would not keep accelerating. In the second place, the reaction products from fusion are *born* with high energy; they are not accelerated to those velocities. Dr. Purcell made two more silly assumptions, probably without realizing their implication. One: he assumed that all the fuel for the trip had to be carried from the start. Why not refuel at the destination, or at convenient antimatter pumping stations established along the way? If one drives from Boston to Los Angeles and back, one does not need to use a huge vehicle, carrying all the fuel for the entire trip. One stops at gas stations along the way. One also does not need to carry a tank of liquid oxygen. One uses air that one gathers along the way, rather than storing it. Remember that there were no gas stations 150 years ago, just as there were no runways on which to land aircraft.

Dr. Purcell also ignored cosmic freeloading: Go past the sun or Jupiter or Saturn to get a free kick. Find a convenient black hole, but make sure not to get too close. Changing the basic assumptions makes enormous difference. Progress comes from doing things differently in unpredictable ways. The future is not an extrapolation of the past. We must recognize that two of the greatest physicists—Lord Rutherford, who explored many nuclei, and Albert Einstein, who determined that E equals mc^2—didn't think that anything useful could be done with the energy of the nucleus; others built new technology on their advanced scientific findings. Incidentally, I discovered that Dr. Purcell was on President Eisenhower's scientific advisory board and had a Top Secret security clearance. He may well have been involved in a highly classified advisory body such as Operation Majestic 12 (described in Chapter 11). His Harvard colleague, UFO debunker Dr. Donald Menzel, was on Operation Majestic 12, and did all kinds of classified consulting work for the CIA, the National Security Agency (NSA), and many companies. None of this was known until my surprising discoveries at the Harvard Archives in 1986.

To summarize: yes, we Earthlings can seriously think of going to the stars before the end of the 21st century, if we are willing to commit the mental and financial resources and are willing to do things differently. Who knows, perhaps we can hitch a ride on an alien spaceship going home? The first North American natives to reach Europe went back with Columbus, not in their own canoes.

The reader will note that I have not discussed faster-than-light (FTL) travel. How often have I heard debunkers say that Einstein's laws say the speed of light is the limit, so going, say, 39 light-years, would require a minimum round-trip journey of 78 years. Right? Wrong! These same travel debunkers casually ignore Einstein's experimentally verified deduction of time slowing down: As the velocity increases, the savings get greater and greater. Of course, as might be expected, these debunkers also set up a totally false premise that visitors must come from other galaxies or across our galaxy, the Milky Way. Even Dr. Michio Kaku, an exciting popularizer of far-out theoretical physics who allows for interstellar travel, starts by talking about trips to other galaxies. Let us get it straight: The Milky Way Galaxy, with its few hundred billion stars (including the sun, our star), is about 100,000 light-years across. Andromeda, the next big galaxy over, is 2 million light-years away. Why not focus on our local galactic neighborhood?

Airborne Propulsion

There are people who suggest that it is silly to worry about star travel when the behavior of so-called flying saucers in the atmosphere clearly violates the laws of physics. They cite noiseless flight and an absence of sonic booms, and that vehicles flying that fast in the atmosphere would burn up quickly because of the air friction, and that the acceleration would smash the people inside, and so on and so forth. To me, as a nuclear physicist working on far-out propulsion systems, these atmospheric propulsion problems were of great interest. The laws of physics set very few limits; our control (or lack thereof) of appropriate technology is the problem. We think very little of taking long journeys on airplanes at heights above 30,000 feet, but there is not enough air up there to breathe. A pressurized cabin solves the problem. Pilots in U-2s and other high-flying airplanes move at more than 70,000 feet, but they use oxygen, they wear G-suits, and so on.

But are there other, different approaches to flight? Because I was working on fusion propulsion systems, I got very interested in plasma physics. Most of the universe consists of plasmas: collections of charged and neutral particles in a gaseous form. It is an electrically conducting fluid. The stars are plasmas. Much of the upper atmosphere consists of plasmas. That is why Marconi could communicate long distances across oceans, as the ionosphere is an electrically conducting fluid. The space between the sun and the planets has a certain amount of plasma. The aurora borealis is a plasma phenomenon. In the mid-1960s, Stuart Way of Westinghouse Research Laboratory in Pittsburgh, working with some graduate students at the University of California, Santa Barbara while on a sabbatical, built an electromagnetic submarine, taking advantage of the fact that seawater is an electrically conducting fluid. It had no moving parts, and it worked slowly and silently slipping through the ocean.

There is a law of physics that indicates that electric and magnetic fields at right angles to each other produce a "Lorentz force" on charged particles, such as electrons, at right angles to both. (Lorentz was a Nobel Prize–winning Dutch physicist.) The force acting on the craft is proportional to the square of the magnetic field. So twice the magnetic field gives four times the force. The process controls flow around the object (the electromagnetic submarine), and reduces drag as well. The same developments of high-strength superconducting magnets that make fusion propulsion attractive apply once again. Way's effort, even noted in *Time Magazine*, inspired Japanese scientists to build a much bigger submarine actually using superconducting magnets. (The movie *The Hunt for Red October* assumes a Soviet electromagnetic submarine.)

Of course, flight in the atmosphere is not the same as motion in seawater. But throughout the years there has been a great deal of effort in the utilization of various techniques to make the atmosphere in the vicinity of a vehicle become an electrically conducting fluid. We can see the plasma when a high-speed incoming meteor heats up to a glow—that is a plasma region around it. When the astronauts come back into the atmosphere, their kinetic energy of flight converts some of the atmosphere into a plasma, which makes it difficult to communicate with them because the radio signals can't penetrate the plasma. These phenomena are directly related to the heating of the craft, the drag (air friction on the craft), the lift, and the sonic boom production by shock waves produced by high-speed flight. Of equal interest is the ability to control the plasmas so as to make them totally absorbing of radar signals beamed at them to detect their presence. No radar lock-on, no anti-aircraft missiles. That there was an enormous government-sponsored interest in the interactions between vehicles and plasmas became quite obvious to me when, in a brief stint at McDonnell Douglas in California (the program was canceled, of course), I had a search done of the technical report literature (as opposed to the general, open scientific literature) in 1969. I received more than 900 abstracts using the key word *magneto-aerodynamics*. Ninety percent of these were classified. There is a related high-technology field of magnetohydro-dynamics that has also received a lot of attention: An electrically conducting fluid passing between two poles of a magnetic field can produce a current at right angles to the magnetic field. Small systems have been operated.

Stuart Way's electromagnetic submarine. Courtesy of the author.

Much of the concern deals with the passage of rocket nose cones at high speeds with onboard nuclear weapons. One needs to know how much drag is produced, what the effect on the radar profile is as seen from the ground, and how much the path of the nose cone is changed by the plasma interactions. Most of this work has been conducted in industry, of course. Avco Corporation actually did a study decades ago showing that a vehicle coming back from Mars carrying a superconducting magnet to control the heating on atmospheric reentry here on Earth, would weigh less than the heat shield otherwise needed. A fact that emerges when one studies many UFO reports is that often a change in the color of the air around the craft occurs when it changes speed or direction. There have also been hundreds of reports of apparently electromagnetic effects on vehicle engines. I discussed this in my Congressional testimony way back in 1968.

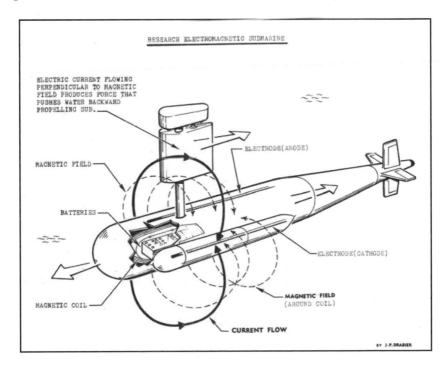

Electromagnetic submarine schematic. Courtesy of the author.

As is so often the case in many areas of cutting-edge technology, one finds well-educated people claiming, "It is impossible," or "That would violate the laws of physics." In fact, instead of saying it is impossible, they should be saying, "Gee, I don't know how to do that. Let us see if we can get some clues from observations." Some of these observations could be sophisticated, such as airborne interceptors, reconnaissance planes, spy satellites, wind tunnels, and so on. All of which data are normally born classified. Just think of how much of the technology we take for granted in the modern world would have been considered totally impossible 200 years ago. There was no electricity system, no flight system, no computers, no satellites, no microwaves, no Internet or telephone or radio or television or iPods. I repeat: Progress comes from doing things differently in an unpredictable way.

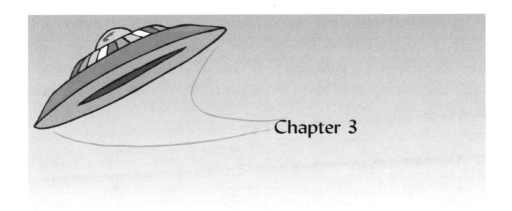

Chapter 3

From Where Do They Come?

There has been talk about the possible origins of alien life for a very long time. Long before flying saucers became a factor in the discussion, writers have talked of men from the moon, of Venusians, of Martians, Saturnians, and Jovians. Some of the more serious discussions were in response to the notion that canals had been observed on Mars by Schiaparelli in 1878. Percy Lowell, around the turn of the 20th century, made a big fuss about these. (It turned out that they weren't really canals.) H.G. Wells, in *War of the Worlds*, a novella published in 1898, talked of strange Martians so advanced they could fly to Earth from Mars before we even had airplanes. They devastated England (not New Jersey, as portrayed in the radio broadcast by Orson Welles in 1938). Others much later talked of hidden civilizations under the earth, maybe in holes at the poles. A myth was created about Admiral Byrd, noted polar explorer, going through the hole at the pole in an airplane and finding a hidden civilization. One of the people spreading the myth was a colorful character named Harley Byrd, supposedly the admiral's nephew (later supposedly his grandson!). I checked years ago with Admiral Byrd's pilot, who told me that he was with Byrd on every mission, and it never happened. He did add that it had already come out that sometimes Byrd drank too much, at which time he might have said anything. I checked with the Byrd family and found there was no nephew or grandson named Harley.

The focus was, of course, on our own solar system, because it wasn't accepted until after 1925 that the universe was much larger than had been thought to be the case. Those nebulae, just "clouds" way out there, turned out to be other galaxies. As the equipment got better we learned more. The 100-inch telescope on Mt. Wilson was a real advance, and then the 200-inch diameter mirror on Mt. Palomar (1949) became the best instrument. Now we have spectacular achievements, such as the Hubble telescope in orbit, that need not worry about the influence of the atmosphere. Soon there will be much better optical and radio telescopes in orbit. Very sensitive electronic devices have overtaken film for monitoring faint light from distant worlds.

It is tempting to forget that our galaxy is only about 100,000 light-years across, about 15,000 light-years thick, and has probably somewhere between 100 and 400 billion stars. There are billions of other galaxies, and the universe is not only very large—we have gathered light that has been traveling a distance of about 13.6 billion light-years—but also very old. The SETI people want to listen for radio signals from all the nearby stars, and to look for powerful optical signals such as those we can send right now—even though we have only had lasers since 1958. I don't think our lasers are the best there will be in even 50 years, no less 5,000 or 5 million.

Now there is general agreement that if there are advanced civilizations out there, they probably reside on planets perhaps similar to ours or others in our solar system. The first discovery of an exoplanet (also known as an *extrasolar planet*, or a planet outside of our solar system) took place in 1992, and was made using a relatively crude technique. By monitoring the position of the star as a function of time against background stars, it was found that there were wiggles in the curves. These were almost certainly due to the fact that the center of gravity of a solar system having some big planets is not in the center of the star, but changes locations as the planets move around it. All heavenly bodies attract each other, but, for example, when Jupiter and Saturn happen to be on the same side of the sun, the center of gravity about which they and the sun revolve moves somewhat. There is a second effect that has been measured, namely that when a large planet moves in its orbit so that it is between the star and our telescopes, it blocks out some of the light from the star, and the intensity of the signal decreases slightly. About 293 exoplanets had been found around about 200 stars by the end of 2007. Yes, there are some solar systems with more than one planet.

"Well," the impatient ones ask, "have we found any Earth-like planets?" Not really, but that doesn't mean they are not there—only that our measuring techniques are still too crude. The stars greatly outshine the light from their planets. An important point here, totally ignored by the SETI people, is that any civilization that has had space travel for a short time, say only 100 years, will have located other Earth-like planets in their neighborhood. They wouldn't be guessing. They would know which solar systems to explore. They would know from analyzing light from those planets if there is biological life there. As Carl Sagan pointed out years ago in *Scientific American*, they would have found at least plant life here a couple of billion years ago. We are still the ignorant ones about where there is life out there. They know there is life of some kind on Earth.

As one can imagine, all this will change drastically when a new generation of space telescopes is orbited. Within 25 years we can expect, barring catastrophes, that we will be able to directly observe Earth-size and Earth-density planets around any of the stars in the local neighborhood, if they are there; the Terrestrial Planet Finder system is scheduled to be lofted within 25 years. Bear in mind that planets differ greatly from each other even in our own solar system. For example, if you had a big enough bucket of water, Saturn would float in it, whereas the Earth is more than five times denser per unit volume than is water. Surface temperatures, atmospheric compositions, density, composition, and so on, all vary from planet to planet. In addition, an advanced civilization might well have established colonies on planets they have noted as being suitable for them, perhaps by first destroying anybody already there, if the emergency need for a new location occurred. Remember that other civilizations in the neighborhood would have already had an equivalent system thousands or millions of years ago, and would know about our solar system. We sometimes act as though no one is more advanced than we smart earthlings—a typical arrogance of a primitive society whose major activity is tribal warfare. It is clear on the basis of those exoplanets already observed that almost all our ideas about how solar systems are formed need revision.

Now that we have sent spacecraft to other planets, we have, not surprisingly, discovered that things are not the way we expected. Venus, once thought to be a tropical paradise (because it is always covered with clouds), rather than being quite a bit like Earth with almost the same size and density, is very hot indeed, and its clouds are not water vapor clouds, but rather something close to sulfuric acid, and at a temperature hot enough to melt lead.

Mars, now that we have explored parts of its surface with the *Pathfinder* and other probes, seems certain to have had plenty of surface water in the past, rather than having been a perpetual desert. Titan and Europa, satellites of Saturn and Jupiter, respectively, could possibly have water. Another important factor is the discovery that conditions for life are much more flexible than had been thought. Despite high pressure, high temperatures, and the absence of light (deep down in Antarctica, and even in places in nuclear reactors that have high levels of "deadly" radiation), or near very hot, very dark locations in the oceans, we have discovered extremophiles (organisms that thrives in extreme conditions). Some have suggested that life is so resistant to natural forces that it can survive long journeys though space, and might travel from planet to planet on meteors or comets or cosmic dust. Apollo astronauts actually recovered some Earth bacteria that had been left behind on parts of the *Surveyor* spacecraft on the moon, despite its exposure to the intense sunlight, space vacuum, and so on, for several years. The point here is that despite our arrogance about how clever we are, we still have a great deal more to learn about our own solar system, our own neighborhood (say, within 50 light-years), our galactic neighborhood (within 200 light-years), and within the galaxy—no less other galaxies. Andromeda, a favorite target galaxy, is more than 2 million light-years away. I don't think we need to worry about visitors from other galaxies. The local galaxy is quite large enough to offer older systems more advanced than are we primitive youngsters on Earth.

Frankly, I can't think of any way to determine the age of the civilizations visiting Earth, especially because the various groups may come from civilizations of substantially different ages. Yes, they seem to have huge mother ships or space carriers equivalent to our aircraft carriers. The earth excursion modules observed to land all over the planet (as described in Ted Phillips's collections of thousands of physical trace cases) seem to be much more maneuverable, faster, and quieter than our atmospheric aircraft. They also seem to be able to suddenly disappear from a location. We don't know if there is a galactic federation in this sector, or if we are the focus of a bunch of civilizations getting ready to join, destroy, or auction off the planet.

Astronomers have their own particular approach to the existence of other civilizations in our neighborhood. In Chapter 5 I discuss the serious problems with the cult of SETI, but first I should probably discuss the work of Nikolai Kardashev, a Russian astronomer who, way back in 1964, suggested that as time moves on, a civilization on a planet will first use up all the energy of the planet (Type 1), then all the energy of the solar system (Type 2), and then finally all the energy of the galaxy (Type 3). Many people have posited that because the energy of a solar system is so much greater than the energy of a planet, a Type-2 civilization should be a bright beacon, and easy to spot.

However, as I look at our technological developments, at least in some areas, I find us using less energy, not more. For example, when I first did computerized radiation shielding calculations about 50 years ago, the computers were relatively slow, used a multitude of vacuum tubes, and required big air-conditioning systems to keep them cool to extend the life of the tubes. My home computer uses much less energy and performs many more calculations per unit time, and has much more data storage. The field of nanotechnology is rapidly developing much smaller, more efficient systems. It takes far less energy to dig up enough uranium to fuel a nuclear power reactor than it does to dig up the fuel for a coal- or oil-fired power plant. How about what happens when we use more and more renewable energy, such as the sun, wind, and breeder reactors? Jet engines for airplanes are far more efficient per unit weight (thrust per pound) than they were 25 years ago. Nuclear-powered aircraft carriers, submarines, and ice breakers use far less fuel and total energy than did the old diesel systems. Sending radio signals to satellites, which then radiate them to receivers on the ground, is in; blasting out in all directions, with little of the signal being picked up by receivers, is going out of style.

I find it interesting that some people are still arguing for hidden civilizations on Earth (perhaps having come here from Mars), as opposed to those of extraterrestrial origin, to explain the worldwide reports of flying saucers, huge mother ships, landed objects, and the like. This is not a new idea: Jules Verne's 562-page *A Journey to the Center of the Earth* was published back in 1864. There have been many followers of the Hollow Earth idea, and a large amount of published material on it is available. They are convinced *something* is happening, but that interstellar travel is impossible, so the visitors must be from Mars, other bodies in our solar system, or underground hidden civilizations. In the first place, interstellar travel, as noted in Chapter 2, *is* feasible. In the second, building high-performance craft requires a substantial manufacturing capacity: both the requisite knowledge and some very large caves in which to build huge mother ships. Could there be bases under water? Surely. But again, where are the signs of the manufacturing facilities, and why build huge mother ships that can fly up, up, and away, if your base of operations is under the ground or the ocean? Whole fleets of saucers have been observed. With today's spy satellites able to spot the launch of a single intercontinental ballistic missile (ICBM), we should certainly be able to spot huge (as big as a mile) craft launched from underground. I am not saying we Earthlings haven't built a lot of underground facilities; of course we have, and for a couple of good reasons: (1) They keep down observations by other countries' spies in orbit, and (2) they protect against nuclear weapon explosions. The best technology for digging and excavating underground facilities in which nuclear weapons can be tested (because of the ban against air bursts), has been developed by nuclear weapons labs such as Sandia, Los Alamos, and Livermore. So it can be kept secret.

Although there have been many sightings of flying saucers heading up, up, and away, they certainly don't allow us to determine the target or home base. But there is one case that provides a clear indication of the star system of origin. That case is the famous abduction of Betty and Barney Hill in 1961, with detailed hypnotic regressions performed by Dr. Benjamin Simon, an outstanding psychiatrist who helped thousands of World War II veterans suffering from "shell shock" (Post Traumatic Stress Disorder) to recover repressed memories. The base stars in the map seen onboard the alien spacecraft by Betty Hill (and evaluated by Marjorie Fish) are only 39.2 light-years away—just down the street. As I detailed in Chapter 2, many noisy negativists insist that travel over such a "long" distance is impossible, because things can't move faster than the speed of light. The technological progress of our society has frequently been delayed by the pronouncements of those who look backward rather than forward. (It is important to note that, as will be discussed later, Zeta 1 and Zeta 2 Reticuli, the stars identified by Betty Hill and Marjorie Fish, are only 1/8 of a light-year apart from each other, are each visible to each other all day long, and are a billion years older than our sun.)

The author, son Sean Friedman, and Betty Hill. Los Angeles, circa 1972. Courtesy of the author.

Another suggestion that is often made is that aliens are time travelers from the future, and perhaps even our descendants coming back to check on things. Maybe they warp space and time to pop in and out—I have no idea how that can be accomplished. It is distressing that so much time and energy and scientific manpower are going into string theory and the supposed multidimensional universe, by comparison with so little, in the open scientific community, into the serious investigation of the flying saucer puzzle. There is a big database for the latter and none for the former.

The author, star map researcher Marjorie Fish, and an alien bust based on the Hill case. Courtesy of the author.

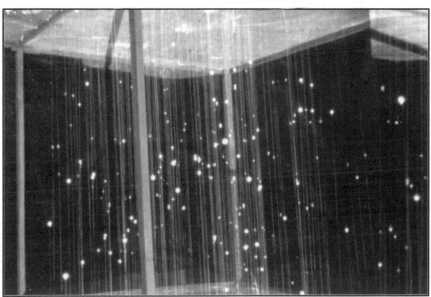

The largest of Marjorie Fish's star models (upside-down). Courtesy of the author.

My own conclusion is that some aliens have come to Earth from a planet around the old southern sky stars Zeta 1 or 2 Reticuli, that there are probably others from elsewhere in the local neighborhood, and that they have known we exist for a very long time. I certainly expect that there is some kind of neighborhood association with rules about interference with other more backward civilizations such as ours until we give signs of being able to bother them. Much as we would like to think we are the center of the universe, I am convinced we are at the edge of the neighborhood. Perhaps a small fish in a big pond?

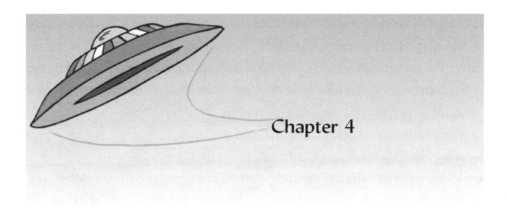

Chapter 4

The Cosmic Watergate

As noted in the Introduction, one of the four major conclusions to which I have arrived, after 50 years of study and investigation, is that the subject of flying saucers represents a kind of Cosmic Watergate. This means that some few people within the governments of major countries have known since at least 1947 that indeed *some* UFOs are intelligently controlled extraterrestrial spacecraft. It certainly does not mean that everybody in government knows what is going on; secrets aren't kept by telling everybody what's happening and hoping that nobody will talk. Secrets are controlled by an elaborate system of granting security clearances and establishing strict criteria for access via need-to-know lists.

A personal example of the limits of need-to-know happened to me in the late 1950s while employed by the General Electric Aircraft Nuclear Propulsion Department in Ohio. I was working on the development, design, and analysis of high-performance radiation shielding. Weight, temperature, and volume were important considerations, because we couldn't use loads of concrete and lead—lead has a low melting point, and concrete is not very effective per unit weight. The air used to cool the reactor and drive the jet turbines could easily be at a temperature above 1,800 degrees. I frequently reviewed *Classified Nuclear Science Abstracts*, a monthly publication listing significant research and development reports produced by government laboratories and industrial contractors. I often saw listings of reports on U.S. Navy work on radiation shielding related to the nuclear reactors used in submarines and planned for aircraft carriers. Most were classified SECRET RESTRICTED DATA. The reports I wrote about my shielding research had the same classification. Unfortunately, I was unable to obtain a need-to-know for access to the Navy work, no matter how relevant it might have been to mine. This process of restriction is referred to as *compartmentalization*. The scientist who stressed the need for compartmentalization early on was Dr. Vannevar Bush, who was also involved with the Majestic 12 program (detailed in Chapter 11).

All programs have classification guides and designated people who can classify or declassify documents. One only has access to what one needs to do one's job. Being curious about what other scientists are doing does not provide access. Being in a high-level civilian position also doesn't guarantee access. For example, when Harry Truman was vice president of the United States in 1945, having been a U.S. senator in the years before that, he did not have a need-to-know about the atomic bomb program. When President Roosevelt died on April 12, Truman had to have a special briefing, and, a couple of months later, had to decide whether or not to drop the A-bomb on Hiroshima. I have seen several indications that egos of people in government and the media are among the major allies of those trying to keep secrets—they think they know about everything going on. "If I don't know, it can't be real" is a widespread sentiment.

The typical security classifications are CONFIDENTIAL, SECRET, TOP SECRET, and TOP SECRET CODE WORD (such as ULTRA, UMBRA, MAJIC, and so on). Usually, the higher the level of classification, the fewer the people who have access. There are also, and for fairly obvious reasons, rules concerning the fact that higher-level material can't be referenced in documents at lower security levels, and there are tough rules for the handling and storage of classified documents. Even if one works in a restricted area with guards at the door, one cannot leave classified documents out on a desk at night. One cannot take them out of the area. Safes in which documents are stored must meet certain fire and other regulations. If the guards, who check classified areas every night, find classified documents, the offending party would be called and will have to come in and do an inventory, no matter how late at night. One quickly became very concerned about following the rules. Furthermore, ending a job does *not* relieve one of the responsibility of not talking or writing about classified materials. Cameras and radios are prohibited in classified areas. Unfortunately, there was also no process for informing people who had had access (such as to documents I had written) that the documents had been declassified. I wrote a number of reports that, so far as I could determine, were still classified long after I left the program. Checking from a new employer, I also found that some documents had been declassified, but the new employer hadn't been informed of that.

I remember that at one point the mention of the material lithium hydride was forbidden. A bit later it could be mentioned, but not the application for the project utilizing it. Even later, one could comment that it was used as a radiation shielding material to protect against neutrons, but not for which system design. I had the feeling that the security officer thought we would discover a magic shielding paint, and therefore he classified information that any college freshman physics major would know.

Often, noisy negativists, usually well-educated academics, have claimed that governments can't keep secrets. These are almost always people who have never had a security clearance and have no idea how security works. I still remember, now 50 years later, how intimidated I felt when I had to act as a courier for my own lecture slides to be used in a presentation at a classified conference on radiation shielding. There had been a delay in getting them prepared, and the official courier had already left. I was called in and told in no uncertain terms how careful I had to be. The briefcase carrying the slides had to be with me at all times: on the plane, in the rental car (not in the trunk), in the restroom, and so on. They obtained my travel itinerary and told me that if the plane crashed, they would try to recover or at least protect the classified material. They didn't care about me. To say the least, I was relieved when I finally turned the material over to the document-control people at the other end of the trip.

Some of the same negativists, usually with a vested interest in SETI or astrobiology, insist that something as important as the discovery of alien life would rapidly be spread far and wide by the media, and that there is no national security aspect to the UFO question. Kent Jeffrey, an airline pilot who originally was a strong advocate of the reality of the Roswell Incident, changed his mind, and, among other statements, claimed (in the MUFON journal in June1997), "The existence of a crashed alien saucer would have been much more of a social and scientific issue than a national security issue." How naïve can one get? I checked and found that Jeffrey had never had a security clearance and didn't seem to have any understanding that classified material can't be disseminated to people who don't have a clearance and a need-to-know. He even claimed that pilots at Roswell, whom he interviewed 50 years later, would certainly have known about a crashed saucer in 1947, and would have told him if they had known anything! This is frankly ridiculous. Knowing about the saucer would not have made him—or anyone else—better pilots. If they had known, they could not have talked to Jeffrey. I was favorably impressed with a number of those pilots whom I met at group reunions. They were particularly aware that planes might be shot down and them taken prisoner—the less they knew, the less they could tell the enemy.

Can I prove that governments can keep secrets about big and very expensive projects? Of course I can. Here are a few example (I am sure some readers know of many others): During World War II the United States spent billions of dollars on the so-called Manhattan Project to develop nuclear weapons in secret. Estimates vary, but all together at least 60,000 people were involved. The first explosion of an atomic bomb was a great success at Trinity site on the White Sands Missile Range in New Mexico on July 16, 1945. It was seen from as far away as 100 miles, at 5:30 a.m. A press release was finally issued, because of the many calls to the police and sheriff's offices, noting that an ammunition dump had blown up, and that fortunately no one was injured. This was a flat-out lie. Less than a month later, after nuclear weapons were dropped on Hiroshima and Nagasaki to end the war, the secret of the existence of the project was revealed, but few technical details of it.

During World War II, the German communications code had been broken by some brilliant mathematicians in England. They couldn't tell anybody because, if the Germans thought their code was unbreakable, they would continue to use it. So for much of the war there was a group of 12,000 people at Bletchley Park in England whose job it was to intercept German military communications (that was fairly easy, considering how close they were), and then decode the messages, translate them, and pass them on very carefully to those few people with a serious need-to know for them. All actions taken on the basis of the decoded messages had to be carefully done so that the Germans could not be aware of this major coup by the allied forces. Was this all released at the end of the war? No. There was no mention of this extremely important development for 25 more years. One reason was that some other countries were still using the same cryptography devices and techniques as the Germans had been. There was no point in letting anyone know about our ability to read their mail. In the Pacific war it was of great importance that the allies had broken the Japanese codes. Intercepting and decoding enemy communications doesn't provide one with ammunition, but it is surely useful to know where and how many enemy ships are sailing and enemy planes attacking.

General George C. Marshall, the chief of staff under President Roosevelt, made a strong private plea to Republican presidential candidate Thomas Dewey, during the 1944 election campaign, *not* to claim that the United States had broken the Japanese codes and knew about Pearl Harbor in advance. He expected that, if the Japanese believed that, they would change the codes we had broken. Dewey, to his credit, agreed, saving thousands of lives.

Not too long after the end of WWII, the cold war was heating up rapidly. Much to the U.S. government's surprise, the Soviet Union tested their first A-bomb in August 1949, their second and more powerful one in 1951, and their third (again more powerful) bomb shortly thereafter. One of the scariest declassified memos I ever read at the Truman Library concerned the minutes of a National Security Council meeting in the early 1950s at which it was claimed that the Russians had made more progress in the development of nuclear weapons, and techniques for delivering them, in the past 18 months than had been expected for five years. But Russia was a closed society, with Joseph Stalin the epitome of a brutal dictator. Getting spies in to find out what was happening was terribly difficult.

The Central Intelligence Agency contracted with Lockheed to design, build, and test what wound up as the U-2 spy plane. It was built on time and on budget. The program was so secret that President Eisenhower personally approved every U-2 flight. The big advantage of the U-2 was that, with its long wings and powerful engine, it could fly higher and much farther than other planes, including the fighter planes and anti-aircraft missiles protecting the Soviet Union. Because of their radar, the Soviets could track the planes, but couldn't shoot them down. They very quietly protested to the United States. The Soviet people were not told of these flights, because that would admit that nothing could be done. The U.S. public couldn't be told either, because we were violating international law. Both sides found out the truth when the Russians finally shot down Gary Powers's U-2 in 1960. There were initial denials made by the United States—bad weather had blown the plane off course; sorry about that. Then Premier

Khruschev showed the wreckage and the cameras and the live pilot who had not taken the cyanide capsule as he was supposed to. Ike finally admitted it was a spy plane that needed to be used because the Soviets had such a closed society, and we had need of knowing what they were up to, so we wouldn't be caught again as we were at Pearl Harbor. The two sides didn't conspire together. Each had good reasons for not revealing the truth.

Well before Powers was shot down, it was obvious that the Russian defenses would improve and that cameras in space, by contrast, would be pretty much invulnerable to destruction, and, because of the Earth's rotation, could spy on the entire Soviet Union over and over again. The Naval Research Laboratory (NRL), working with some Johns Hopkins scientists, and others, developed the Corona spy satellite, in secret. Believe it or not, the first 12 failed for one reason or another. Finally, number 13 was successful in 1960. It obtained more information about the placement and character of Soviet military systems than all the U-2 flights that had preceded it. Many others were flown. The first public discussion of the Corona spy satellite was not until 1995, when the NRL, in a 75th anniversary celebration booklet, spoke of their role in the program—35 years and several billion dollars later.

A somewhat similar example involved the design, development, launch, and operation of seven Poppy satellites used by the highly secretive National Reconnaissance Office (NRO), whose very existence was classified for almost a score of years. The purpose was to monitor Soviet ships at sea. The seven were launched between 1962 and 1971. NRO satellites are very expensive, and often the business end could cost close to a billion dollars each. The first public discussion of them was in 2005. Another example is the Stealth Fighter, developed mostly in Nevada around Area 51 throughout a period of 10 years and at a cost of $10 billion, in secret. The SR-71, a high-performance successor to the U-2, but many times as fast and able to fly much higher, was also developed there, in secret.

In November 2007, the *New York Times* and *U.S. News and World Report* discussed the impending cancellation of the Future Imagery Architecture program funded at Boeing by the NRO to develop an entire new generation of spy satellites. Apparently $18 billion had been spent without success in a TOP SECRET CODE WORD program. I am absolutely certain there have been other so-called black budget programs about which we have not heard anything. The point is: Secrets can certainly be kept. It may be that some of these programs have made detailed measurements of flying saucer secrets. But we can, with some effort, definitely lay out proof that there has indeed been a Cosmic Watergate by reviewing the false claims and disinformation released by various agencies of the U.S. government about flying saucers.

That the government would cover up observations of strange airborne vehicles during WWII makes sense. There were reports from military pilots in both the European Theater of Operations and in the Far East. Fortunately, the craft, though clearly having high-performance capabilities, did not seem to be overtly hostile. They seemed to be monitoring rather than attacking. If they were being flown by enemy pilots, perhaps they were under remote control or lacked armaments. If not, then there were much more important problems to worry about. Many Americans are not aware that the Germans and Japanese were good fighters, had high-tech equipment, and came very close to winning the war. The intelligence effort was of extraordinary importance in the allied victory, including, wherever possible, the use of disinformation to mislead the enemy. For example, Hitler refused to let his reserves rush to Normandy after the allied invasion on June 6, 1944, because he had been convinced by clever disinformation that the real invasion would actually come at Calais. Once he realized he had been duped, it was too late.

In 1946 there were more than 1,000 observations of "ghost rockets" in Sweden. These had some publicity in the United States, and, according to the *New York Times* (August 20, 1946), General David Sarnoff and

General James H. "Jimmy" Doolittle apparently talked to Swedish defense authorities about those observations, perhaps how their radar surveillance could be improved. A major concern was whether or not they were related to new rocket developments being done by Soviet scientists, perhaps using some of the German technicians and scientists who had worked on the V-1 and V-2 efforts. To the best of my knowledge, no one has seen the report that had to have been filed by Doolittle. Many years later I found out Doolittle was still alive and located him in Carmel, California. I told Bill Moore, who lived in California by then, and he went to visit him. A secretary was there during the entire conversation. General Doolittle remembered everything about the 1946 trip, except what he did in Sweden. He admitted having been close to Dr. Vannevar Bush, a key scientific advisor and a member of Majestic 12. A little checking established that he actually had obtained one of the first PhDs from MIT, where Bush was, in aeronautical engineering way back in 1925. He was really *Doctor* Doolittle and had a great career during WWII, which included leading the aircraft carrier–based bomber raid on Tokyo, Japan, in April 1942. He had been a vice president of Shell Oil after the war, and his contract provided that he could spend up to half his time on government work. He served as chairman of the National Advisory Committee on Aeronautics (NACA), and later of the Air Force Scientific Advisory Board, succeeding Dr. Theodore Von Karman. Much less well known are two intelligence jobs he did for Ike: A West German intelligence agent had traveled all over the United States talking to various U.S. intelligence groups, and then went back to Europe and defected to East Germany. Doolittle was asked to clean up the mess, which included talking to all the same people to find out what might have been told to the agent. Ike also asked Doolitle, who had come to know him well during the war, to do a report on the CIA. I have letters that discuss the task, but I have never found the report. In other words, he was discreet, extremely knowledgeable about technology, one of the world's greatest pilots, and well respected for his discretion. He was also well known to Generals Twining and Vandenberg, who were members of Majestic 12. Vandenberg was the second director of the Central Intelligence Group (later named the CIA), and also the second chief of staff of the USAF. Twining, who later became the chairman of the Joint Chiefs of Staff, was head of the Air Materiel Command (AMC) at Wright-Patterson Air Force Base near Dayton, Ohio, in July 1947.

In a widely disseminated newspaper article on July 8, 1947, Twining was quoted as saying that the flying saucers being observed all over the United States were not the result of a secret government project. This is on the same front page of the *Roswell Daily Record* with the famous headline "RAAF Captures Flying Saucer on Ranch in Roswell Region." In the late 1980s I was able to prove that General Twining had gone to New Mexico on July 7 and returned to Ohio on July 11, per his flight log and that of his pilot, William McVey. One of the reasons for focusing on Twining as an important part of the government UFO activities was a SECRET (Not TOP SECRET) memo he wrote to General George Schulgen on September 23, 1947, with these strong claims: "A. The phenomenon reported is something real and not visionary or fictitious. B. There are objects probably approximating the shape of a disc, of such appreciable size as to appear to be as large as man-made aircraft..." and then "H. The lack of physical evidence in the shape of crash recovered exhibits which would undeniably prove the existence of these objects." I have had to point out many times that General Twining could not have talked about an alien crashed saucer in a SECRET memo. Basically, this is disinformation to assuage concerns of any spies at the AMC. This memo first appeared, declassified, in the University of Colorado Final Report on UFOs (the Condon report) in 1969. Attention was later focused on him when he was listed as a member of the MJ-12 group on the roll of film received in 1984 (see Chapter 11). The group that launched (in Alamogordo, New Mexico) the Mogul balloons that the Air Force finally decided were responsible for Roswell— despite the complete lack of a connection with witness testimony—was under his AMC. In addition, Air Force General Roger Ramey claimed on July 8 in the afternoon that it wasn't a flying disc that was recovered, but a weather balloon/radar reflector combination. Twining's Alamogordo AMC people actually staged a launch of such a combination for the press on July 9. The front page of the July 10 *Alamogordo News* had the headline "Fantasy of Flying Disc Explained Here," three pictures of the launch, and a long article. I know from the firsthand testimony of retired General Thomas Jefferson Dubose, chief of staff to General Ramey in Fort Worth, that DuBose took the call from Ramey's boss, General Clements McMullen in Washington, instructing him to get the press off the Army Air Force's back, saying, "I don't care how you do it." In short, then, the U.S. Army Air Force was lying through its teeth as it smoothly pulled a bait-and-switch by first claiming, in Walter Haut's press release of July 8, that a flying saucer had been recovered, then replacing that idea with the radar reflector/weather balloon explanation that held good for 47 years. They replaced this with the lies about Project Mogul (see Chapter 9), and then explained away reports of small alien bodies with crash test dummies not dropped until 1953 weighing 175 pounds and being 6 feet tall, as opposed to big-headed skinny little aliens. Time travel comes in handy when one is lying. But of course our knowledge of these deliberately dishonest shenanigans came long after the events in question.

Meanwhile, there have been many other examples of a careful effort to cover up the truth about flying saucers. The infamous Washington, D.C., press conference on July 29, 1952, with Major General John A. Samford and (now Major) General Roger Ramey explaining away the myriad sightings of flying saucers over D.C. and elsewhere in 1952 as caused by temperature inversions was very well done. The press didn't follow up effectively, though the radar controllers have long since indicated that what was observed visually and on radar could not have been caused by temperature inversions. A detailed account of the sightings of the summer of 1952 is given in the 2007 book *Shoot Them Down* by Frank Feschino, Jr. Deception was clearly the order of the day.

In Chapter 1, I noted the totally false claim from the secretary of the Air Force on October 25, 1955, that "Even the UNKNOWN 3 percent could have been identified as conventional phenomena or illusions if more complete observational data had been available." It surely was deliberately deceptive for the press release not only to lie about the percentage of UNKNOWNS, saying 3 percent instead of 21.5 percent, and ignoring the fact that there was a separate category called "insufficient information"—neither giving the title of the report: *Project Blue Book Special Report No. 14* (the press would probably then have asked about reports 1 through 13), nor the name of the group that did the work (the Battelle Memorial Institute), nor the names of the researchers, and so on. Equally distressing is the fact that apparently no journalists asked for this information, or for the data to support the false 3-percent claim. Besides these egregious deceptions, the annual reports issued after 1955 about the activities of Project Blue Book were obviously crafted to keep the number of UNKNOWNS minimal. One example is that if a sighting couldn't be identified, but only had one witness, it was automatically listed as *insufficient information*. The sightings "still under investigation" at the end of the report period were not included. If one added these back in, the usual supposedly low percentage of UNKNOWNS grew to be close to the 21.5 percent of *PBBSR 14*. I should mention that I made numerous trips to Wright-Patterson Air Force Base, Foreign Technology Division, in the early 1960s, and met with Major Robert Friend—the officer in charge of Blue Book. During most of those trips I also visited the Battelle Memorial Institute to review their huge holdings of Soviet technical literature for a project on which I was working for Aerojet General Nucleonics. It had nothing to do with UFOs, but involved both FTD and BMI.

Of course, there are at least two other important facts that demonstrate a commitment to falsehoods rather than truth on the part of the Air Force. One would certainly expect that the best and most significant flying saucer reports would be those by sophisticated military crews using radar, gun cameras, and other instrumentation such as is used by reconnaissance planes trying to evaluate foreign aircraft capabilities and to obtain hard data. However, we know from the October 20, 1969, formerly classified statement (obtained by the late Robert Todd using the Freedom of Information Act—FOIA) by General Carroll Bolender that "Reports of UFOs which could affect National Security are not part of the Blue Book System." According to documents obtained by John Greenewald (available on his Black Vault Website, *www.theblackvault.com*, and reported in his book *Beyond UFO Secrecy*), these were to be reported by making CIRVIS reports (Communications Instructions for Reporting Vital Intelligence Sightings). Blue Book wasn't even on the distribution list for these reports. Funny that the public was never told this. It has always been claimed, since 1969, that the USAF no longer is involved with the collection or evaluation of UFO reports. As John Greenewald determined using FOIA, pilot manuals for our most advanced interceptors, well after 2004, still have instructions for promptly making CIRVIS reports about unidentified flying objects separate from observations of unidentified aircraft, ships, submarines, and such.

The second major difficulty is that those who have spent a lot of time with Blue Book files, such as Dr. Bruce Maccabee, Dr. James E. McDonald, Brad Sparks, and members of Project 1947, have found case after case for which the supposed explanation absolutely doesn't fit. It is a pity the major media have never done so, nor the debunker community, nor the SETI cultists claiming so loudly that there is no evidence. Very often, if one doesn't look, one doesn't find.

There is an additional difficulty: Propagandists have been very successful at stating or implying that the United States Air Force, and its predecessor, the U.S. Army Air Force, were the only government organizations concerned with the UFO problem. Considering that flying saucers represent a significant political, technological, and "foreign" intelligence problem, this frankly seems ridiculous. What about the United States Navy, which has observers all over the world, and, because ships are pretty self contained, can control leaks relatively easily? Trying to get UFO information from the Navy is very difficult. (Remember that 3/4 of the planet is covered with water.) I wrote to a Navy history office for UFO information, and was told they had none. I sent them a formerly TOP SECRET Air Intelligence Report No. 100-203-79 entitled "Analysis of Flying Object Incidents in the U.S.," jointly authored by the Air Force Directorate of Intelligence and the Office of Naval Intelligence. They thanked me for the interesting document, but continued to insist that, as they had told me earlier, they had no information about UFOs. Nonetheless, I have talked to many former Navy officers who have told me of sightings at sea.

It appears that there are least 16 different American intelligence agencies. Can we be expected to believe that *none* of them are involved in collecting and evaluating data about flying saucers? Wouldn't the FBI be hearing things? They certainly had files on UFO organizations, rock stars, and so on. Wouldn't the Central Intelligence Agency be trying to determine what other countries know about flying saucers? For example, the National Security Agency has been estimated to have an annual budget exceeding $10 billion. They listen to military and other communications traffic from all over the world, using sophisticated ground-based and space-based listening systems. One would think they would be hearing something about sightings of flying saucers over foreign nations such as Russia by their radar and aircraft observers. The fact of the matter is that both the CIA and NSA do collect plenty of UFO information, even if they are reluctant to release it. If they do, then one would also expect the NRO spy satellites to pick up a lot more. How do I know? The facts are reasonably clear, even if little detailed information is released.

CAUS

Back in the late 1970s a group known as Citizens Against UFO Secrecy (CAUS) made a request under the relatively new Freedom of Information

Act for UFO information collected by the CIA. The response was that the CIA had nothing to do with UFOs other than having had the Robertson Panel of scientists meet for a few days in early 1953. The CIA's negative response was appealed, and it was ordered to do a search when it turned down the appeal by CAUS. Attorney Peter Gersten led the battle. Finally the CIA was kind enough to release about 900 pages of documents concerned with UFOs. Strangely, none were classified higher than SECRET. In addition, they released a list, by date and title, of more than 50 other UFO-related documents originating from other agencies, which the CIA, by law, could not release. Only the originating agency could do that. The list included 18 documents from the NSA, some from the State Department, the Army, the Defense Intelligence Agency, and so on. Unbeknownst to the public, everybody was collecting UFO info.

An FOIA request was filed with the NSA for their 18 classified UFO documents as listed by the CIA. It was turned down on the grounds that "sources and methods" information—information concerning how, where, and from whom such data could have come—could not, by law, be released. Gersten filed an appeal, and Federal Court Judge Gerhart Gesell instructed the NSA to do a search. Much to our surprise, the NSA came back to court admitting it had found not 18 but 239 UFO documents! The agency noted that 79 were from other agencies—including 23 from the CIA that somehow had been missed by the CIA in fulfilling the earlier CAUS request, apparently because some were TOP SECRET. Of course the NSA could not release these. We said we would settle for the 160 NSA UFO documents. Again, this request was refused on the basis of sources and methods information not being releasable. We appealed to the judge and tried the legal ploy of requesting that the 160 files be shown to the judge who had already received a special security clearance to deal with the matter. Now the NSA prepared a 21-page legal-size TOP SECRET CODE WORD affidavit justifying the withholding. Judge Gesell was so impressed by the affidavit that, even though he was not allowed to see any of the 160 NSA UFO documents, he agreed with the NSA. In his ruling of November 18, 1980, he stated, "The *in camera* affidavit presents factual considerations which aided the court in determining that the public interest in disclosure is far outweighed by the sensitive nature of the materials and the obvious effect on national security their release may well entail." National security and UFOs!

Gersten filed an appeal with the U.S. Court of Appeals in Washington, D.C. I was there for the oral hearing. Frankly, having worked under security for 14 years, I was not impressed with the primary argument that the public and scientific communities have a need-to-know for everything, as I believe there are many national security secrets that should not be revealed. In any event, the Court of Appeals agreed with the lower court, having also had access to the affidavit. The Supreme Court wouldn't hear the case. So naturally we filed an FOIA request for the affidavit. It was sent, though, perhaps not surprisingly, about 75 percent was blacked out. (For those wondering why we didn't scrape off the black to see what was underneath, I should add that we got Xerox copies of the blacked-out version, so there was nothing under the black ink!) The government agencies may be lying and cheating, but they are not stupid. I must admit that I took great delight in showing the blacked-out affidavit on TV and to my lecture audiences, turning the pages and getting laughter in response to page after page of blacked-out text.

I also filed an FOIA request for their copies of 23 CIA UFO documents noted by the NSA. These had somehow been missed by the CIA when they did their search for CAUS. The NSA list of CIA UFO documents gave no clue as to their content. It took two years for me to get a response, even though the FOIA rules require a 10-business-day response time. What I received were 12 documents that, believe it or not, were Eastern European Newspaper articles about UFO sightings, fortunately translated into English. Why it would take more than a few days to release newspaper articles the Russians had the day they were published, I have no idea. With these clippings I was also told that if I wanted to

CIA UFO document released under FOIA. Courtesy of the U.S. government.

appeal their rejection of my request for their own 11 UFO documents, and had other questions, I was to call a certain number and ask for Chris (no last name). It sounds rather silly, but it is consistent in that their letters had no letterhead, which I suppose would keep me and other requestors from creating false documents. Naturally I called and asked for Chris. He told me the procedure to follow and asked, "You aren't really going to appeal, are you?" I said I was. He asked if I expected to get anything. I said "I don't know, but if I don't, Phil Klass will say I was too lazy." So I filed my appeal. Three years later I received portions of four documents. They were heavily censored. On two pages one can read eight not very exciting words. My favorite was the page showing only the words *Deny in Toto*. They couldn't even find eight words to declassify! I realize this sounds pretty darn silly. But now I had proof that the NSA and CIA were withholding UFO documents.

Things changed when President Clinton signed Executive Order 12958 in 1996, designed to reduce the huge government inventory of classified documents, some of them many decades old. They take up a lot of space, require being kept in vaults, inventorying, guards, and so on. Also it would seem contrary to the basic idea of FOIA to keep documents classified that should have long ago been declassified. The rule provided that all documents more than 25 years old automatically be declassified in 2001, unless the holding agency could justify the withholding on national security grounds. This means all documents would have to be reviewed to assure that some weren't wrongly declassified. Most agencies did little, because they expected Clinton wouldn't be reelected in 1996, and the Republicans would trash the order. They were wrong, so there was a mad dash to review. I was told the Air Force was reviewing 100,000 documents a month. In 1997 I heard a rumor that the NSA would be releasing some of its documents. I called, and the woman with whom I spoke knew who I was because she had an article in front of her from Phil Klass complaining about my supposedly showing the documents on TV without saying anything about sources and methods info that was required to be withheld. This wasn't true. But she sent me the new package. Would you believe that now the affidavit was only 20 percent blacked out? In addition, the NSA released all 160 pages of its TOP SECRET UMBRA documents previously totally withheld. There was a small kicker: White-out had been used. All but one or two lines per page were whited out rather than blacked out, presumably because it would be less striking on TV. Again the withholding exemption was "sources and methods." It was apparently mostly intercepts of Soviet radio transmission about UFO sightings. I don't think any reasonable person would believe that the other 97 to 98 percent was sources and methods information. Audiences still get a kick out of the whited-out documents.

The date for automatic disclosure kept being shifted forward in time.

Then another strange thing happened. Several ufologists contacted me to say that the NSA was no longer withholding UFO information! I politely asked if they could read what was under the white-out, because I surely could not. Of course they couldn't either. Some people have asked me if I didn't feel frustrated because so much UFO information was being withheld, even though it was all old. I have said that I would like to have the information that's not being released. However, having worked under security, I can appreciate the need for withholding some information. But at least with the blacked-out CIA documents and the whited-out NSA documents, no one in or out of the government can say that all government UFO information has been released. Still, there are noisy negativists who still insist there is no cover-up.

Another area rarely discussed is the role of NASA on the UFO scene. Some have told me that, after all, NASA is a civilian organization. Their work isn't classified, is it? Some of it is. NASA was a direct outgrowth of the old NACA, created in 1959 in response to the Soviet launch of *Sputnik* in October 1957 that caught the Eisenhower administration—and presumably the intelligence community—off guard. The big Soviet lead in space activities (the first satellite, the first animal in space, the first man in space, the first flight around the moon, and so on) was of great concern because these would indicate the ability to launch intercontinental ballistic missiles carrying nuclear weapons against the United States. NACA, for example, ran all kinds of classified wind-tunnel tests for the military. The NASA Space Nuclear Propulsion Office at Lewis Labs in Sandusky, Ohio, was cosponsor of the NERVA nuclear rocket program with the old Atomic Energy Commission. It was also involved in the design and testing of small nuclear reactors for space vehicle applications. I worked on both. Again, there was a lot of classified technology. The technical data, and measurements obtained when the nuclear rockets were tested, were classified. All people working on the program required a security clearance. Don't forget, there is a great deal of spy satellite technology about which NASA was surely consulted. Frequently, Cape Kennedy has launched classified payloads. I am certain all the astronauts had security clearances.

I had an interesting experience at an annual meeting in San Diego in 1968 of the American Nuclear Society. I was working for Westinghouse Astronuclear Laboratory and was chairing a session at the meeting. William Anders, whom I had met while working on the development of small nuclear reactors for space applications, had become an astronaut (he later flew on *Apollo 8*, the flight that went around the moon), and was also chairing a session at the meeting. We got to talking, and spent two hours discussing UFOs. I had some copies of UFO documents with me because I was giving a piggy-back lecture during the trip. He bought one of each. I said that I had heard rumors about astronaut sightings, and asked him about them. He was guarded in his response, indicating that he didn't think there had been any astronaut observations that couldn't be explained. He said it in such a way that I was convinced that I was touching on a classified subject. Yes, I had a clearance, but certainly no need-to-know for his UFO information. I have another colleague who had a similar conversation with another astronaut, who probed for what my colleague might know, but told my colleague nothing. I learned more about those astronaut sightings from the Condon report than Anders had told me. I had several long conversations with astronaut Gordon Cooper, who provided written testimony to the UN General Assembly at which I also spoke in New York. Dr. Edgar Mitchell, the sixth man to walk on the moon, also spoke openly to me about his conviction that flying saucers are real.

After a lecture I gave to a McDonnell Douglas Management club near the Los Angeles airport, a member of the large audience approached me and asked if I would speak some time later to his NASA group at North American Rockwell Downey, where the Apollo Command Modules were designed and built. Of course I said yes. I was given a nice tour of the facility. My picture was taken with the *Apollo 12* Command Module that had been to the moon and back. I gave my lecture to a NASA-only group; none of the North American Aviation personnel had been invited. I was asked lots of questions, but it was very much a one-way street. They told me nothing. I have also spoken to groups at both the Houston and Cape Kennedy NASA facilities.

The author and the Command Module of Apollo 12.
Courtesy of the author.

In late 2007, a federal court judge directed NASA to finally fulfill their obligation under FOIA to look for documents dealing with the Kecksburg, Pennsylvania, UFO crash and retrieval of December 9, 1965, after a four-year legal effort. Investigative journalist Leslie Kean and the Coalition for Freedom of Information (CFI) had been battling for four years to get this action. The Army had pointed them to NASA for more information, but NASA held back, I suppose hoping the CFI would forget about it. Kean had been persistent in her efforts to dig deeply into the UFO question. She did the first major discussion in the American press about the French COMETA report, and worked with the Sci-Fi TV network people on several of their UFO shows. She also worked with movie producer James Fox (*Out of the Blue*) to coordinate the important press conference at the National Press Club in Washington, D.C., on November 12, 2007, which was moderated by former Arizona governor Fife Symington, himself a pilot (and witness to the real Phoenix lights observed around 8:30 p.m. by thousands of people on March 13, 1997, about 90 minutes before the observation of military flares dropped that evening). The press has somehow managed to confuse the two events, and TV programs have often shown film of the flares as though they were the huge, silent, triangular-shaped craft seen earlier.

Military and government officials from such countries as Iran, Chili, Peru, England, Belgium, France, and the United States spoke out at the conference. Retired Iranian Air Force General Parviz Jafari was one of those who testified. He had been one of the Iranian pilots of an F-4 interceptor chasing a UFO in Iran on September 18, 1976. He attempted to shoot it down. All his controls went out temporarily. The detailed classified report about this fascinating event was published by the Defense Intelligence Agency, not the U.S. Air Force. It was widely distributed in Washington.

It is amazing that journalists and the general public often act as though the old USAF Project Blue Book with its miniscule staff was the sum total of the U.S. government's efforts to get at the truth about flying saucers. In the course of lecturing and responding to questions, I have found that most people have no idea how much old classified information is still around. The Eisenhower Library, for example, still had 300,000 pages of classified material a few years ago, despite the fact that President Eisenhower left office in January 1961. They still had drawers full of TOP SECRET CODE WORD material.

Disclosure Project

There has been much public discussion about the Disclosure Project, headed by Dr. Stephen Greer. There was a big Washington, D.C., press conference on May 9, 2001, at which testimony was presented by numerous former military people claiming that indeed flying saucers were real, and the information about them was being withheld. There was plenty of good testimony. The leaders of the Disclosure Project have talked about wishing for Congressional Hearings, but they have unfortunately mixed in a supposed cover-up of truly advanced technology back-engineered from wreckage recovered at Roswell in 1947. Supposedly, free energy was now a reality, but being withheld to protect oil companies. No evidence to substantiate this claim has been provided. Greer was selling stock in a company that had supposedly been successful. He didn't use government documents to prove either saucer reality or the cover-up.

I provided information to Congressional hearings held on July 29, 1968, by the House Science and Astronautics Committee, along with 11 other scientists. There was no formerly classified information presented. As far as I have been able to determine, no committee would have a need-to-know for TOP SECRET UFO information. What would be the point of the hearings? A bizarre twist was that Greer was offering to give a seminar at his farm in Virginia about everything he knew. The cost of admission would be $600, and a nondisclosure agreement would have to be signed.

Another individual who has supposedly released classified information about flying saucers being back-engineered at the infamous Area 51 in Nevada is Robert Scott Lazar. He claimed to have been a nuclear physicist working at Los Alamos National Lab. He had supposedly obtained a job at Area 51 through the good offices of Dr. Edward Teller, a leading physicist who worked on atomic bombs and the Star Wars program. There really is an Area 51, where such systems as the Stealth Fighter, U-2, SR-71, and loads of unmanned aerial vehicles (UAVs) were developed. Underground facilities there keep activities out of sight of spy satellites, and to protect them in case of nuclear war. However, none of Lazar's claims have stood up. He claimed he had an MSc in nuclear physics from MIT in Cambridge, Massachusetts, and an MS degree in electronics from the California Institute of Technology in Pasadena. John Lear, a pilot who had made flights for the CIA (son of the John Lear who had developed the Lear Jet and other advanced equipment), stood behind Lazar's claims without providing evidence. Because I was being asked about him, I did some checking, and found (with the help of investigative journalist George Knapp at KTLA-TV in Las Vegas), that he was in the bottom third of his high school class on Long Island, had taken only one science course, and had graduated in August, not with his class. This almost certainly indicates that he couldn't have been accepted at MIT, as they only take students in the top 10 to 20 percent of their high school graduating classes, and who have had many science courses. Lazar has produced no diplomas from any college—he claimed his records had been erased by the government. I checked with the MIT registrar's office, the office that holds MS theses, the physics department, and the Legal Counsel. No one had ever heard of him. The counsel said there was no way to erase all of one's records. Cal Tech never heard of him either. Lazar, when asked to name some of his professors, mentioned Bill Duxler, who was said to recall him from the physics department at Cal Tech. I located a physicist by the name of Dr. William Duxler, who indeed had Lazar in one of his courses, but at Pierce Junior College outside Los Angeles. Duxler had never taught at Cal Tech. Pierce is the one school that acknowledged Lazar's attendance. Quite obviously, if one can go to MIT, one doesn't go to Pierce. Lazar was at Pierce at the very same time he was supposedly at MIT more than 2,500 miles away.

Lazar's name appeared in a telephone directory at the Los Alamos National Laboratory. The top of the page says the directory lists employees of the Department of Energy, the Los Alamos National Lab (LANL), and various subcontractors. After Lazar's name it says "K/M Kirk/Meyer." He worked for *them*, not the lab. He was apparently a technician at the big Meson accelerator and worked with professors coming there from all over to do experiments. I checked with the personnel department at LANL, giving them Lazar's name and that of an old colleague of mine that I knew had worked at the lab. They found my guy, but not Lazar. Working for a subcontractor is not the same as working for the lab.

He had claimed at one time to have figured out how saucers work using element 115 and gravity wave amplifiers. Year later I was deluged with people letting me know that an announcement had been made that indeed element 115 had been created at a big accelerator, and, therefore, that Lazar must have been telling the truth. Unfortunately, it took almost a month of operation of a huge accelerator to produce four atoms of 115, and the half-life was less than a millisecond. Lazar had claimed that Los Alamos had 500 pounds—not possible with that short of a half-life. One also needs a million billion billion times as much. His scheme was science fiction. I received a call from a friend of his, asking what it would take to convince me about Lazar. I mentioned things such as a diploma, the title of his thesis and the name of the thesis advisor, a resume, and a listing of professional papers and memberships. I sent copies of my diplomas, a detailed resume, and copies of listings in professional group directories and alumni associations from the University of Chicago. I never got anything back. I have yet to meet a person who doesn't still have his or her college diploma.

Not everything Lazar has ever said was a lie—just most of the disinformation about his background and what he learned about UFOs. I am constantly being asked about Lazar and why he would lie. I point out that I am a physicist, not a psychiatrist. He is bright and speaks well and is handy with devices, and runs a company selling technical equipment. Many copies of a video in which he tells his story have been sold. But when he declared bankruptcy, he listed his job as "self-employed film processor"— a bit beneath his supposed professional background.

I hate to say it, but lying about educational credentials is not uncommon. I have checked up on many people, and usually ask the registrar if they get many calls about people claiming to have graduated from there, but hadn't. The response? "All the time."

In summary, then, it is easy to prove that there has been a major cover-up. I have often said that if any media group would spend half as much time blowing the lid off the Cosmic Watergate as the *Washington Post* and other media have done with the political Watergate or the Monica Lewinsky debacle, it could be done in six months if they started with those of us who have collected so much evidence.

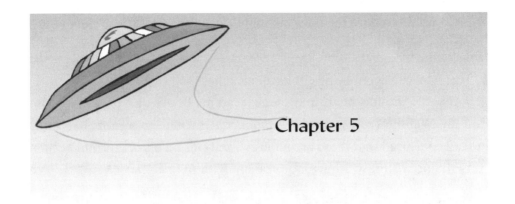

Chapter 5

The Cult of SETI

Many people are surprised when they learn that (despite my strong conviction after 50 years of study and investigation that some UFOs are of extraterrestrial origin) I think the acronym SETI really should stand for Silly Effort To Investigate, rather than the accepted Search for Extra-Terrestrial Intelligence. People expect me to be a big fan of SETI. Usually they are unaware of the generally unscientific basis for the SETI movement, and the strong negativity of its comments about UFOs, despite its clear ignorance of the subject. Yes, I recognize that the leaders of the SETI movement (*cult* might be a better word, as I will discuss) are card-carrying scientists, such as the late Carl Sagan, Frank Drake, Seth Shostak, and Jill Tartar. It is quite clear that their negativity, because of their prominence and widespread public claims, has had a major effect on the news media, the public, and other scientists. The ridicule so generated has helped keep people from reporting their sightings, professors from teaching classes or sponsoring theses, and journalists from digging deeper.

It is useful to note the basic assumptions of the SETI Search, and my responses to them.

1. There are intelligent beings at locations other than Earth.

Anyone who has heard me speak, read my books and papers, or visited my Website (*www.stantonfriedman.com*) would be aware that I am indeed convinced that there are alien civilizations on planets around other stars than our sun, so I have no problem with item 1.

2. No alien visitors are coming to Earth.

Those same people would also be aware that I am convinced that there is indeed overwhelming evidence that aliens have been visiting Earth, are being tracked by military radar systems, are abducting earthlings, and are being observed by pilots and others all across the Earth. Therefore, item 2 is false.

3. The only way to find out about alien civilizations is to listen for radio signals or pick up laser signals with optical telescopes. (The optical and radio telescopes are located on the surface of the planet and rotate with it, and the signal must penetrate through the atmosphere.)

If aliens are visiting us, then item 3 is nonsense. Perhaps it would make more sense to learn sign language or telepathy to communicate with representatives of advanced civilizations? The data indicates that the visitors can communicate with earthlings. For all we know, they may have communicated with various planetary leaders. It would appear that they haven't talked to the SETI gang. Remember that the SETI community is not actually seeking ET intelligence: They are seeking signals—not intelligence, and not beings. In an October 1994 article in *Scientific American*, Carl Sagan defined SETI as "an attempt to use large radio telescopes, sophisticated receivers, and modern data analysis to detect hypothetical signals sent our way by advanced civilizations on planets around other stars." The respectable part of the UFO community deals with the overwhelming evidence that ETI has visited Earth; I can find no reason to believe *any aliens* are merely sending signals to us.

4. Aliens wouldn't know we were here until they picked up background signals from us.

Item 4 is pretty silly if aliens have been capable of interstellar travel for some time, perhaps as little as a billion years. We were probably listed as an interesting planet with a primitive society in all the libraries in the neighborhood—until we started exploding nuclear weapons and sending up rockets and slaughtering each other. Columbus and other explorers didn't send signals to the new world (smoke signals?) before heading out. Our local neighborhood, after all, is at least 4.5 billion years old. Earth was suitable for life a billion years ago, and our technological society, crude as it must be compared to that of societies just a little older (maybe only by a million years), is only a little more than 100 years old. If there is anyone out there, some will be much more advanced, because 100 years is nothing on a cosmic time scale.

5. The infamous Drake equation is a good way to determine how many alien civilizations able to send radio or laser signals here are out there.

The Drake equation is worth discussing at greater length. Some claim that it gives us a good idea of how many advanced civilizations there are in the galaxy, starting with the basic number of a few hundred billion stars of all kinds in the Milky Way galaxy. One estimates the number of stars created per year, the fraction of all stars that have planets, the fraction of the planets on which life develops, the fraction of life-bearing planets that also develop communication technology, and the lifespan of those civilizations.

We have a pretty good idea of how many stars are created per year. We can't be too far off as to the number of planets per solar system and what fraction have life, and what fraction of them have civilizations, and the lifespan of a civilization—or can we? We have a database of *one* planet in *one* solar system that has only recently developed long-distance communication skills. We have no data on how many appropriate planets there are in the neighborhood, what fraction of them developed life and technology, or how long those civilizations—including our own—have lasted, or will last. It is pretty silly to refer to the Drake relation as an equation, as though it was scientific in the way of $E=mc^2$. Many people have used the equation to compute the number of civilizations. The results vary from a few thousand to millions. Frankly, I would say the number is probably in the many billions in our galaxy alone, primarily because there doesn't seem to be anything special about Earth. Why not just put numbers on a dart board and throw darts at them?

A major problem with the Drake equation, and SETI in general, is that it is assumed that not only is no one traveling here now, but that there has been no colonization and no migration anywhere in the 13-billion-year history of the galaxy! And yet when we look at the distribution of intelligent life on Earth (don't quibble by asking "is there any?"), we find that migration and colonization have been the major means of establishing communities. Furthermore, we have no clue as to how many civilizations more advanced than ours have been here in the past. Earth certainly had an appropriate atmosphere a few billion years ago. Dinosaurs, as astonishing as it may seem, were here hundreds of millions of years ago, and lasted for far longer than has man. We know very little about past civilizations here from tens of thousands of years ago, let alone millions. Heinrich Schliemann, a rich amateur anthropologist who studied the stories about the ancient city of Troy, used Homer's *Iliad* as a guide, and concluded that it was located at a particular spot in the Middle East. Historians of the day, in the 1870s (as might be expected, based on their rejection of the notion of dinosaurs), told him that Troy was mythical. If it had been real, the historians would have known about it. This reflects one of the tried and true rules for resistance to new ideas: If X were true, we smart guys would have known about it. Therefore, absence of evidence is evidence for absence, and there is no point in looking. That conclusion is pseudoscience, not science.

Schliemann, being wealthy, *did* look, and found Troy down 75 feet. Very little of the surface of Earth has been explored down 75 feet. So-called scholars are still arguing about Atlantis, and that would have stood less than 100,000 years ago. It took decades to convince geologists that continental drift was real. For a very long time historians believed in the notion of circumstances on Earth having changed slowly and steadily—not via disasters. Now we know that there seem to have been many abrupt and sudden changes on Earth in the past, which might have been caused by the impact of an asteroid or comets, global warming, tsunamis, nuclear warfare, massive earthquakes and volcanic eruptions, and so on. Past civilizations may well have been covered up by such events.

6. Signals would be sent here to attract our attention, rather than merely seeming as background noise, or signals sent out in all directions.

One has to ask, with regard to item 6, just why would somebody out there a long way away, and, according to SETI, never able to visit or be visited, bother trying to communicate with a primitive society, such as ours, whose technology is unknown (if there are no spies in the neighborhood)?

7. We are so smart that we can determine their communication techniques and devise appropriate signal-reception capabilities.

Item 7 is pretty silly. What egos we have that, knowing nothing about ETI, we can figure out how they would communicate! At the time an alien signal would arrive, if the sender was 500 light-years away, the sender would have to be able to accurately predict our technology 500 years in advance! We ourselves were certainly unable to predict our technology even 100 years in advance. Look at the changes in the past 60 years: space stations, the Internet, lasers, microcircuits, H-bombs, cell phones, and more. A factual story helps illustrate the silliness: In 1938, just before the Germans started World War II, one of their generals was told that Great Britain was building a series of towers more than 200 feet tall along the English Channel. They had cross bars near the top facing toward Europe. The general concluded that because Germany was working in secret on a new technology (radar) able to spot flights of British aircraft, these towers must represent secret British radar research and development systems.

There was only one way to find out. The huge Graf zeppelin was equipped with what was, for the day, sophisticated radio-receiving gear and flown slowly over water and along the coast to measure the frequency, pulse width, and other attributes of the British radar as the zeppelin passed by the towers. Then techniques for jamming it could be developed. The vehicle flew at 70 miles per hour, and didn't pick up one signal. The Germans repeated the observations just to make sure. This time they wandered over England and caused an international incident. As one might expect, the excuse was that the zeppelin had been blown off course. Either way, again: no signals. As it happens, the Brits were indeed tracking the Germans. But the Germans concluded, like rational SETI cultists, that the Brits weren't developing radar because the smart Germans would have detected it. Throughout the war, fortunately for the allies, the Germans remained ignorant of the fact that the Brits were indeed operating radar, and with no German jamming. It turns out the Germans were off by a factor of 10 in their estimates of what frequencies the Brits would use. Remember that there had been much contact between scientists of both countries in the period between the wars. There had been travel back and forth, publications in the same journals, and so on. So, if the Germans couldn't correctly predict the British frequencies, how in the world can the SETI cultists expect to guess the characteristics of technology from an alien world only 39.2 light-years away (the distance to Zeta Reticuli), let alone the 500 or 1,000 light-years away, which the SETI prognosticators assume the nearest communicating society would be? It is truly mind-boggling. (As it happens, Seth Shostak claimed that Zeta Reticuli had been listened to 10 years ago and no signal was found; therefore we should ignore the ideas of these UFO types. Give me a break.)

8. Alien societies do not engage in colonization or migration.

The notion that there has been no alien colonization or migration has no basis in fact. As soon as a society developed interstellar travel, maybe only a billion years ago, they would also be aware of the many catastrophes that could cripple a society. There could be asteroid impacts, or a supernova. They would work out techniques for moving on, and perhaps, instead of conquering a nearby society, terraforming a suitable planet so they could move in. Within a few decades of developing local travel techniques within a solar system, they would develop space-based planetary detection systems, such as the space-based Terrestrial Planet Finder system to be launched from Earth within 25 years, which will be able to directly observe Earth-like planets around all the stars in the local neighborhood. This could easily have happened a billion years ago for nearby civilizations.

For all we know, intelligent life on planet Earth was settled here in a colony or two a long time ago. I like to suggest that perhaps Earth was started as a penal colony where the bad boys and girls from other settlements were left behind to fend for themselves, and that is why we are so nasty to each other. (I consider 50 million deaths in WWII an indication of that nastiness.) For those who chortle at the thought, don't forget that some of the earliest settlers in the state of Georgia and on the continent of Australia were indeed convicts.

9. There is no national security aspect to the question of alien life. All information about alien civilizations would be immediately revealed.

I admire the way the SETI cultists make such proclamations as item 9. Surely anyone thinking about it would recognize that every country on Earth would be concerned about alien spacecraft able to outmaneuver and out-fly anything we have flying. Consider that at least two saucers crashed in July 1947 in New Mexico (see Chapter 9). There would have been major national security concerns: Are the visitors friend or foe? Are they aligned with any other country on the planet? How can we determine how they operate from the crash wreckage and measurements we can make of flight characteristics from interceptors? How can we be sure that other countries can't determine what we learn? After all, the Soviets had spies in our nuclear weapons labs. How can we determine where other crashes on Earth might have occurred, and what those countries have learned about what *we* have learned? How can we use disinformation and misinformation to fool our enemies and perhaps convince them that we are doing nothing? The Robertson Panel set up by the CIA in 1953 to consider the UFO question recommended the use of Walt Disney and other educational outlets to fool our enemies by fooling our friends. As I have repeatedly pointed out, based on my 14 years of experience working on classified R & D programs, one cannot tell one's friends without telling one's enemies. The best data would be that obtained by military defense systems, so there would be no need to clue in the public.

I demonstrated in my book *TOP SECRET/MAJIC* that Dr. Donald Menzel, an outstanding Harvard astronomer and the first major UFO denier back in the 1950s, actually had a TOP SECRET UMBRA clearance with the CIA, NSA, and various other government intelligence agencies. His colleagues were not aware of this, as demonstrated by the absence of mention of his many post-war highly classified activities (including work for the NSA as a cryptographer) in an eight-page appreciation article ("An Appreciation of Donald Howard Menzel," by Leo Goldberg) in *Sky and Telescope* after his death, and in a special issue on the 100th anniversary of his birth. Furthermore, he was almost certainly a member of the highly classified Operation Majestic 12 group established by President Truman in 1947 to deal with the flying saucer problem. His anti-UFO books and articles might well have taken advantage of his skills at writing science fiction. His first book in 1953, *Flying Saucers*, was translated into Russian, and probably kept a lot of Soviet scientists from digging into the UFO problem.

I have been asked my opinion as to who might have taken Menzel's place. Perhaps Carl Sagan? Sagan did serve on government committees and did have a security clearance. However, he had picketed government installations about various activities with which he didn't agree, and he was never in the military. Menzel had been a Navy commander during WWII, and a cryptographer, and was commander of Naval Reserve Communications Unit No. 1 in Cambridge, Massachusetts, after the war. A better bet to my mind might be Frank Drake, now of the SETI Institute in California. After completing his undergraduate degree, he spent three years in the Navy working on electronic countermeasure techniques, which required that he have a high security clearance. He remained in the reserves for at least 10 years after that, having gone from the Navy to Harvard to get his PhD in radio-astronomy. Menzel was his Naval Reserve commander. The Naval Reserve likes to make use of highly talented professors, with high security clearances, for various summer projects. Drake, in his book with Dava Sobel, *Is Anyone Out There?*, claims several times that he is sure no one is coming here, but suggests there are 100 million civilizations in the galaxy. Of course, no factual basis is given. Methinks he doth protest too much.

10. There is no convincing evidence and there are no large-scale scientific studies about so-called flying saucers or the Cosmic Watergate.

Item 10 is one of the factors that bothers me the most. I read the books of the SETI buffs. For example, I had read two books by Seth Shostak before we each gave three lectures on the *Queen Elizabeth 2*. He hadn't read either of my two books then available, nor any of the five large-scale scientific studies I discussed in my lecture. I guess this is a good example of ignorance being bliss. He still hadn't read any of those when, six months later, we did a three-hour debate on *Coast to Coast Radio* with George Noory. The vote of the listeners was 57 percent for me, 33 percent for him, and 10 percent calling it even. If one looks at the SETI community's books, mention of the large-scale scientific studies noted in Chapter 1 is completely absent. If any of them are aware of the studies, they surely have decided not to mention them or read them so they can continue to make their silly claims that there's no evidence. They also seem to have intentionally avoided dealing with the substantial literature on interstellar travel. Again a demonstration of the attitude, "don't bother me with the facts, my mind is made up." This is silly, and not the way of science.

The author and SETI specialist Dr. Seth Shostak on the Queen Elizabeth 2. *Courtesy of the author.*

11. The great majority of scientists and other intellectuals do not believe in flying saucers.

I will discuss in detail the public opinion polls about flying saucers in Chapter 8. Judging by these polls and the responses I have had from many dozens of professional groups to which I have presented my illustrated lecture "Flying Saucers ARE Real," the majority do accept the notion that flying saucers are real...when they can express their opinions in private.

12. The SETI community can speak for planet Earth, should communications be received.

I think it is laughable that the SETI specialists think they can speak for the planet. I doubt if the big shots in government (heads of intelligence agencies) who know about alien visitations are concerned about SETI messages. Foreign affairs are normally conducted by the state departments or bureaus of foreign affairs. In December 2007 there was a bit of a fuss at the International Astronautics Federation about whether radio astrono-mers should be able to send out messages to other star systems to try to get a response—without seeking approval from the other experts (they don't seem to worry about governments). Alexander Zaitsev has sent out pow-erful signals (Active SETI) toward particular stars less than 100 light-years away. The concern is that maybe it isn't a good idea to announce our pres-ence to the neighborhood, because there might be bad guys out there who would do bad things to us if they found out we were here. Think about that for a minute. If we assume they can do bad things to us, that certainly suggests they can get here. If they can get here now, couldn't they have thousands or millions of years ago? Couldn't they just check the galactic Internet to see what is happening on Earth? The locals would certainly be concerned. If they can't get here now, then why worry about them? Of course, there is the additional problem that if they are 50 light-years away, we couldn't get a response for 100 years. This time period may be impor-tant for us, with our burgeoning technological capabilities, but other plan-ets must be well ahead of us. We might even be the only "civilization" going through the brief transition from being stuck on one's own planet to being able to bother other planets.

13. The reception of a signal from an alien transmitter would be one of the most significant events in the history of the planet.

With regard to the importance of receiving a signal, there are several considerations. First, I have no reason at all to expect that we will be able to receive and interpret an alien signal sent from afar. (Would it be AM or FM?) Secondly, we would have no way of knowing if it is coming from an automatic device, possibly left to respond when they hear from us. Possibly the civilization that sent it is no longer around—especially if one assumes they are a long distance from here. If they are 1,000 light-years away, it would take the signal 1,000 years to get here. Also, could we believe anything they said, even *if* we can interpret it? Why would they waste their time and energy sending a signal to such a primitive society? Frankly, I think most people would not be very excited by a signal, because it isn't local. Now, if the story is that aliens have abducted three people from the next county, that would get our attention, because then it could happen here. As noted in the book *Shoot Them Down*, it appears that not only were military pilots in 1952 ordered to shoot down UFOs if they didn't land when instructed to do so, but it appears that we lost a number of planes to the UFOs. I have seen no evidence that the public has been told about these. This type of thing would be far more significant than receipt of a radio signal.

14. The number of advanced signal-sending civilizations within perhaps 1,000 light-years is very small.

I find it fascinating that estimates of how close the nearest sender is have slowly but steadily increased with time. Sir Martin Rees (born in 1942) is now the Astronomer Royal of the UK and Royal Society Professor at Cambridge University, and was elected president of the Royal Society in 2005. He is a very distinguished astrophysicist. He has published more than 500 papers and is considered an expert in such areas of science as black holes, quasars, the formation of galaxies, and so on. In a May 31, 2002 BBC News article, he said that "aliens could exist possibly as balloon-like creatures floating in dense atmospheres. Attempts to find them had suffered from 'flakey' associations with UFOs." He said, "We should stop transmitting messages to outer space [meaning closing down all the FM, TV, and radar installations] and instead listen for signals from super-intelligent computers in the form of strings of prime numbers or digits." He added, "You might find intelligent life so far away that signals take maybe 10 or 20 years to get here."

Less than four years later he contributed a guest column to the *Times of London*, on October 15, 2005. He began by talking about new spacecraft trying to find some kind of life on Mars or beneath the ice on Europa, a moon of Jupiter. He asked, "Could some of the planets orbiting other stars have life forms far more interesting and exotic than anything we might find on Mars? Could they even be inhabited by intelligent beings?" So far so good, but then he wrote: "The claims that advanced life is widespread must confront the question posed by Enrico Fermi, the great Italian physicist: If intelligent aliens were common, shouldn't they have visited us already? Why aren't they or their artifacts staring us in the face? Shouldn't we have seen so many UFOs that there is absolutely no doubt about them?" For those who look, so many UFOs *have* been seen that there is no doubt. I will discuss the so-called Fermi Paradox shortly.

Rees went on to say, "But the fact that we haven't been visited [which is not what Fermi said] doesn't imply that aliens don't exist. It would be far harder to traverse the mind-boggling distances of interstellar space than to transmit a signal. That is perhaps how aliens would reveal themselves first." He went on: "If we found such a signal, could we build up communication? Intelligent aliens would probably be hundreds of light-years away or more. Can we communicate with beings whose messages may take hundreds, thousands, or even millions of years to reach us?" So in three years, according to Rees, the communication distance had gone from 10 or 20 light-years to hundreds. Truly amazing with no evidence provided. Rees walked in the footsteps of other British Astronomer Royals such as Sir Richard van der Riet Wooley, who in January 1956 stated, "Space travel is utter bilge." (This was 22 months before *Sputnik*.)

15. There are probably no advanced, signal-sending civilizations within 100 light-years.

Seth Shostak, on December 6, 2007, on Space.com, claimed that "distances between adjacent civilizations, even assuming there are lots of them out there, are measured in thousands of trillions of miles—hundreds of light-years." Not a shred of supporting evidence is provided. So at best we can call it more dartboard physics. He also made another silly comment: "To hop from one of our starry neighbors at the speed of our snazziest chemical rockets takes close to 100,000 years." Why would anyone care about chemical rockets any more than they would care about slide rules for doing computations? I surely didn't walk instead of flying to China from eastern Canada. Way back on October 23, 2003, he claimed that "it is very unlikely that there is any civilization within 50 light-years." One would think that some terrible disease had decimated all life on planets around the roughly 2,000 stars within 50 light-years. This isn't even good science fiction.

Dr. Jill Tartar waxed almost poetic when, in February 2006, she made the following statement: "SETI is the only research program looking for life beyond our solar system. It is the way we are going to understand where we are coming from and how we are going to survive as a species...the search could yield headlines within a few decades." In fact, ufology has plenty of evidence of life out there now—SETI has provided none, and won't look at the ufological evidence. This is cult thinking, not science. It is fairly obvious to anyone but the SETI cultists that no signal received today could help us through our present problems, when it had to be based on info or questions received from us tens or hundreds of years ago.

Now, in December 2007, in a YouTube interview, Dr. Tartar has said that she wouldn't rule out there being alien artifacts (not live aliens, of course) somewhere in the solar system. In one of the sillier moments of the Peter Jennings ABC-TV mockumentary on February 24, 2005, Dr. Tartar had quite seriously described an encounter with a bright light while she and her husband were flying their plane at night. Could it have been a UFO? Oh, no, they finally realized it was the moon, with clouds moving across the face. This was the best she could do for a UFO sighting? There are many excellent cases involving multiple witnesses, visual and radar daytime observations of metallic craft moving in very special ways, as anybody would note who read Dr. James McDonald's Congressional testimony way back in 1968.

16. The SETI community doesn't need to provide any evidence whatsoever that there are intelligent beings sending messages to Earth that we can intercept and interpret.

Less than two years ago Shostak said, "It is a common canard that the SETI community's skepticism is simply due to their failure to be open to the idea [of UFOs]. That's wrong. Their skepticism is rooted in the lack of good evidence." A truly amazing and self-serving statement, because the community, judging by its own publications, hasn't even looked at the evidence. In a May 2007 *Discover Magazine* article, Shostak says Frank Drake had it about right in 1961 when "Drake and his compatriots plugged their best guesses into the [Drake] equation. They came up with an answer in the thousands—meaning that intelligent life is common enough that there should be a technological civilization within about 1,000 light-years." This is science, using "best guesses"?

Considering that there are at least 8 million stars within that distance, and that about 400,000 are similar to our sun, that means we are extraordinarily special, because we could predict alien technology, and match it. This is science fiction, not science. For those who need more examples of fiction in the guise of science, here is what Carl Sagan said on the enormously successful *COSMOS* TV series, seen by 600 million people back in the 1980s. On the "Encyclopedia Galactica" segment, in which he trashes the Betty and Barney Hill case and Marjorie Fish's excellent work, he says, "What counts is not what seems plausible, not what we would like to believe, not what one or two witnesses claim, but only what is supported by hard evidence. Extraordinary claims require extraordinary evidence." We ufologists have provided such evidence. The SETI people have provided none. Amazingly, Sagan's next statement was, "There must be other civilizations far older and more advanced than ours." Neither he nor any of the other SETI cultists have provided *any* evidence, much less extraordinary evidence, to support this extraordinary claim.

In his *Scientific American* article, he noted that a quite sophisticated Harvard University radio telescope search by himself and Professor Paul Horowitz found 37 interesting signals, of the billions collected by the Megachannel ExtraTerrestrial Array (META). None panned out. The 600-plus UNKNOWNS of *Project Blue Book Special Report No. 14* just don't count, apparently—they involve real people rather than just instruments. SETI folks can't deal with witness testimony, physical trace cases, radar visual sightings, abductions, government secrecy, interstellar travel—a lack of communication, to them.

The Cult of SETI

I am sure that some people are offended by my use of the term *cult* for the SETI practitioners, collectively. Let us look at the evidence to back me up. Cults usually have charismatic leadership—Sagan, Drake, Tartar, and Shostak certainly qualify as highly trained and effective charismatic communicators on science topics. Cults normally have a strong dogma—SETI surely has one: "There is advanced life out there somewhere sending signals that we will be able to intercept and decode. Nobody from there is coming here. We just need to keep listening with ever-improving instrumentation, and we must ignore any evidence that anybody is visiting." Cults do their best to ignore or repress testimony that is opposed to their beliefs— no shortage of that from the SETI community. Finally, cults tend to have a terribly enlarged view of their own importance and significance as compared to that of the rest of the world. Case closed.

The Fermi Paradox

A quick Google search yields 72,600 hits on "Fermi Paradox." Obviously, it has been a topic of discussion. The basic story, for those unfamiliar with the terminology, is that in 1950 at the Los Alamos Scientific Laboratory in Los Alamos, New Mexico, a group of scientists were talking at lunch and decided that once interstellar travel was feasible, it shouldn't take more than a few million years (a tiny fraction of the galaxy's age) for the galaxy to be colonized. As they were walking out, Enrico Fermi supposedly said, "So where is everybody?" There have been innumerable interpretations of what he meant. Some would like to believe that he was saying there are no aliens—if they are not blatantly here, perhaps landing on the White House lawn. I am convinced that is not what he meant at all. I should stress that, as noted by Martin Rees, Fermi was a great scientist. He was awarded the Nobel Prize in physics in 1938 for work he had done in Italy in exposing various elements to neutrons (neutrons weren't even discovered until 1932), and measuring the isotopes that resulted from the absorption of the neutrons.

Because his wife, Laura, was Jewish, and Mussolini was going along with Hitler and putting pressure on Jews in Italy, the Fermi family left for the United States after the Nobel ceremony in Sweden, and never returned to Italy. He was at Columbia University for a while, and then went to the University of Chicago to lead a small group of outstanding scientists to try to develop the first chain-reacting nuclear pile. After his departure from Europe, some German scientists had discovered that sometimes when a neutron was captured by a uranium nucleus, new species, having much lower atomic weight than uranium, were produced. Two key scientists who were involved were Lise Meitner and Otto Frisch. They published a paper, and shared information with Nils Bohr, the great Danish physicist. He brought the details to the United States. It was then determined that fission had actually taken place with the release of an amount of energy indicating that the difference in the weight of the new atoms and the original uranium atom had been converted to energy by the famous $E=mc^2$ equation. (E stands for energy, m for mass, and c is the speed of light.) A key discovery was that the fission also produced more neutrons immediately, indicating that a nuclear chain reaction was possible.

Fermi directed the construction of the pile (reactor), succeeding, in total secrecy, in going critical, self-sustaining, on December 2, 1942, on the squash court under Stagg Field at the university. He then became a key figure at Los Alamos in the design of the actual atomic bombs that were used against Japan in 1945. Fermi was an extraordinary scientist, one of the few equally at home in experimental and theoretical work. He went back to the University of Chicago after the war, and was one of the reasons I switched to UC in 1953 after two years at Rutgers in New Brunswick, New Jersey. Unfortunately, he soon had exploratory surgery, which found him riddled with cancer, undoubtedly produced by all the neutrons to which he had been exposed, and he died in 1954. It is somewhat ironic that one rarely hears of exploratory surgery nowadays, because of all the radioisotope and other tests the medical world now uses in place of surgery—these are a direct outgrowth of Fermi's nuclear physics activities. What particularly impressed me, after Fermi's death, was the enormous esteem in which he was held by his colleagues, who themselves were outstanding scientists. He was known to be an outstanding teacher. One of his techniques was to ask questions that forced students to think. I think that is why he said, "So where is everybody?"

The paradox is that if the calculations were right (Fermi was very rarely wrong), then shouldn't there have been many aliens about? Some say that if they are not obviously all over the place, then there are none out there. Others have suggested that we have been intentionally avoided. There are many other solutions offered. The one I think is most appropriate is that aliens *have* visited the planet, are seen all throughout the world, are detected by sophisticated instruments whose output is kept classified, and the government has plenty of reasons (as discussed in Chapter 4) for keeping the data secret. It is important that Fermi, unlike the SETI cultists, had been involved for several years during and after the war in highly classified scientific work. The Manhattan Project involved tens of thousands of people in secret. Los Alamos was a secret city. Fermi was, of course, a consultant, along with many other of the wartime scientists, for years after the war, again with a high-level security clearance. I have no idea whether he was actually aware of the Roswell Incident in New Mexico in 1947.

For sure, Los Alamos was then one of the finest laboratories in the world, and Vannevar Bush and others involved in Operation Majestic 12 would have certainly made use of their top people and expensive, sometimes unique, analytical tools. I have been there a number of times on classified activities related to nuclear rockets, in addition to when I lectured to the local chapter of the American Nuclear Society (there was an enthusiastic crowd of 500 present for my "Flying Saucers ARE Real" lecture in 1968). I know that their library at that time had an excellent collection of books about flying saucers. The first copy of *Project Blue Book Special Report Number 14*, which I had seen at the University of California Library in Berkeley, was a privately published version published by Dr. Leon Davidson, an LASL scientist, when he worked at the lab. There had also been secret meetings of representatives of a number of intelligence agencies, such as the FBI, CIA, and Air Force Intelligence at Los Alamos to discuss flying saucers in the late 1940s. Typically, in recent years, Los Alamos employed about 8,000 people, of whom about 2,500 were engineers and scientists. Its annual budget was running about $1 billion. Compare that to the typical academic project. A few years back I checked and found that the total combined annual budget for our three major nuclear weapons labs (Los Alamos, Sandia, Livermore) was more than $3 billion, and more than the annual budget for *all* National Science Foundation research programs.

Predictions in Astronomy

It is important to note the rarely advertised fact that the astronomical community has been wrong time after time in its claims about a wide variety of astronomical topics. These include the size, age, and energy production processes of the solar system, the galaxy, and the universe. Until measurements were made, the astronomical community had made factually in-error claims about all these, about the conditions on the surface of Venus and Mars, about Mercury keeping the same face towards the sun, about the lack of significance of electromagnetic fields within the solar system, about the possibility of ever determining the composition of the stars, and so on.

One of the better books about planets and the neighborhood is *Lonely Planets: The Natural Philosophy of Alien Life* by Dr. David Grinspoon of Colorado. His father, Lester Grinspoon, MD, was a Harvard psychiatrist, and had been a close friend of Carl Sagan. Lester had published a paper suggesting a Freudian explanation for UFOs in general and the Hill case in particular: Round discs, believe it or not, were symbolic of the female breast, and the large cigar shapes were obviously phallic symbols! The Hill case was a folie a deux—one person's mental construct accepted by the other member of a couple. Not an ounce of data was presented to support these quaint notions, as discussed in *Captured*. David noted that he, as a graduate student, had observed the total astonishment of the scientists present at the Jet Propulsion Laboratory in Pasadena on July 9, 1979, as the data came back from the *Voyager 2* spacecraft passing by the planet Jupiter. Its cameras were focused on the satellite Europa. The theories had predicted an ancient, dead, cratered landscape on the small ice planet. Instead they saw a smooth, bright surface crisscrossed by strange dark lanes. The theories were dead wrong.

Throughout his book, David cites examples of reality conflicting with theories and the need for a certain amount of humility about predictions. He said, "As you might expect, many comfortable preconceptions had been completely overturned. Much of what we thought we knew about comparative planetology turns out to be wrong." I wish his elders could be so honest and humble; he is much less negative about UFOs than are they. He was unaware of *Project Blue Book Special Report Number 14*, the Congressional hearings of 1968, the physical trace cases, and of the facts about Roswell. David cites only two Roswell books, one being the gross Air Force volume *The Roswell Report: Fact vs. Fiction in the New Mexico Desert—Case Closed* and Karl Pflock's book *Roswell: Inconvenient Facts and the Will to Believe*. He seems to have accepted the notion that 6-foot-tall crash test dummies weighing 175 pounds and dropped in 1953 or later were somehow responsible for reports of small, big-headed, strange beings observed in 1947 near Roswell. The late Karl Pflock did a lot of research, but resorted to character assassination about the people involved, and took the absence of documented evidence (about Roswell and Majestic 12) to mean there *was* no such evidence.

Space Travel Networks

I find it quite surprising that none of the SETI literature seems to make any serious attempt to compare our airline industry with what we might expect aliens to put together, to account for the comments made to Betty Hill by her abductors. She was told that the heavy lines on the star map she saw (probably as a hologram) onboard a flying saucer were heavy trade routes, lighter lines were normal trade routes, and the dashed lines were occasional expeditions. The heavy trade routes were between the base stars Zeta 1 and Zeta 2 Reticuli, which are only 1/8 of a light-year apart from each other. That is 35 times closer to each other than our sun is from the nearest star of any kind. They are also a billion years older than the sun.

There is a direct analog with the air and space industries on Earth: Major airlines carry hundreds of passengers on large planes over long distances. There are smaller, mid-size planes, and there are small planes carrying one or two persons but able to move at high speeds employing oxygen at high altitude. There are small commuter planes carrying 15 to 120 passengers that fly with pressurized cabins (the crew and passengers don't normally wear oxygen masks). There are planes that carry only cargo—think Federal Express and UPS. There are planes that carry only destructive weapons (of mass destruction), and have offensive guns and rockets to use for air-to-air destruction. Note especially that the passenger and cargo planes do not fly at random. There is a great deal of traffic between certain pairs of cities. There are many airports at which the biggest planes can't land; there are many towns and villages that have no airports; there are long runways and shorter ones and even underground runways and hangars. The biggest airports seem to be near large cities. We can also notice that only a few countries have big booster rockets used to launch various satellites, and that some satellites are launched atop other countries' rockets. Only a few countries have launched men into space. We further notice that some countries have very busy networks of trains and of ships, some carrying cargo, some carrying passengers. There are highways carrying a huge variety of large and small vehicles. The transport systems are organized. We notice that there are even huge varieties of ships, from submarines to battleships to aircraft carriers. The huge carriers carry dozens of small high-performance aircraft and cruise missiles. The subs carry missiles that can attack with nuclear weapons. Some ships (and some planes) can be refueled while moving.

SETI doesn't talk about sun-like stars. It never discusses special places where sun-like stars are close to other sun-like stars, and how those distances vary. They seem to be quite happy to check out each star from the Earth for certain-frequency signals. They don't look for situations in which a signal bypassing one of the target commerce stars might be headed right toward us. Radio communication systems on Earth have been evolving: Instead of just having each station broadcast in all directions, signals are being sent up to satellites, which then redirect the signals back down to Earth, saving a great deal of energy. So future visitors may be lucky to pick up *any* signals coming from Earth, because the signals will be coming back down to us instead of spreading to the heavens.

SETI people don't seem to want to discuss the simple notion that technologically advanced civilizations must either learn to live at relative peace with other civilizations or be destroyed by that advanced technology. Any visitors here would quickly realize that there are many different defense radar installations, many different interceptor planes and rockets, and different types of communications systems. They would further recognize that, despite serious problems of distribution for food, clean water, medical help, and transport systems, an enormous fraction of the resources on planet Earth are being used for military purposes. Enrico Fermi clearly recognized that there aren't fleets of alien vehicles landing at airports on Earth or visiting seaports or landing on the White House lawn, which implics, not that they are not coming here, but that they recognize the reality of the political and military differences and enmities on Earth. I can't imagine any galactic federation allowing the membership of such a primitive planet whose major activity is tribal warfare, no matter what the cost to the planet's well-being, and that of its inhabitants. The rule is: Shoot first, ask questions later.

SETI is an exercise in futility foisted off by charismatic scientists on the press and some of the scientific community. I am sure the intelligence agency personnel in the know about alien visitations think SETI is a great system for misdirecting the attention of everyday people and the media interested in space and visitors from it. I expect there will indeed be a day of reckoning, and SETI will sound as silly as the Astronomer Royal.

Some of this may sound like an academic exercise. I beg to differ. Our society is dependent on space assets such as satellites; there are about 4,000 in orbit right now, involved in all aspects of our society— GPS systems, navigational satellites, weather forecasting, communications, and national defense to a huge degree. Unmanned aerial vehicles are operated over Iraq by controllers in the United States, and our protection against nuclear-tipped ICBMs from overseas is based on detection from space within a very short time of launch, and taking immediate decisive action while the ICBM is in its boost phase—near-Earth space, between the ground and low Earth orbit, is absolutely vital. It is of interest to me that all alien spacecraft, whether the small Earth Excursion Modules or the huge space carriers, must pass through this region of space. We must be able to distinguish between them and our space-based enemies. Some countries, including the United States, China, and Russia, have already developed the capability of destroying satellites in orbit. Will we attack flying saucers as well?

I wrote an article when Carl Sagan died, giving him credit for doing more than anybody else to get earthlings to think about extraterrestrial intelligence. It is truly sad that he didn't use his scientific skills to become educated about the flying saucer data, and his great communication skills to make the world aware of that data.

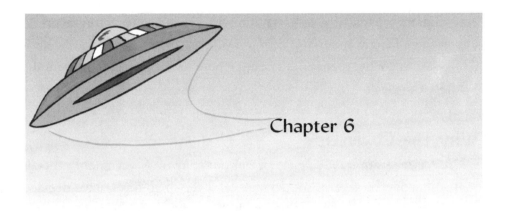

Chapter 6

The UFO "Why" Questions

In the course of my 40 years of lecturing about flying saucers I have found very little resistance to the evidence I present, such as data from the large-scale scientific studies discussed in Chapter 1. Probably the major reason is that most people have never heard of these studies, and the data pretty much speaks for itself. However, in the question-and-answer sessions that always follow my lectures, and in many classroom visits and radio interviews, I find that what really concerns those doing the asking is my reaction to various specific cases I haven't touched on, and a host of "Why" questions. As a physicist, and not a psychiatrist, I don't always have any understanding of *why* individuals behave the way they do. I am still mystified by grown men sexually attacking young girls, by priests molesting choir boys, by parents grossly mistreating their children, by serial killers, by mass murderers, by people who go on a rampage and kill a number of innocent people at a school or shopping mall. What I *can* try to do is answer more general questions about flying saucers, such as, Why would the government not tell us what it knows about flying saucers? Why would aliens come here in the first place? Why do astronomers tend to be anti-flying-saucer? Why, if aliens are coming here, don't they just land on the White House lawn?

Why the Cover-Up?

It is clear from the evidence of flat-out lying by government officials that somebody, or several somebodies, at a very high level, have decided that the public cannot be told the truth that some flying saucers are alien spacecraft. I am not talking about casual evasiveness such as a comment that "I don't think any astronaut sightings haven't been identified." I mean statements such as, "Even the UNKNOWN 3 percent of the cases in this study *Project Blue Book Special Report No. 14* could be explained as conventional phenomena or illusions if more complete observational data had been available," by the secretary of the Air Force. The UNKNOWNS were actually 21.5 percent, and they were separate from the 9.3 percent for which there was insufficient information. Clearly the secretary of the Air Force, Donald Quarles, who made these blatantly bogus claims, did so for a reason. Because I am not privy to high-level classified documents from the USAF, I can only speculate:

1. It seems pretty clear that the most important aspect of the reality of flying saucers, to any government, is their advanced flight technology. They are more maneuverable, can fly higher, faster, slower, quieter, and stealthier than anything any country on this planet had then and most likely has now. That has serious national security implications, as does the apparent ability of the huge mother ships to get here from other, presumably nearby, solar systems.

2. Should they decide to attack us, we would likely be unable to defend ourselves against them.

3. If we, or any other government on this planet, could duplicate their flight capability, we could defeat the military forces of any other country. That governments care about such capabilities is proven by the vast sums of money spent on advanced propulsion, detection, communication, electronic, and intelligence systems, for military applications.

4. We would be concerned that those controlling the saucers might join forces with any of the relatively primitive societies here on this planet. The United States, as the most successful, richest, most polluting, largest resource-utilizing country, would be a natural target for everybody.

5. If we, or anybody else, have recovered saucer wreckage, and done scientific measurements of the flight capability of these objects and their apparent ability to control the behavior of humans from a distance (as demonstrated by the many good abduction cases), we would try to make sure that no one else could find out what we have managed to learn. We would also be very serious about trying to determine, with the use of spies, satellite observations, and electronic eavesdropping, what others have learned on their own, and what they have learned about what *we* have managed to achieve in these areas. For instance, the National Security Agency is a large and competent worldwide eavesdropper, and sophisticated reconnaissance satellites operated by the National Reconnaissance Office monitor all kinds of foreign activities in secret. Past experience says the use of disinformation and misinformation would be standard practice, as in all military confrontations. It doesn't take much study of all the wars to see this. An important part of many sports is the ability to fake out one's opponents. Remember that the basic rule is that one cannot tell one's friends without telling ones enemies, because they also read the papers, watch TV, and so on.

6. The people in charge in all countries would be trying to predict what would happen if statements were publicly made that indeed aliens are visiting. It would be dependent on the framework in which the information was presented: Would all countries have to join together to make such an announcement? If they did, how would earthlings respond?

7. Over and over again people have suggested that the major reason information has not been revealed is fear of panic, as dramatized by the Orson Welles's radio broadcast in 1938 of H.G. Wells's *War of the Worlds*. Right? Personally, I don't think it is. First of all, *War of the Worlds* was presented as Martians *destroying* earthlings. What could we (before the space age, nuclear weapons, jet fighters, and so on) possibly do against Martians? If the story had been true, people would have had a legitimate reason to panic. But what if the existence of aliens were presented as peaceful visits by powerful, advanced societies who could obviously have long since destroyed us if they had a mind to do so? Suppose we were told that they were here for a variety of peaceful reasons from a variety of civilizations, all much more technologically and sociologically advanced than we are. For, if they hadn't learned to live in peace with other civilizations, they would have already been destroyed themselves—or, much more frightening, they would have subjugated or destroyed all the others.

8. If the persons making such an announcement were highly respected, or at least not considered threatening in the way that the presidents of the United States, USSR, and China might be considered (say, the Queen of England or the Pope), and added that international conferences were planned to consider the religious, economic, and political implications of the visitations, that might help. If there were suggestions that the aliens

could help us heal the sick, feed the starving, and redistribute the wealth, this would be a threat to the powerful and a boon to the weak. You see, I presume that in all areas of technology (because we are so young on a cosmic timetable), our visitors are superior; not just in flying, but in eavesdropping, communications, medicine, and computation. I wonder what their reaction would be to the cover story on *USA Today* on November 6, 2007, noting that the average annual salary of major college football coaches exceeded $1,000,000. But 30,000 children died yesterday of preventable disease and starvation. No front-page headlines for them.

9.   I presume that if such an announcement were made, no matter how carefully, church attendance would go up, mental hospital admissions would go up, and the stock market would go down (as uncertainty is always the enemy). I further expect, based on more than 600 college lectures, that many in the younger generation would immediately push for an earthling orientation, rather than the nationalistic ones that are the rule on this planet. To some, that would be great. After all, we are *all* earthlings. But, unfortunately, I can't think of any national government that would want its citizens to owe their primary allegiance to the planet instead of that individual government. Nationalism is the only game in town. People in power have a nasty habit of wanting to stay in power.

10.   Some extremists in the Christian fundamentalist movement, such as Pat Robertson and the late Jerry Falwell, have loudly proclaimed that there is no intelligent life anywhere but on Earth, and that this UFO stuff is the work of the devil. Kind of an insult to God to think that this is the best she can do. They would be up the creek politically if an announcement of alien visitations were made. But not all religions have this

attitude: Muslims, Hindus, and Mormons, among others, claim that there are other worlds out there. Father Balducci, who works at the Vatican, has appeared at some UFO conferences and made it clear that there is no fundamental reason to reject the notion of visiting aliens. Dr. Barry Downing, a religious leader with scientific training, has found UFO sightings in both the Old and New Testaments, as described in his intriguing book *The Bible and Flying Saucers*. He is a MUFON consultant.

11. Many people have told me that if aliens are visiting here and we are not visiting there, they must be much more technologically advanced than are we. Surely that means that soon we would discover new methods of energy production...which would do great damage to the oil, gas, and coal industries. We would discover new methods of ground and air transportation, and new and improved techniques for communication and computation. In other words, there would be economic chaos. I recall that in the late 1980s the Western countries were urging the Russians to have elections and democracy and capitalism, and everything would be great. They achieved those ends, and economic chaos ensued, because they had no middle management and no built-in systems. For some time, until world oil and gas prices went through the roof, they were not better off.

12. I have personally heard of seven instances in which military planes chasing flying saucers were never heard from again. The chasing isn't surprising, in view of the official USAF 1952 orders to "shoot them down if they don't land when instructed to do so." If I have heard of seven such events, then surely there have been a great many more. (More details are given in *Shoot Them Down* by Frank Feschino, Jr.) One can perhaps understand the reluctance of the government to admit that such

losses had occurred (even though Major General Roger Ramey admitted in 1952 that more than 300 interceptors had been scrambled). Impotence in the face of intruders is not something that governments want to admit. The military didn't tell families of lost airmen what happened to the pilots, and pilots, hearing that their colleagues had been zapped, might have been very reluctant to take offensive actions against aliens.

Why Would Aliens Come to Earth?

In a paper I wrote 32 years ago, I listed 25 reasons for aliens to come to Earth, from the sublime to the ridiculous. After all, although we do know a lot about how governments behave, and, sometimes, even understand their motivations, we can only speculate about the motivations of aliens. We can get some clues from the myriad of activities reported in abduction books by Budd Hopkins, David Jacobs, Yvonne Smith, and Ray Fowler. Certainly, as described in *Captured!*, we can get a good glimpse, because of the extensive efforts of Dr. Benjamin Simon, to determine what was done to Betty and Barney Hill, and the behavior of those particular aliens. I have not spoken with any aliens, and might be wary of believing any clues they might give.

I think aliens have many reasons to visit us, partly because I am convinced that there are many civilizations in the local neighborhood. The SETI specialists, as noted in Chapter 5, seem to think, with each passing year during which they (not surprisingly) don't pick up any radio or optical signals, that there is no one around in the local neighborhood. Dr. Seth Shostak, one of the loudest voices in the SETI cult, noted that distances between adjacent civilizations, even assuming there are lots of them out there, are measured in hundreds of light-years—a truly extraordinary claim. In the first place, he has no data on any civilization out there. Not one. In the second place, there are roughly 2,000 stars within a mere 54 light-years, roughly 16,000 within 100 light-years, and 128,000 within 200 light-years. The incredible and entirely baseless implication is that no civilization even as "advanced" as ours is within 200 light-years! That means we are extraordinarily unique, despite our star, the sun, being run-of-the mill, and besides there being about 50 sun-like stars in the local neighborhood (within 54 light-years). We have already, despite the primitive nature of our instrumentation, discovered about 290 exoplanets. Also, we are well aware that although the nearest star to the sun is 4.3 light-years away, Zeta 1 and Zeta 2 Reticuli (39.2 light-years from us) are only an eighth of a light-year apart from each other, and a billion years older than the sun. I am absolutely certain that within hundreds of light-years there are other pairs of sun-like stars that are relatively near to each other, and at least as old as the sun.

Having near neighbors provides a huge incentive for interstellar travel, compared to our situation. A far more logical conclusion than Shostak's is that advanced civilizations, as discussed in Chapter 5, are simply not using our type of radio or laser communication anymore, if they ever did. Why would they send us messages, and why would we think we can predict their communication techniques? After all, we don't use Wright Brothers–type airplanes anymore...

I travel a lot, as does Seth Shostak, to lecture and educate and communicate. Some people travel to visit, do business, perform, compete, or hide. When Charles Lindbergh flew solo to France in May 1927, his 33.5-hour trip was unique, and he won a huge (for the time) prize of $25,000. Nowadays, 10 million or so people cross the Atlantic each year. Practically none but the pilots on the huge airliners making the journey are intrepid flyers as was Lindbergh. In other words, it seems pretty clear that the number of people traveling between point A and point B is very much dependent on how long it takes, how frequent the flights are, and what they cost. The cheaper and faster, the more travelers and the easier it is to find an excuse for making the trip. Many million people per year fly to tourist centers such as Las Vegas, Hawaii, and Paris. We must also look to our own past to trips, often difficult ones, made by large numbers of people to hard-to-reach places. Think of those seeking gold in California in 1849, or in Alaska in 1897–1898. In contrast, think of sports fans today flying to the World Series, or to soccer or hockey championships. Plane loads of tourists fly from Japan to Prince Edward Island every summer to see *Anne of Green Gables*, the Canadian musical, because they consider it a Japanese story. They wouldn't, if they had to go by a slow boat. It is easy to forget that Magellan's ship took three years to go around the world. Now, the International Space Station flies around the world about every 90 minutes. It covers the distance of Lindbergh's flight in less than 15 minutes. A hundred years ago, millions of immigrants came from Europe and Asia to the United States. It wasn't a fun trip, especially in steerage. I enjoyed a week-long voyage on the *Queen Elizabeth 2* from Southampton to New York. I gave three lectures to earn my way, as did Shostak. We wouldn't have done so if the trip had been the hardship it was for, say, Columbus to travel to the New World in 1492.

Think of how confusing it must have been for natives of the new world trying to make sense of the various groups of white men visiting in their large ships for the next 300 years. There were people from Spain, Portugal, Holland, France, Italy, England, and more. Some were there to find gold. Some were looking for new lands for their kings. Some were looking to convert the Heathens. Some were looking for new commercial goods to take back, such as potatoes and tobacco. Some of the first settlers in Georgia and Australia came from debtors' prisons. My grandparents and many others came from Eastern Europe in the time frame between 1900 and 1910 to evade the oppression under the Czar and to make new homes for their families. Their passage took much longer and was far less comfortable than was mine.

I believe it is useful, in dealing with claims of the noisy negativists that there would be no reason for advanced beings to come here, to review what is special about Earth.

1. It is at this time the only planet in the solar system mostly covered with water.

2. It is the only planet in the solar system to have a high level of oxygen in the atmosphere.

3. It is the densest planet in the solar system (not the heaviest or the biggest). On average, a cubic centimeter of the Earth weighs more than a cubic centimeter of any other planet in our solar system. This means that one would expect to find a greater abundance of heavy metals here than on any of the other planets. We know from star spectra that heavy metals are fairly rare in the galaxy. By *heavy metals* I mean such elements as uranium, gold, tungsten, osmium, rhenium, platinum, and so on. They are much denser than lead, and many have special properties, some of which were unknown even 100 years ago. The major use for uranium back then was as a yellow coloring agent for glazing china dishes! Zirconium and titanium are comparatively light metals, but also have properties of no interest a century ago. The piping and plumbing in nuclear submarines and other nuclear-powered vessels is mostly made of zirconium alloys, because of its combination of low neutron-capture cross-section and corrosion resistance. Neutrons were not even discovered until 1932. Titanium is a relatively light but strong metal, used, for example, in the high-speed SR-71 reconnaissance aircraft, and in cases for laptop computers. An entire new metal-forming industry was created for each of these metals.

Table 1: Element Densities (Grams/cc)				
Element	**Density**	**Element**	**Density**
Aluminum	2.7	Gold	19.3
Lead	11.35	Rhenium	21.02
Tantalum	16.65	Platinum	21.45
Uranium	18.95	Iridium	22.42
Tungsten	19.3	Osmium	22.57

4. It should further be noted that there are many resources, such as metallic nodules, at the bottom of the oceans. Many diamonds that have been recovered off the coast of Africa have special properties (besides beauty). A wide variety of interesting poisons and potentially beneficial biological agents have been recovered from sea creatures, and certain biological materials (drugs, for example) have an enormous value per pound.

5. Earth has a wide variety of plant and animal life conceivably of interest to other-worlders for improving their stocks.

6. With many different races and more than 6 billion earthlings, there is a huge variety of human genetic combinations. For example, we have been improving domestic animals by crossbreeding and artificial insemination. Soon it will be by cloning and genetic manipulation. Aliens might be doing a huge survey of gene combinations, looking for the unusual characteristics that can improve or harm hybridization activities.

7. Many genetic diseases are relatively rare, occurring in only one in a thousand, 10,000, or million earthlings. Aliens would have to pick up a host of specimens to find the special ones.

8. The Earth-moon combination is unique in the solar system. The moon is larger, compared to the Earth, than is any other planetary satellite compared to its planet. Because it keeps the same face toward the Earth, the other side would be a great location for an alien communication system to contact other bases, with no background interference from the Earth, as well as a good place for huge mother ships, because it has no atmosphere, as opposed to the much higher surface gravity and dense atmosphere of the Earth.

9. From a tourist viewpoint, Earth has many fine and remote locations for hunting, fishing, swimming, hiking, and mountain climbing for air-breathing creatures.

10. Unique within the solar system, Earth, throughout the last 100 years, has rapidly increased its production of radio, TV, and radar signals that leave the planet and provide information (as well as infomercials) to visiting intelligence agents.

Primary Alien Motivation

I wish to make only one assumption about all advanced technological civilizations: I believe they are all concerned about their own survival and security. Therefore, they must keep tabs on the primitives in the local neighborhood to assure they are not becoming a threat. Close tabs would be necessary only when the newbies show signs of being able to bother them. It is one thing to develop blast furnaces to produce steel from iron ore and a number of other metals. But by the end of World War II we had provided three clear signs that soon (in less than 100 years) earthlings would be capable of traveling to nearby solar systems, indicating that we would be a threat on the basis of our war-making tendencies, which certainly didn't stop in 1945 at the end of the war. We collectively killed 50,000,000 of our own kind during that war.

The three clear signs of potential for interstellar travel in the very near future were:

1. The development and use of nuclear weapons. Only two were used in anger, but hundreds were exploded as they rapidly increased in power. Their use is easy to detect using radiation-detection equipment and air sampling, but probably not using Mogul balloons. Hiroshima involved an atomic bomb releasing the energy equivalent of 12,000 tons of TNT in August 1945. By 1952 we had exploded the first H-bomb (using nuclear fusion as well as nuclear fission), having the power of 10 million tons of TNT and creating a fireball three miles across. Russia later exploded one with energy equivalent to 50 million tons of TNT. As noted in Chapter 2, despite the apparent ignorance of the SETI cultists and other noisy negativists, fission and fusion could be used for deep-space travel. As I commented in Chapter 2, appropriate fusion reactions in a rocket can exhaust particles having 10 million times as much energy per particle as in a chemical rocket. Progress comes from doing things differently in an unpredictable way. It should also be noted that the fuel/propellant for fusion rockets are isotopes of hydrogen and helium, the lightest and most abundant elements in the universe. Every advancing civilization will discover fusion, because it is the energy source of all the stars. We did it in 1938. Only 14 years later we exploded an H-bomb.

2. The development of ever more powerful rockets as demonstrated by the many V-1 and V-2 rockets used by the Germans to attack England. They were loaded with explosives, not airmail. These were followed by ever more powerful intermediate-range ballistic missiles, then intercontinental ballistic missiles, and huge behemoths such as the peaceful *Saturn 5*. Progress has been rapid, but, again, primarily for military utilization.

3. Finally we have the amazing growth in the development of electronic systems. Radar developed in secret during WWII by the Germans, English, Americans, and Russians puts out ever more powerful signals leaving the Earth, unlike AM radio signals. Miniaturization, so that radar systems and then computers could be installed in aircraft and then on rockets, followed very rapidly. We quickly went from vacuum tubes to transistors to integrated circuits to micro-integrated circuits. Computer circuitry continues to evolve. Costs and weight and power consumption go down, and capability rapidly improves. Some people want to give the credit for the incredible progress to back-engineering of Roswell or other alien wreckage. I don't. I want to give credit to the expenditure of huge sums of money for improvement in military capability.

I find it very interesting indeed that the only place on planet Earth where all three areas of new threatening technology could be checked out in July 1947 was southeastern New Mexico. Our first nuclear explosion took place at Trinity site on White Sands Missile Range July 16, 1945, leaving a radioactive spot. That is also near where we were testing a bunch of captured German V-2 rockets, and where we had our best radar to track the rockets, which sometimes went well off course. Roswell, of course, is also in southeastern New Mexico. An English astronomer tried to say aliens could have gone to the Soviet Union for the same purposes. Sorry, but they didn't test their first atomic bomb until August 1949.

In summary, I think every civilization in the local neighborhood, and any local subset of the galactic federation, has put out the word that Earth is a serious threat to the neighborhood. Of course they would be concerned about us. Also I should note that the transition from low-tech to high-tech can be amazingly short on a cosmic time scale. That means that we may well be the only planet in the local neighborhood at this intermediate stage of development between being able to make a mess of our own planet and being able to wreak our brand of havoc elsewhere as well. The bottom line to me is that a major reason for aliens to be checking us out is to quarantine us if we show no progress in acting as responsible galactic citizens. I am only grateful that they haven't yet wiped us off the slate and decided to start again. Throughout the years I have asked a lot of people, "If you were an alien, would you want earthlings out there?" The answer has always been no.

I should stress that, considering all the good reports of huge space carriers (mother ships), each carrying many smaller Earth Excursion Modules, that each EEM may be here for a different reason: graduate students, communications experts, genetic sample–gatherers, mining engineers, vacationers, honeymooners, specimen gatherers, and so on.

Reasons for Visiting

Here is a list off the top of my head of reasons for aliens to visit us, in no particular order:

1. Graduate students doing their thesis research on:

    a. The development of a primitive society.

    b. Geology, meteorology, sociology, biology, icthyology, entomology, religion, and so on, on a primitive planet.

    c. Foreign languages.

    d. The success or failure of colonization or interference from many years ago. (Perhaps Earth was used as a penal colony, a sort of Devil's Island of the neighborhood, and that is why we are so nasty to each other.)

2. Broadcasters with a weekly show: Idiocy in the Boondocks.

3. Specimen-gathering for an ET zoo.

4. Participation in galactic chess competitions (recall Bobby Fisher and Boris Spassky meeting in Iceland).

5. Corporations planning for the equivalent of a new coaling station for the local galactic transportation system.

6. Mining engineers seeking new supplies of special items such as gold and platinum.

7. Preparing remote storage sites for weapons to be used in a future war with other aliens or with earthlings.

8. Gas, food, and lodging.

9. Punishment for space miscreants: two weeks near Earth is punishment enough for a lifetime.

10. Space electronics experts checking on new sources of interference for their space communications systems, as used by asteroid miners.

11. Planners for the equivalent of the Olympic Games to be held on neutral ground.

12. Advance men for space missionaries (just as many missionaries went to China and Africa to convert the locals).

Why Don't Aliens Land on the White House Lawn?

This is a simplistic question, and I need to give my overview of the situation before answering it. Firstly, I think that all galactic federation intelligence agencies would do a lot of surveillance as soon as they recognized how rapidly our technology is changing and how warlike earthling societies have become. Look at the changes in flight capability between the Wright Brothers and the rapid increase throughout the next 43 years in the speed, altitude, range, and payload capability of aircraft. Look at the increase in destructive capability of the bombs and antiaircraft shells and rockets, and the cleverness of our radar and proximity fuses. Note that propellers were replaced by jet engines; 10-ton blockbusters by 12-kiloton nuclear weapons. Wars evolved from trench warfare of the First World War involving mostly military combatants, to the mass bombings of the Second World War mostly on civilians. (A single mass bombing of Dresden or Tokyo killed tens of thousands of noncombatant civilians.) Estimates vary, but there is a general consensus that WWII saw the destruction of 1,700 cities and about 50 million earthlings. It was followed, not by worldwide peace and prosperity (despite the Marshall Plan in the immediate post-war period to help starving civilians in Western Europe), but by a cold war involving two major nations building ever more powerful armaments (nuclear weapons), ever more sophisticated means for delivering them, and ever more sophisticated sky monitoring systems (such as radar) to protect against incursions by the other side.

Clearly, alien visitors would have to be totally stupid— hardly likely— not to collect detailed information on the location of airborne military radar systems, airfields with military interceptors, antiaircraft guns and rockets, and so on. They would make it a point to determine the maximum velocity, maneuverability, altitude, and offensive weapon capabilities, from machine guns to air-to-air missiles, airborne radar, and so on and so forth. Rule number one for intruding aircraft must be to try to avoid the local defenders. As a general rule, despite all the airborne encounters between earthling aircraft and flying saucers, the aliens don't seem to show signs of wholesale retaliation. (For those who aren't aware of the many encounters between flying saucers and earthling aircraft, both military and civilian, I would refer readers to the files of NARCAP [National Aviation Reporting Center for Anomalous Phenomena]. Dr. Richard Haines, a scientist with NASA Ames Research Center for many years, had already collected more than 1,000 pilot sightings when he appeared in my documentary movie *UFOs ARE Real* in 1979. The number is up to more than 3,000 now.)

Back to landing on the White House lawn. Firstly, the White House and environs are in a no-fly zone. There is a lot of radar coverage, and many interceptors ready to chase away intruders, as they did during the huge wave of radar visual sightings over D.C. in the summer of 1952. The message, loud and clear, is STAY AWAY. Secondly, though I hate to bring it up, the president of the United States does not speak for 6.5 billion earthlings! Clearly he doesn't even always speak for 300 million Americans. Is there anybody who *does* speak for Earth? I don't know of anyone who does, not even the head of the General Assembly at the United Nations. Some people might suggest that, as a democratic society, we should elect a leader to represent the planet. Surely the galactic federation would only allow for planetary representatives. A real problem with the American notion of "one person, one vote," is the simple fact that China has 1.3 billion people, India 1 billion, and so on. The United States, with only 300 million, would never agree to such a system.

Why Are Astronomers Generally So Anti-UFO?

I have had many opportunities to observe astronomers and read or hear their views on UFOs. For the most part they are indeed generally negative. I think two words provide the reasons: ignorance and arrogance. They are almost completely ignorant about the UFO evidence, not just the studies noted in Chapter 1, but the more than 4,000 physical trace cases from more than 70 countries collected by Ted Philips, the detailed photo analysis of UFO pictures, and accounts of alien abductions. They are not just ignorant about advanced technology that might be used for deep-space propulsion or for highly maneuverable systems in the atmosphere. They are also ignorant about the national security aspects of the UFO problem. They presume that because their concern is the universe outside Earth, they would know about alien visitors, who would most likely want to talk to them. The history of astronomy is full of false claims by the leading lights. I have on occasion noted that astronomy seems to be sort of a democratic science: The leading lights get together and decide on truth, and woe be unto he who disagrees. There is no place to publish, and academia is characterized by publish-or-perish.

Good examples include the size and age of the galaxy and universe, both of which greatly expanded in the 20th century, as did knowledge of the physical processes that produce the energy of the stars. It was physicist Hans Bethe who, in 1938, figured out that it was nuclear fusion that powered the stars—not an astronomer. Generally speaking, there is nothing in the training or education of astronomers that provides a basis for their frequent claims that aliens can't get here because it would take too much energy. There is no question that the amount of energy it takes to travel from say Zeta Reticuli to Earth is entirely dependent on the path taken, and the energy source. All our deep-space probes take advantage of clever engineering, cosmic freeloading, and more. It is absurd that astronomers refer to the use of chemical rockets or coasting for star travel. Of all people, they should know about nuclear fusion. I was truly shocked when Dr. Tyson, head of the Hayden Planetarium in New York, claimed on the Peter Jennings mockumentary of February 24, 2005, that our fastest craft, the *Voyager* spacecraft, would take 70,000 years to get to the nearest star. This is true, but totally irrelevant. No mention was made of the fact that *Voyager* has been essentially coasting since it left Earth. It has no propulsion system.

I have also found it laughable that astronomers often act as though they would be experts on the behavior and motivation of aliens. Not only are they not professionally knowledgeable about UFOs or propulsion systems, but surely they are not experts about the behavior and motivation of earthlings, much less aliens. Perhaps psychiatrists, social workers, doctors, nurses, and even lawyers would be better suited—all are professionals accustomed to dealing with living, thinking beings. But astronomers? One astronomer told me that he couldn't imagine aliens visiting just to stop automobiles. I can find no indication that the purpose of the visits is to stop engines, any more than that people drove automobiles in the late

1890s for the purpose of scaring nearby horses. Stopping cars could easily be for the purpose of controlling the drivers, or, as in the Iranian jet case of 1976, for preventing missile attacks. It could also be an unintentional consequence of the presence of sophisticated energy production or communication systems.

One peculiar aspect I have found is that, perhaps because they are more interested in the huge universe rather than the local neighborhood, astronomers often act as though visitors would have to come from another galaxy. In a radio discussion, one famous astronomer started by saying he just didn't think people knew how much energy it would take to get here from another galaxy, as Andromeda is more than 2 million light-years away. Zeta Reticuli is 39.2 light-years away, which is a very different transportation problem. If we need a loaf of bread for dinner, I simply am not concerned about it being 9,000 miles to a fine bakery in Sydney, Australia; there is a good one less than two miles away.

Another problem is that at least some astronomers think linearly. Allen Hynek used to point out that if the thickness of one playing card represented the distance to the moon from the Earth, than the nearest star is 16,000 miles of playing cards away. In addition, twice as far takes twice as long. For space travel this is simply not true. If we could double our rocket's speed at burnout when heading toward the moon, we would get there 20 times faster. The effective thrust is the difference between two similar quantities: the thrust of the rocket pushing up, and the gravity pulling down. If they balanced, the rocket wouldn't go anywhere. If the thrust is a bit bigger at the start, than the rocket will accelerate because it is losing weight (propellant). The difference is steadily increasing. I tried with no success to get Allen to look at the vast literature on interstellar travel. Admittedly, not much of it is published in astronomical journals. Information about flying saucers almost never appears in such journals. But then, studies of stars, galaxies, and satellites don't involve unexpected observations without instrumentation by non-astronomers of activities controlled by intelligent beings. I wonder how many astronomers subscribe to the MUFON journal or *UFO Magazine*, or the *International UFO Reporter* of the Center for UFO Studies.

I often ask during college class visits how long it takes, at one G acceleration, to reach the speed of light. Many professors guess 1,000 years. In reality, it is only one year. Ignorance may be bliss, but having it pointed out is not.

I can't find any reason for thinking, per some astronomers, that knowledge of alien visitations would be immediately spread far and wide. Admittedly, the SETI people would probably make a noisy announcement should they ever pick up a signal, but that would certainly not change things as much as admission of an alien presence here and now. Think of how upset astronomers will be when the government finally provides proof of alien visitations. The famous Brookings Institute Report on the impact of contact with extraterrestrials noted that the egos of scientists would be greatly bruised by recognition of how little they know.

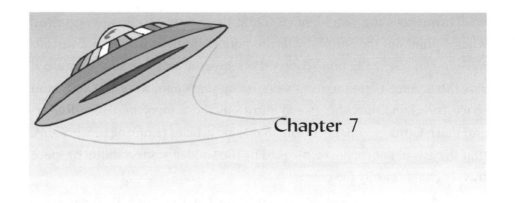

Chapter 7

Science, Science Fiction, and UFOs

Several groups (besides government-paid disinformation specialists) can be cited as being most responsible for the general ignorance of the public about flying saucers, and the strongly negative attitude shown by a number of public figures. They are the members of the media who haven't done their jobs, the science fiction writers who can't accept the idea of UFOs, and the SETI specialists who feel it necessary to attack the notion of space visitors in order to gain support for the strange idea of listening for signals instead. There are also the academics who publicly express strong views against UFO reality without bothering to study the evidence. There is, of course, another group: the kooky element that gets far more media attention than it deserves, as well as some apologist ufologists and closet ufologists. The more they apologize and stay in the closet, the less likely the public and scientific communities are to come to understand how much evidence there really is. In addition, the government has created a substantial mythology (as described in Chapter 4).

Throughout the years I have found that many people are surprised when I point out the antipathy to the notion of alien visitation of various well-known science fiction writers. People seem to think that because it was the science fiction writers who, many years ago, were talking about space travel and publishing such stories as those involving Buck Rogers and Flash Gordon, and those pulp magazine articles featuring space aliens, that they would normally be pleased by the sudden respectability of space travel. That is hardly the case.

I will deal in detail with three of the best-known science fiction writers: Dr. Isaac Asimov, Ben Bova, and Arthur C. Clarke. Their views have unfortunately been widely spread because of their status, and have had a strong negative influence among the general public—not just the relatively small sci-fi community. Almost never have they been held to account, though I have tried.

Isaac Asimov

Dr. Isaac Asimov (1920–1992) was a prolific writer of nonfiction books and science fiction novels and stories. His book total is more than 400 (with some uncertainty due to the inclusion of some coauthored books, anthologies, and so on). He also wrote many articles. Though his PhD is in chemistry, he has always earned his living as an author. I had discussed his anti-ufological attitudes as expressed in his book *Is Anyone There?* in my 1973 MUFON symposium paper "Ufology and the Search for ET Intelligent Life." Someone unknown to either of us sent him a copy of the symposium proceedings. He noted the comments I had made, and was stimulated to write a supposedly scientific article entitled "The Rocketing Dutchman" for the February 1975 issue of *Fantasy and Science Fiction*. A much shorter version appeared as a "Background" article in *TV Guide* for December 14, 1974. Both articles deserved awards for massive misrepresentation, lack of awareness of the relevant data, arrogance, illogicality, and irrationality. They were fine examples of the pseudoscience of anti-ufology. I will focus on the *Fantasy and Science Fiction* article because it was more detailed, although, considering that *TV Guide*, at that time, had a weekly circulation of 18 million, it undoubtedly did far more damage.

Asimov began by casting aspersions at me and other UFO "believers." He quoted my statement that "Many people are surprised that two of the noted science fiction and science writers Isaac Asimov and Arthur C. Clarke are both quite vehement in their anti-UFO sentiment." He responded: "That Friedman meets people who are surprised at this indicates, I suppose, the level of the circles he moves in. After all, why should the fact that Arthur and I are s.f. writers lead people to suppose that we have forfeited our intelligence and must surely believe any mystic cult that seems to have some elements in common with science fiction?"

The people to whom I was referring were the students and professors at the hundreds of colleges at which I had spoken, as well as the scientists and engineers at the many dozens of professional engineering and science organizations that had sponsored my programs. He obviously hadn't noted the background sheet about me, which appeared on page 10 of the same MUFON volume as my paper. If he had, he would have noted that we were both members of Mensa, and that I belonged to the American Nuclear Society, the American Physical Society, the American Institute of Aeronautics and Astronautics, and was then a Fellow of the British Interplanetary Society— of which Arthur C. Clarke had been a founder. I had worked for 14 years as a professional nuclear physicist for such major companies as GE, GM, Westinghouse, TRW System, Aerojet General Nucleonics, and McDonnell Douglas. I worked on a whole host of highly classified advanced research and development projects, including nuclear aircraft, fission and fusion rockets, and nuclear power plants for space applications. I think a dispassionate observer might consider those circles at least the equal of those of a science fiction writer who had never worked as a scientist, despite the PhD. It was pretty silly for him to suggest that only people of low intelligence belonging to mystic cults accept the notion of flying saucer reality.

As detailed in Chapter 8, there was plenty of data then, as well as now, indicating that the greater one's education the more likely one is to believe in flying saucer reality, and that a majority of engineers and scientists involved in R&D activities do as well. I have seen no poll of science fiction writers. Asimov obviously hadn't either, because he gave no evidence at all to support his negative position.

His article was written in question-and-answer format. Unfortunately, he asked the wrong questions, studied no relevant data, provided no references, and came to foolish conclusions because of his bias and ignorance. He started by focusing on the unanswerable question of whether or not there are other intelligent life forms in the universe. He starts with the assumption of 640,000,000 Earth-like planets in the galaxy—no basis is given for this number. We know that there are roughly 256,000,000,000 stars in the Milky Way galaxy (plus or minus 100 billion). So he is saying only 1 in 400 has an Earth-like planet. At that time no exoplanets (planets in other solar systems) had been discovered. From whence cometh his number? Throwing darts at a dartboard? We have not yet found any truly Earth-like planets in our neighborhood, but our techniques are primitive, and will certainly improve as new instruments are launched within the next 25 years (as discussed in Chapter 5 on SETI). We have already found more than 290 exoplanets around 200 stars—a fairly significant percentage compared to 1/400. Asimov whittles his number down by an amazing sequence of assumptions having no basis in fact. He notes that Earth has had life for about 3 billion years, a civilization for about 10,000 (1/300,000 of its history), and an industrial civilization for about 200 years (1/50 of the time for civilization). He therefore reduces the supposed number of Earth-like planets in the galaxy by dividing 640 million by 300,000, and then by 50, to give 43 industrial civilizations, and assumes (he claims) that we are roughly average, so that there are 21 civilizations more advanced than we, and perhaps capable of space travel. He doesn't seem to know the difference between calendars, which measure time, and maps, which show the distribution of things in space. Knowing the fraction of available time for which there has been a civilization here (we actually do *not* know that) tells us nothing about what fraction of planets have civilizations now, in the past, or in the future. For all we know, there could have been 50 different civilizations on Earth alone throughout the past billion years. It took digging down 75 feet for Heinrich Schliemann to discover the "mythical" city of Troy, though it existed just a few thousand years ago. We also recognize that catastrophic events that could change the surface of the planet, can occur, such as being hit by an asteroid, or a comet, or a nuclear war. Very little of Earth has been explored down 75 feet.

When I first wrote about this, I noted that I had been married to my wife for only 7 percent of my life. Now it is about 45 percent. Did that mean that only 7 percent of the male population was married? My father at that time had been bald for 2/3 of his life. Did that mean that 2/3 of men are bald? Of course not. But Asimov wasn't even assuming that Earth was average. He was assuming that nobody got started sooner than we did at having an industrial civilization. That is frankly absurd, especially when one notices that the galaxy is about 13.6 billion years old, and that the Earth has been around about 4.56 billion years. An error of only 1/10 of one percent in the 3 billion years would be 3 million years. He was also totally neglecting colonization, migration, the exiling of prisoners, or the dispersal of civilizations by those who started earlier.

Asimov then compounds totally false reasoning with more of the same in trying to determine the distance between civilizations so that he can show how terribly far away the nearest one supposedly is. He imagines the 21 advanced industrial civilizations distributed randomly throughout the galaxy, which means, he says, that they would be, on average, 13,500 light-years apart from each other. He doesn't give any details about the calculation, and seems to assume that the conditions are the same throughout the volume of the galaxy. His next statement is a truly unscientific claim: "With the nearest home planet of flying saucers 13,500 light-years away, the chance of visiting us would seem small." But as any real scientist would note, the only way to convert the average distance between civilizations to the distance to the nearest one is to assume uniform distribution. But he said he distributed them randomly. That means the nearest one could be 15 light-years away, or 39.2, as in the case of Zeta 1 and Zeta 2 Reticuli in the constellation of Reticulum, as discussed in *Captured!* In other words, his approach was totally unscientific and illogical. Any high school student would know that because the average distance from my home to the 10 largest metropolitan areas in the United States at that time was 1,800 miles, certainly didn't mean the nearest one was 1,800 miles away. As it happens, it was only 30 miles.

Then Asimov, realizing that he may be treading on thin ice with his pseudoscientific calculations, becomes magnanimous and says that maybe the Earth is only 100 light-years from a very advanced civilization. "This would be tremendously unlikely," he said. This is a scientist? He has no data at all about the distances to any other civilization, but he knows what is unlikely? He never bothers to mention how many stars are within 100 light-years, or even 50. We know that very few people are 7 feet tall. Does that mean that there would never be two 7-footers in the same area at the same time? Obviously not, if one looks at National Basketball Association games, in which there are often two 7-footers on the court at the same time. I should note that there are between 8,000 and 15,000 stars within 100 light-years, of which roughly 360 are sun-like stars, and might, not unreasonably, be expected to have planets of some kind. Their distribution is certainly not uniform. The nearest star of any kind to the sun is 4.3 light-years away. But Zeta 1 Reticuli and Zeta 2 Reticuli, both sun-like stars, are only 1/8 of a light year apart from each other. This is 35 times closer to each other than the sun is to the next star over. Of course, though just down the street from us, they are also a billion years older than the sun. Inhabitants on planets around either star would have had far more incentive for the development of interstellar travel with a target so close, and with so much more time at their disposal.

It is bad enough that Asimov was irrational about the distribution and number of planets having a civilization, but surprisingly, for an outstanding science fiction writer, he seems to have no imagination about the motivations of alien beings. He wrote:

> If we ignore the question of distance, there remains that of motive. If these Rocketing Dutchmen are buzzing around Earth deliberately and for some rational reason, it must be because Earth interests them. But what on Earth can possibly interest them? It is natural (if perhaps egotistical) to assume that to any outworlder the most interesting thing about Earth is man and his civilization. But if the flying saucers are investigating us, why don't they come down and greet us? They should be intelligent enough to work out who our spokesmen are and where our centers of population are and how to go about making contact with our governments.

I would suggest that anybody thinking this makes sense review my list of reason for aliens to come to earth in Chapter 6. For one thing, neither Asimov nor I can be sure that there haven't already been many contacts between aliens and government leaders. At that time (in the 1970s), thousands of people made their way to Alaska to help build a pipeline—not to socialize with the Eskimos. The same goes for those thousands who made a much more difficult trip to the Klondike in 1887 to seek out gold deposits. Columbus wasn't an anthropologist. He had to deal fairly with the natives because he needed them to provide food and water, and not to be aggressive toward him and his crew. However, the aliens seem to be able to do their thing without any help from us. Furthermore, aliens would have to be totally stupid not to realize that ours is a primitive, warlike society. We Earthlings operate many radar systems to detect enemies and UFOs, and interceptors to try to destroy or capture them. Military types would love to be able to duplicate alien technology, not for social purposes, but to destroy other civilizations. Very little effort went in to Project Plowshare, to try to build canals and lakes with nuclear weapons, as opposed to threatening destruction with them. It cost about a billion dollars to land the *Viking* spacecraft on Mars in 1976, and there were no translators on board to deal with friendly Martians. The rule here is shoot first, ask questions later...at least when a Texan is president. That 3-mile-wide mushroom cloud when the first H-bomb was tested in 1952 spoke volumes about what earthlings were all about: war.

But let us be magnanimous and accept Asimov's suggestion that the aliens are here to investigate earthlings and our "civilization," such as it is. He assumes they haven't contacted Earth governments, apparently because he isn't aware of such contacts. We now, by Asimovian logic, have the notion, popular amongst UFO deniers, that absence of evidence can be presumed to be evidence of the absence of it. I must admit that I have been unable to find any evidence that he ever had a high-level security clearance or a need-to-know for such data.

Surely even a science fiction writer would admit that rule number one for any alien explorers has to be to try to be sure you can get home. It seems quite clear that every air force, zoo, TV talk show host, and so on, would love to get its hands on a flying saucer and its crew. The first government able to duplicate flight behavior of the saucers would be well on its way to ruling planet Earth, because they would make wonderful weapons-delivery and defense systems. Surely Asimov would have been aware that billions of dollars are being spent by Earth governments every year to develop better weapons systems, such as the B-1, the SR-71, the stealth fighter and bomber, and cruise missiles. Surely he was also aware that there was no leader (then or now) who speaks for the planet and could negotiate with aliens on behalf of the planet.

In the real world we make use of silent sentries in space to determine the capabilities of our enemies, as opposed to asking them what systems they have. Surely a civilization would find out more about its opponents with instrumentation, and by monitoring our TV, radio, telephone, and now Internet signals, than by landing in Times Square or the Kremlin. Perhaps Asimov wasn't aware of the big-budget agencies such as the NRO and NSA. They and the CIA, KGB, and FBI try to gather as much information as possible without risk to the agents.

Asimov said: "Nor is it conceivable they can be afraid of us." He was actually serious! However, a blow-gun dart can be just as deadly as a laser. Perhaps Asimov has forgotten our nuclear weapons, conceivably directed by our radar systems? We certainly tested not only nuclear weapons, but antimissile missiles. He said that if aliens find the place unpleasant, they are surely intelligent enough to communicate with us. Furthermore, he said, "On the other hand, if they are interested in us but do not wish to make contact with us, if they do not wish to interfere, they are certainly intelligent enough and advanced enough to be able to study us in whatever detail they need without ever letting us be aware of them. No, they should either come down and say hello, or they should go away. If they do neither, they are not intelligently guided spaceships." I was totally shocked when I read this. Since when did Dr. Asimov become an expert on the behavior of real aliens and of planetary governments? He set up a straw man, and expects rational, thinking people to blindly accept his incredible conclusions. Surely there is a middle ground between saying hello and hiding from us. We don't take either extreme in our dealings with strangers. I don't normally talk to the squirrels in my backyard. But then, I don't hide from them either.

Surely even an outstanding science fiction writer would recognize that:

1. Rule number one for visitors ought to be to try to get home. It is obvious that weapons of mass destruction are here in the hands of people who don't mind slaughtering military personnel and civilians. This is a hostile planet.

2. Every military group would like to get its hands on advanced systems in secret to try to figure out how they work and to keep others from finding out what they know.

3. Usually negotiations occur between groups at roughly the same level of power. They can come and go as they please, though apparently destroying aircraft that are too bothersome, as reported in *Shoot Them Down*. We are not their equals.

4. No advanced visitors would trust earthlings with their alien technology, especially because it could be used against them.

5. Those in our galactic neighborhood would be concerned about earthlings who shortly will be able to take our brand of friendship (generally known as hostility) to the stars, to make as big a mess out there as we have here.

Dr. Asimov then proceeded to what a psychiatrist would describe as a projection. He asks a question about alien motivation and then claims that it is the believers who are piling up too many conditions, such as assuming "at least one civilization improbably near to us," "the achievement of faster-than-light travel," and "that they find Earth interesting enough to pester repeatedly, but ourselves of so little interest they won't talk to us, while on the other hand they don't care if we see them."

There is no need to make such assumptions. It is the worldwide data that convinces those willing to study it that aliens are visiting Earth. Except for the outstanding work of Marjorie Fish with the Betty Hill star map, pointing to Zeta 1 and Zeta 2 Reticuli, we have no clues as to from where they are originating. Just as I don't need to know how digestion proceeds in order to eat dinner, I don't need to know where they originate to say they are from off the Earth. If we don't have an atlas showing the locations of other civilizations, we can't say whether the visitors originate probably or improbably near to us. Why suggest that faster-than-light travel is required, when Einstein's laws of relativity, well established by experimentation, indicate that as one gets close to the speed of light time slows down for things moving that fast? (This was discussed in Chapter 2.) There is also no reason to say that everyone coming here must have come directly from another solar system as opposed to from a base much closer to us. My longest lecture trip involved speaking at 25 campuses in 35 days in 15 states (when I was much younger). I was gone the whole time, rather than going out and back and out and back. Captain Cook, in his voyages of discovery, went from one new place to the next.

Next Dr. Asimov admitted that he has not investigated even one report of extraterrestrial spaceships or of beings on board the ships. In a phone conversation, he further admitted that he had not read much of the UFO literature and that he does not receive any publications of the UFO groups. I should have thought that would have automatically disqualified him from writing a supposedly scientific article. I find it difficult as a scientist to accept the notion that a writer, supposedly also a scientist, should express an opinion about a subject about which he apparently knows nothing besides what he reads in the tabloids. His justification for dismissing such reports out of hand is that "eyewitness evidence by a small number of people uncorroborated by any other sort of evidence is worthless." Here is yet another straw man. Because he hasn't examined any of the evidence how is he justified in claiming there isn't any? One of my major rules for UFO deniers is "Don't bother me with the facts, my mind is made up." He certainly followed the rules.

The fact of the matter is that there are many good reports, in documents such as both volumes of *The UFO Evidence*, in J. Allen Hynek's book *The UFO Experience*, in *Project Blue Book Special Report No. 14*, in the Congressional Hearings of 1968, and even in the Condon report, as discussed in Chapter 1. There are a myriad of physical trace case, radar visual cases, and photographs that have passed muster. If Asimov had bothered to read Ted Phillips's paper, "Landing Traces: Physical Evidence for the UFO," in the very same volume of MUFON papers as mine, he could have read of 546 physical trace cases. A later volume from Phillips, *Physical Traces Associated with UFO Sightings*, would have provided him with data on more than 800 cases. Now Phillips's files include more than 4,000 cases from 70 countries. About 1/6 of these cases involve reports of creatures, usually diminutive, associated with the landed craft. Even back then there were dozens of cases of abductions on file. Asimov could have checked with Dr. Jacques Vallee's computerized catalog of close encounters between UFOs and earthlings. More than 1/3 involved observations of humanoid creatures. I am certainly convinced that if writers such as Asimov had been less negative, despite their ignorance, we would be aware of many more such cases. He might also have looked at the excellent paper, "Basic Patterns in UFO Observations," by Vallee and Dr. Claude Poher, a French scientist, comparing American and French cases, to find great similarities. As it happens, Poher made a strong presentation at the National Press Club in Washington, D.C. on November 12, 2007, based on his many years of investigation.

Asimov went on to say that he wanted "something less prone to distortion and less subject to hoaxing than eyewitness evidence is. I want something material and lasting, something that can be studied by many. I want an alloy not of Earth manufacture. I want a device that does something by no principle we understand. Best of all I want a ship in plain view, revealing itself to human beings competent to observe and study them over a reasonable period of time." So do I. And why not? All alien civilizations would turn over their craft to us nice, curious, peaceful guys on Earth, right? This is truly science fiction. Surely most people don't turn over loaded guns to 3-year-olds to play with. Asimov presumes that no such material is studied in secrecy. Thus the real test seems to be to find a saucer that he can climb around. I am not surprised that he is not demanding a ride, though, because he was well known for his unwillingness to fly in airplanes.

It is strange, but I don't think Asimov has worked with many police forces, or radar operators, or secret U.S. military groups that evaluated captured enemy equipment such as cryptographic machines or crashed airplanes. Such things were not put on display. The information obtained by the Soviet Union about the Manhattan Project, from spies who worked at Los Alamos, certainly wasn't. It was definitely believed in, even though apparently no volume of fissionable material was turned over with it. We also don't have pieces of a black hole or neutron star either, but I would bet he didn't reject them.

Asimov went on to state that, "If flying saucers are spaceships, this must be proven by direct evidence. It can never be proven by wailing 'but what else can it be?'" Here, I agree with him. None of the many scientists who agree with me that there is overwhelming evidence that some UFOs are manufactured craft behaving in ways we can't duplicate, and therefore originating off the Earth, wail, "But what else can it be?" After all, we don't know much about the aliens or whether they are cyborgs or servants or big shots. Perhaps they are being punished for past transgressions and are serving a sentence to spend two weeks working on Earth. Bad crimes get three-week sentences. I should point out that the first living things put into orbit around Earth were a dog and a monkey—hardly the builders of the craft in which they flew.

In response to his own question, "What do you think, yourself, that flying saucers are?" he states, "My own feeling is that almost every sighting is either a mistake or a hoax." At least he admits that this is a *feeling* and not the result of any investigation. He follows the second rule for UFO deniers: "What the public doesn't know, I won't tell them." As I have discussed, in *Project Blue Book Special Report No. 14*, 21.5 percent of the 3,201 sightings investigated by the USAF could not be explained, completely separate from the 9.3 percent listed as insufficient data. Fewer than 5 percent were listed as hoaxes, and fewer than 2 percent as crackpot cases. The special UFO subcommittee of the American Institute of Aeronautics and Astronautics noted (in "UFO: An Appraisal of the Problem" in *Astronautics and Aeronautics*) that 30 percent of the 117 cases studied by the Condon Committee could not be explained, and that one could come to the opposite conclusions from Dr. Condon on the basis of the data in his report.

Asimov did have some nice things to say about Dr. J. Allen Hynek, apparently because he knew him personally, and because he approved of Hynek's noncommittal, non-controversial attitude about UFOs. Speaking of the cases available for Hynek's study, he says: "These reports are so riddled with hoaxes, and the flying saucer enthusiasts have so many cranks, freaks, and nuts among them, that Hynek is constantly running the risk of innocently damaging his reputation by being confused with them." Here again we have assertions completely unsupported by any evidence and contradicted by readily available data. Rules number 3 and 4 for deniers are demonstrated in spades: "If one can't attack the data, attack the people," and "Do one's research by proclamation, not investigation. It is easier, and most people won't know the difference."

Dr. Asimov finishes his parody of the scientific method by noting how difficult it would be to study the genuine puzzlers, "because they appear unheralded, unexpected, and with the utmost irregularity in space and time. There is no way of laying a trap for them short of setting up a worldwide monitoring system that would be fearfully expensive." Again we have incredible naivety: There are definitely numerous radar monitoring networks set up all over the world. There are spy satellites covering the world for the United States and the Soviet Union, and now other countries, in secret. They surely don't come cheap and are intended to catch the unexpected, in secret. I must remind the reader of the National Reconnaissance Office, the National Security Agency, the Aerospace Defense Command, and their Soviet and Chinese equivalents, and so on. Dr. Asimov closed his article with, "We end up with anecdotal half memory of something half seen." This may indeed be true for someone so dazzled by his own brilliance and knowledge of everything important that he can't admit his own ignorance, or see that the real world is loaded with data to be seen by those with vision instead of prejudice.

I sent a tightly packed letter to *Fantasy and Science Fiction* with specific criticism and references to the sources of data. Much of it was published in the May 1975 issue, but with none of the references. His response was, "Mr. Friedman's letter is the typical lucubration [I had to look that up] of the professional ufologist who makes a good living by lecturing to the naïve. The worst thing that can happen to him is to have a real space-ship land—for then conventional scientists will take over. I dare say he doesn't worry about that much." As I wrote in my 1977 paper for MUFON, "Science Fiction, Science, and UFOS": "I think that the reader, learning that I have lectured at more than 350 colleges in 47 states and four provinces, and to dozens of professional groups, and that I spent 14 years working as a scientist in industry, might agree with me that this is a good example of psychiatric projection."

It was Dr. Asimov's article that is the typical bit of prose by a professional writer who makes a good living writing for the naïve. The worst that could have happened for *him* would be to have had a real spaceship land, and for the scientists, such as myself, to take over. I dare say he didn't worry about that very much. I should add that his *Fantasy and Science Fiction* article was reprinted in a book of his "science articles" without my critique. He certainly had plenty of chutzpah.

I also had sent an article to *TV Guide* specifically criticizing his supposed "background article" in the December 14, 1974, issue, giving data and references. They sent me a note saying that my material had been sent on to Dr. Asimov (we wouldn't want to educate the 18 million readers of his unscientific fiction, I guess). There was no response from him...until I sent him a copy of the 1977 MUFON paper. He is famous for replying to all communications, and I got back a postcard saying, "I don't want you to think I didn't get your letter—so that you would be forced to write again. I received your letter. I do not wish to answer, and in future I will not even acknowledge." There's nothing like arrogance and ignorance.

I have gone into detail about Dr. Asimov because his approach is so typical of the nonsense that has led so many scientists, journalists, and the public to denigrate anything about flying saucers. There is no doubt he was a fine writer, and (unfortunately) had enormous influence about this subject on so many people.

Ben Bova

Ben Bova (1931–?) is a noted science fiction writer who had been editor of *ANALOG* and then editor of *OMNI*, a quite fancy publication that mixed science fiction and science. He has published more than 115 futuristic novels and nonfiction books. He had worked in industry, is president emeritus of the National Space Society, and is a past president of the Science Fiction and Fantasy Writers of America. Late in life, he earned a PhD from California Coast University in 1996. He made his view about flying saucers clear in a comment in the Brass Tacks section of *ANALOG* on December 25, 1975, in response to a letter suggesting that *ANALOG* open its pages to a responsible debate on the UFO evidence within the framework of the scientific method. Bova said:

1. "It's been well established that most UFO sightings are unusual, but perfectly natural phenomena."

2. "The unexplained sightings are simply those for which there is too little information to provide a solid factual basis for an explanation."

3. "To date there has been no (repeat NO) valid evidence for extraterrestrial visitations."

4. "Would that there were."

His first sentence is true—as are the facts that most isotopes aren't fissionable, most stars aren't supernovas, and most chemicals cannot treat any disease. Item 2 is absolutely false. I would thoroughly disagree with item 3, and the fourth is window dressing that my contacts with science fiction writers clearly have been shown not to be the case: If they wanted visitations to be real, the best they could do would be to study the readily available data instead of ignoring it and making totally false statements. I wrote a letter to Bova spelling out why item 2 was false, giving 14 references to data and including the summary tables of data from *Project Blue Book Special Report No. 14* about the categorization and quality evaluation of 3,201 sightings. Bova must be given credit for responding promptly, though he obviously didn't look at the tables or any of the references. He wrote:

> I've been into the UFO controversy for many years. The thing that impresses me the most is not the fact that there are so many unexplained sightings, but that so many people are willing to leap from such sightings to the conclusion that we are being visited by extraterrestrials—the lack of explanation of the sightings in question is actually a lack of information. Whenever enough information about a sighting has been obtained the phenomenon has turned out to be terrestrial in origin.... It would seem there would be a few with enough information about them to show that no terrestrial explanation is sufficient.... I've never seen such a report. I'll be glad to revise my opinion.

Here we go again with false proclamations and window dressing. The data I sent proved that the sightings that could not be explained were absolutely *not* those for which there was insufficient information. Obviously, he really wasn't "into" the UFO controversy, or he would have looked at the evidence. If he had, he would not have come to the same conclusion, especially noting that the better the quality of the sighting the more likely to be unexplainable—meaning that it had characteristics that cannot be explained by terrestrial phenomena.

I did send another letter, but nothing was published. Again we have the basic tenet of debunkdom: Don't bother me with the facts; my mind is made up. Bova at least is consistent. He wrote an article in the Naples, Florida, *Daily News* of October 13, 2002, 27 years later. This time there were insults. He uses the term "UFO Faithful" three times, totally ignoring the fact that even in 1977 the greater the education, the more likely to accept UFO reality. He stated that Walter Haut's press release about Roswell referred to the wreckage as a disk. Certainly. The terminology in use at the time in hundreds of articles subsequent to Kenneth Arnold's June 24, 1947, observation, and prior to Haut's July 8, 1947, story, was either *disk* or *flying saucer*. These were generic terms. Bova added, "The disk was definitely a flying saucer. Three alien crewmen had been recovered, two of them dead and the third badly injured." I would be happy to pay $100 to anyone who can provide any article from July 1947 talking about alien crewmen. This is truly science fiction.

He added further nonsense with this comment: "For nearly half a century Roswell has stood as a classic example of the government hiding 'the truth' about flying saucers." Funny that the first such claims appeared in *The Roswell Incident* in 1980, only 22 years earlier. Bova then admits there was a cover-up (lasting 47 years), because Roswell, he claims, was a Mogul balloon, citing Karl Pflock's book *Roswell: Inconvenient Facts and the Will to Believe* (2001), even though nothing about Mogul fits the wreckage, the timing, or the location of what was found near Roswell. Pflock himself was active in science fiction circles, and the introduction to his book was written by another science fiction writer, Jerry Pournelle. Bova also commented about his "investigative efforts" re UFOs when he was editor of *OMNI*. He said, "It is all too easy to fall for unsupported stories that tell us what we want to believe." This is an excellent description of the nonsense being spouted by anti-UFO science fiction writers. They want to believe there is no evidence so they won't have to admit they have been ignoring such an important story for so long. They create scenarios to back up this plot line, having no basis in fact.

Bova went further, rather surprisingly for someone who has spent so much time with fiction. He said, "Why the government would try to cover up alien visitors is something I don't understand." He really can't imagine the effect it would have on our society, and the development of advanced weaponry from duplicating the technology? He also said, "How a government that leaks like a sieve could possibly cover up such a story for nearly half a century is beyond my comprehension." I believe he was being truthful, and naïve, because he seemed not to be aware of the many multibillion-dollar black budget programs discussed in Chapter 4, which had not been publicly discussed until decades after coming to fruition. Naturally he added, ala Asimov, "I would like to see some scrap of hard palpable evidence." Here we go again with the foolish notion that absence of evidence in his sight or hand is evidence for absence, and that he would have a need-to-know to see it.

Arthur C. Clarke

Arthur C. Clarke is certainly one of the best-known science fiction writers of the 20th century. He was the author of *2001*, and, perhaps surprisingly to some, of a number of books relating to space travel. He wrote an early study demonstrating that the claims of Dr. Campbell back in 1941 (about the difficulty of getting to the moon) as discussed in Chapter 2 were nonsense. He was the first to suggest that satellites in high orbits could be used as communication-relayers. He was one of the founders of the British Interplanetary Society (I doubt he knew that I had been a fellow of the BIS). Its journal had published several extensive bibliographies on interstellar travel. He was, therefore, much more knowledgeable about advanced space technology than were Asimov and Bova. Unfortunately, for whatever reason, he chose to speak out about flying saucers, demonstrating a surprisingly unscientific attitude in a general magazine: the summer 1971 issue of the *Saturday Evening Post*, which had a large circulation at the time. The title was, "Whatever Happened to Flying Saucers?" The article occupied a full page. As with Asimov and Bova, he impugned the mental competence of those who claim to have observed UFOs. He said, "The Public is no longer worried about them—no longer news. The hysterical credulity of the late '40s has been replaced—except in the minds of the few surviving cultists—by a realization of the fact that the heavens are full of extraordinary sights (astronomical, meteorological, and electrical)." I suspect he was also influenced by the false claims by the USAF when Project Blue Book was closed at the end of 1969, as well as the totally misleading and widely publicized words of Dr. Condon when the final report of his study was released in early 1969. What Clarke said, surprisingly, was that what killed the visitors-from-space concept was the International Geophysical Year (IGY), a period from July 1957 to December 1958, dedicated to scientific efforts around the world. "They never discovered a single flying saucer," he said. No basis is given for that statement. UFO aficionados are well aware that an excellent set of four daytime pictures of a flying saucer were taken on board the Brazilian ship *Almirante Saldanha* on January 16, 1958, by an official naval photographer. The ship was there off the Island of Trinidade participating in International Geophysical Year activities. There were more than 40 witnesses on the deck of the ship to the pictures being taken, and they were finally released to the public by the president of Brazil, Juscelino Kubitschek. I have no reason to presume that Clarke would have had a need-to-know for any official observations made for the United States or other governments by

The best of four Trinidade Brazil UFO pictures, relased by the Brazilian president. Courtesy of the author.

military participants in the IGY (though it is certainly true that he was very much involved in the secret development of radar in Britain in the early 1940s). The launch of *Sputnik* on October 4, 1957, as part of the IGY, put the United States very much on edge about any space-related phenomena.

In his article, Clarke discussed the Ballistic Missile Warning radar system and the fact that it is capable of detecting individual nuts and bolts. He implies that such systems have never detected UFOs—or, in the fancy intelligence-community language, "uncorrelated targets." I can't find any reason to believe that he would have had a need-to-know and appropriate security clearance for such observations about intruders in U.S. airspace in the late 1950s. There were no regular, open publications about uncorrelated targets. William Moore had tried using the Freedom of Information Act to obtain such reports for a particular period of time, and was asked for a search fee of more than $100,000. One of my fantasies used to be, what would have happened if such a payment had been made?

Clarke states that we won't hear any more about "encounters with little green men from Venus" now that we know about the conditions on the surface of Venus. I must admit, I haven't heard any legitimate accounts of little green men from Venus. That may be a staple of science fiction, but hardly of scientific ufology. But there have certainly been many fascinating and apparently legitimate encounters between earthlings and aliens from outer space, ranging from the Betty and Barney Hill case (New Hampshire in September 1961), to the case of Charles Hickson and Calvin Parker (Pascagoula, Mississippi, on October 11, 1973), to the Travis Walton abduction (November 5, 1975). These and many more have been investigated by such men of science as Dr. Leo Sprinkle of the University of Wyoming, the late Dr. James Harder of the University of California at Berkeley, and the late Dr. John Mack of Harvard. Clarke claimed, "No—flying saucers are dead." He surely wasn't much of a prophet, judging by the myriad of cases that have occurred since his article was published, and before it was written (about which he apparently was ignorant). I think of the 41 excellent cases reported by Dr. James E. McDonald in his Congressional testimony of July 29, 1968.

Clarke said, "We and our world are in no way unique." I certainly agree with that, though it may turn out that we have more than our share of vicious, evil folks. He then asks, "Well, why aren't there any visitors from space? Where is everybody?" Obviously I don't know where everybody is. I do know that there is overwhelming evidence that some of the beings from out there have been reconnoitering Earth for some time, gathering and evaluating specimens, destroying aircraft when attacked, monitoring the flight capabilities of our interceptors, and apparently ignoring such science fiction legends as Asimov, Bova, and Clarke.

In another good example of psychological projection, he says, in discussing why we haven't been visited, that we should wait patiently, "rather than get involved in any more of the half and wholly baked speculations, which, for the last 15 years, have hindered the serious scientific approach to the most important question that man can ask of the Universe." Presumably he is talking about whether or not aliens exist. Unfortunately, it is the Clarke, Bova, and Asimov writings about UFOs that must be considered half-baked; not those of professional people such as McDonald, Harder, Vallee, Hynek, Sturrock, and the like, who have studied the data indicating that Earth is being visited.

I found it intriguing that in Clarke's 1968 book *The Promise of Space*, he stated that "after 20 years of the wretched things, I am bored to death with UFOs. Any letters on the subject will not be forwarded by my publishers. If forwarded, they will not be read. And if read, they will not be answered." One has to ask why he wrote the article in the *Post*. He has also dabbled on TV, making negative remarks on a Dick Cavitt network TV show on November 1, 1973. As a matter of fact, the subject was broached on a program of the TV series hosted by him several years later, and he was not nearly so negative. Early on he had apparently indicated interest.

Dr. David Rudiak, an outstanding researcher, recently dug out a *New York Times* article of June 22, 1952, which included a review of Clarke's just-published book *The Exploration of Space* by rocket expert Willy Ley. "Even the possibility of trips to other solar systems is given some attention," Ley writes. "Nobody, Mr. Clarke notes, will come out and say that he considers it a future possibility, but if anyone attempts to prove the total impossibility of interstellar flight, there is a great show of indignation and calculations are promptly produced refuting the critics." In connection with this idea, Clarke carefully enters the flying saucer controversy. The question: If even interstellar travel seems ultimately possible, why have none of the other intelligent races presumed to exist ever visited Earth? His answer is that this may have happened before recorded history: "...the most reasonable attitude toward them would seem to be one of open-minded skepticism." I buy that, though one would hope that strong opinions wouldn't be expressed without serious examination of the relevant data.

Again we have certainty expressed about no visits, despite no effort to look at the very evidence indicating the planet is being visited. It is perhaps fitting that on his 90th birthday, on December 16, 2007, Clarke was quoted in the *London Observer* as having three wishes about what he would like to have happen before he died. First, he would like evidence of extraterrestrial life. "I have always believed that we are not alone in the universe," he says. "But we are still waiting for ETs to call us—or give us some kind of a sign." The second was, "I would like to see us kick our addiction to oil and adopt clean energy sources." The third was, "I dearly wish to see lasting peace established in Sri Lanka as soon as possible." (He has lived there for 50 years.) In my view, the signs of ET are all about. If one doesn't look, one will not see.

Many other comments about flying saucers have been made by science fiction writers. One I very much approve of was made by Robert Heinlein (1907–1988), a truly outstanding science fiction writer. He was asked for his views by J. Neil Schulman in one of many written questions he posed to Heinlein in June 1973. "Does Heinlein think any of the Unidentified Flying Objects have been actual contacts with beings from outer space?" he asked. Heinlein responded in a scientific fashion, not a fictional one: "I don't know," he answered. "I simply don't have data. There have been some UFO sightings that are extremely hard to explain. I'm reminded of something Willie Ley said to me, oh, 20 or 25 years ago. He said, 'Vun. Dere is something dere. Two, I do not know vat it is.' I'm just about where Willy Ley put it then; there is something out there and I do not know what it is." Sounds like he placed the question in what I would call his "gray basket." There is nothing wrong in saying "I don't know."

A number of years ago I visited a science fiction book store in Berkeley, California. I asked where the UFO books were. I was informed, with great disdain, "We don't carry any of that garbage." Perhaps it would be much more honest if the term was science *fiction*. I have often suggested that there really is a need for more doctoral theses related to UFOs, besides the dozen or so that have already been done. A good one would deal with the intersection between flying saucers and science fiction. The Internet certainly makes it easier now than it would have been 30 years ago: A recent Google search for "science fiction and flying saucers" returned more than 200,000 hits.

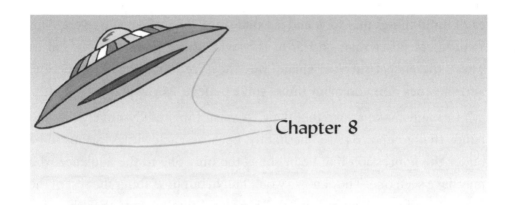

Chapter 8

UFOs and Public Opinion

Some readers may be surprised to find a chapter on public opinion about UFOs in a book entitled *Flying Saucers and Science* by a nuclear physicist. The fact is that people's opinions (no matter how inaccurate) about flying saucers are an important part of the mix, especially when they are (often) completely incorrect. Opinions have a strong influence on both the press and the scientific community. For decades I have been asking this first question in the question-and-answer session after my more than 700 lectures: "How many people here believe they have seen what I would consider to be a flying saucer?" I define my terms at the beginning of my lecture, which is entitled "Flying Saucers ARE Real." I stress that I am only interested in reports by competent observers of strange phenomena in the sky or on the ground that the observer cannot identify, and which also remain unidentified after investigation by competent investigators. Furthermore, their appearance must indicate they are manufactured, and their behavior that they are manufactured elsewhere than on Earth (because we can't build things that look and act that way). Therefore, they were built somewhere other than on Earth. However, these cases may not tell us where the alien visitors originate, why they are here, how they operate, and why they don't do many things some believe they would or should.

I usually make a joke that the CIA wasn't invited. Normally the first hands that go up are raised hesitantly, because each witness seems to be under the impression that he or she is the only one in the audience who may have seen one. They know I won't laugh, but how about the rest of the crowd? I point and count hands:1,2,3...when I finally get to the other side of the hall, the hands go up much more readily, apparently out of relief that each witness obviously isn't the only one. Typically, the number of witnesses is about 10 percent of the audience. So if I have 500 attendees, that's about 50 UFO sighters. Then I ask, "How many of you reported what you saw?" Typically, 90 percent of the hands go down. If there seem to be appropriate hands left (not too young), I ask, "How many of you were in the military at the time?" If some hands are still left, I ask, "Do you want to tell us about it?" I get some very interesting answers. One man, in front of 1,350 people at East Texas State University, said, "I can't; they told me not to say anything." Another, at Indiana University in Indianapolis, said, "They took my pictures." I waited, and then said, "I won't ask your name and you don't need to stand up, but I am sure the audience would like to hear the rest of the story." Everybody clapped. He remained seated and said, "I was piloting a four-engine USAF plane over the Pacific when the plane 20 miles ahead radioed that there was a saucer heading our way. We had gun cameras and managed to get some pictures. We radioed the base to which we were heading, since the film is handled by intelligence people at the base, not the crew. When we landed, they took the film, and the crew was debriefed and told never to say anything."

I have heard many similar stories. One former military man told me he would tell me about it later. He related this, near my table: "I was flying a helicopter in Vietnam when a sleek saucer flew around us twice.

We thought it must be a new Russian vehicle and we would soon be dead. It just dashed off. So back at base, as required, I reported the observation. The command likes to know about new enemy technology. The next day the base commander came over and asked, 'You didn't see anything strange yesterday Lieutenant Jones, did you?' I said, 'Yes, sir. I did and I reported it.' He said, 'You didn't hear me, did you Lieutenant Jones?' 'Well, sir...,' [I said.] 'Do you like flying, Lt. Jones?' [he asked me]. 'Yes, sir.' 'You didn't see anything strange yesterday did you?' 'No, sir.'"

The point of relating these stories is that most people seem to feel that sightings are very rare, and some still think there is no cover-up or intimidation of witnesses. Furthermore, when people quietly tell me of their sightings, often for the first time, I ask why they hadn't reported it. The answer is usually, "They would think I was some kind of a nut." Fear of ridicule seems to be a powerful human concern. Concern with national security is another, for people who have had security clearances.

Once, in a campus classroom, many hours before my lecture, I told a class of about 100 students that I wanted to know their feelings about some things, but didn't want their votes to be influenced by their classmates, so I asked them to respond by raising their hands, but with their eyes closed. Their instructor and I would count the votes. I wanted to find out first what they thought *other* people thought about flying saucers, and then what they themselves thought. About 80 percent felt that most people didn't believe that any UFOs were intelligently controlled ET spacecraft. When asked for their own opinions, however, 80 percent said they did think some UFOs were alien spacecraft. My observation is that people's behavior is far more determined by their perception of how others will react than by their own beliefs. Most people, perhaps understandably, are sheep, not shepherds.

This perception of setting oneself up for ridicule has some serious consequences: Most people are clearly unwilling to report their sightings; most people are likely to laugh when someone else brings up the subject; most professors are not willing to teach a course about UFOs, and are reluctant to sponsor a graduate thesis. Fortunately there have been a number of courses taught by courageous professors, and at least a dozen PhD theses done on UFO-related topics. For example, my talk at East Texas State University was sponsored by the physics department professor, who was teaching such a course, and had me speak to his class as well as at the large public audience. The funny thing is, after it was determined that many students were interested, the English department tried to get the course and entitle it "UFO Literature." (Department income was partially related to the number of students taking a course.) The physics department won the battle.

Perhaps of more concern is the fact that many people in the media are afraid to cover a UFO lecture or a sighting report in a serious fashion because their bosses have indicated they want a light story, as there is nothing to this silly stuff about UFOs. This also means the reporters see no point in getting educated about the topic. I can guarantee ignorance is widespread.

I frequently run across comments such as, "Of course most people don't believe in UFOs," and "Certainly most scientists don't." I know that most people are unfamiliar with the several large-scale scientific studies discussed in Chapter 1, because I ask, after I show a slide and talk about each one, "How many here have read this?" Typically it is only 1 or 2 percent. I was asked to speak to a group of Canadian journalists having an annual conference in St. John, New Brunswick. The letter I received later indicated that there had been a huge change in attitude after my lecture. Attendees had had no idea there was so much solid information, as opposed to the tabloid nonsense they thought was the primary source of UFO data.

A good example of how important perception of attitudes is came in October 1994 when I was on the outdoor set of a two-hour *Larry King* broadcast from way out near Rachel, Nevada (population about 105), more than 100 miles north of Las Vegas, and not far from Area 51. There were four live guests: Dr. Steven Greer, researcher Kevin Randle, local Area 51 expert Glenn Campbell, and myself. The show was due to start at 5 p.m. local time for the Turner Network. In midafternoon I asked one of the producers (not the one I had been dealing with) whether we would be taking phone calls in this remote place. She said, "Oh, yes. They will come into Atlanta and be transferred by satellite to that truck way over there. We will, of course, screen them very closely, because most people don't believe in UFOs." I reacted very strongly, saying that the polls (discussed in a moment) showed that that simply wasn't true. Not only were believers in the majority, but also the greater the education, the more likely a person is to accept flying saucer reality.

She was shocked, but the important impact of the false perception was that, of the roughly 10 short clips shown of various "experts," the great majority were from noisy negativists. The reason was that if, for example, *Time* magazine gets 50 letters about an article and 80 percent are favorable, they might only publish 10, but eight would be favorable, to reflect the attitudes of the responders. One of the "experts" was Canadian actor William Shatner (apparently some thought of him as a space scientist or astronaut!). He made a foolish comment to the effect that witnesses are only wishful thinking by people who want Big Brother from the sky to come down and save them! In short, false perceptions took the place of reality.

Public opinion polls are often difficult to interpret, because the interpretation depends on how randomly the respondents were selected, the size of the sample, how the questions were worded, and how the media often presents a quickie or even quirky version of a complex situation. For example, what do you mean if you say, "UFOs are real?" A skeptic might say, of course there are "real" unidentified flying objects in the eyes of the beholder, but they can all be explained. Some might take the word *UFO* to be a short form of "Extraterrestrial Space Ship." In a moment you will see a question asking, "Do you think there are beings similar to us on other planets?" Well, does that mean humanoid, with two arms, two legs, a head, and a body? Would little guys under 4 feet tall with big heads, skinny bodies, large eyes, practically no ears, a slit for a mouth, and grayish skin be considered "similar to" us? Once, after a lecture to a packed auditorium at the University of Manitoba in Winnipeg, the first questioner in the audience (I select totally at random from raised hands) asked me to poll that audience, as I had earlier shown a slide of some of Gallup results (shown on page 207). I indicated that I wasn't accustomed to asking the attendees to stick their necks out. He responded that he didn't think people would mind. The audience clapped, so I asked, "How many think some UFOs are alien spacecraft?" and "How many think no UFOs are alien spacecraft?" Only about 10 percent said no UFOs are ET craft. This was hardly a fair poll or random sampling, because they had just sat through a fact-loaded 90-minute illustrated lecture entitled "Flying Saucers ARE Real," but it should encourage those who want to speak out—with facts in hand first, of course.

Publicity in the press can be misleading as well. In 1966 the press coverage focused on only 46 percent believing in UFOs, clearly implying that 54 percent did not. In fact, only 29 percent didn't believe. The other 25 percent weren't sure. One can't count the uncertain votes on either side of the question.

It seemed strange to me that many scientists are under the false impression that most people, and especially most scientists, don't believe. Dr. J. Allen Hynek, then the chairman of the astronomy department at Northwestern University, and Project Blue Book scientific consultant until 1969, once told me in his office, "Stan, the problem is that 90 percent of scientists don't believe in UFOs." He may have been right if he had restricted his comment to astronomers, but physicists, chemists, biologists, geologists, and so on, are also scientists. I did point out that I had a good response from various engineering societies. Amazingly, debunker Phil Klass similarly claimed in *UFOs Explained* that the ratio of believers to nonbelievers is about 1 to 11. Though both authors strongly disagreed about UFOs, they were also both totally wrong about what percentage believes some are real—as the data shows. I was certainly convinced that one of the reasons Hynek had been so reluctant to take a strong public stand for any UFOs as alien spacecraft is the false perception that the scientific community would come down hard on him. I was present when he was introduced at a UCLA lecture by Professor Abell of the UCLA astronomy department, with a number of negative comments about the subject. Hynek did not respond at all, other than being apologetic about even talking about UFOs. I felt for a long time that one of the reasons scientists were reluctant to speak out was a combination of Allen's failure to speak out and the noisy negativism from another astronomer, Dr. Donald Menzel, of Harvard. The thinking would be that if there was anything to this subject, they would have spoken out positively.

Dr. James E. McDonald, an atmospheric physicist whom I consider to have been the top ufologist ever, was totally shocked when he visited Project Blue Book in the 1960s in Ohio and found case after case that was challenging, and yet had been casually dismissed. He blamed Hynek for not alerting the scientific community. (Their battle is described in Ann Druffle's outstanding book *Firestorm: Dr. James E. McDonald's Fight for UFO Science.*) A number of his best cases were presented at the Congressional hearings of 1968. It should be noted that Menzel's first book, *Flying Saucers*, had been published in 1953 (and even translated into Russian). Hynek had favorably reviewed Menzel's book, despite its being unscientific and biased. McDonald, in contrast, wrote papers scientifically destroying Menzel's "scientific" explanations, but not many general articles. As I will discuss in Chapter 11, Menzel had been involved in highly classified intelligence activities with the NSA, the CIA, and so on, and was a member of the TOP SECRET Operation Majestic 12. He was the only one of the 12 original members who had written science fiction, so he would have been perfect for debunking and influencing the scientific and journalistic communities. His negative views were presented in depth in the June 9, 1952 issue of *Time* magazine. (This was before the huge flap of sightings over Washington in July 1952.) Perhaps this was in accordance with the comment in the November 18, 1952, Eisenhower Briefing Document (see Chapter 11) about "a significant upsurge in the surveillance activity of these craft beginning in May and continuing through the autumn...."

A series of Gallup polls using the same questions each time were conducted throughout a period of many years, with results shown in Table 1 on page 207. Because of the unsure vote, I have also included the percentage of those who expressed an opinion, leaving the votes for "not sure" out of the picture. I really don't like the word *believer*, but I am stuck with it. Notice that the believers outnumbered nonbelievers each time, except for those with only a grade-school education in 1978. James Oberg, who worked in the space program for many years and has been consistently anti-UFO, claimed that the reason for the high number of believers was all the tabloid TV programs and tabloid newspaper articles touting UFO reality. Dr. Carl Sagan surprisingly cited the tabloid *Weekly World News* more than any other source about UFOs in his book *Demon Haunted World*. This is a testable hypothesis. Presumably, the greater the education, the less likely to be influenced by tabloids. The polls normally included results as a function of the education and age of the respondents as well as by sex and region of the country.

Do note that the greater the education, the more likely a person is to be a believer! In general, the older the individual, the less likely to be a believer, at least back in the 1960s, '70s, and '80s. This may well have something to do with the fact that many years ago most scientists assumed that the process that produced the planets in our solar system was a rare near-collision of two stars. Considering how far apart stars are from each other, this wouldn't happen often (aren't we lucky), and there may well be no other planetary systems in the neighborhood. Much newer astronomical science indicates that planetary formation is part of the life history of

Table 1 Gallup Polls
Q: Are UFOS something real, or just people's imaginations?

	Year			
	1966	**1973**	**1978**	**1987**
Percent Real	46	54	57	49
Percent Real (omit Not Sure)	61	64	68	60
Percent Imaginary	29	30	27	30
Percent Not Sure	25	16	16	21
Ratio Real/Imaginary	1.59	1.8	2.16	1.63

Note: First Lunar Landing was 1969

Table 2 Gallup Polls (Same Question as Table 1)

Factors	% Real		% Imaginary		% Not Sure	
Age	**1978**	**1987**	**1978**	**1987**	**1978**	**1987**
Less than 30	70	53	20	32	10	15
30–49	63	57	23	21	14	22
over 50	40	36	38	39	22	25
Education (1978)						
College	66		23		11	
High School	57		27		16	
Grade School	36		38		26	
Education (1987)						
Attend College	56		26		18	
No College	44		33		23	

many stars. We know that more than 290 exoplanets have already been discovered, despite the crude observational instruments that are presently in use. As noted in Chapter 2, new techniques for measuring the distances to stars in the neighborhood have improved enormously as we have used instruments that are outside the atmosphere, on satellites, rather than on the surface of the Earth. Within 25 years it is expected that new satellites will be in space and able to discern planets around all the stars nearby, if there are any there. This means, of course, that an alien civilization a little older and more technologically sophisticated than ours (say a mere thousand years) would have been able to do that a relatively long time ago. I think every library in the local galactic neighborhood would know that there is advanced technological life on Earth. Also, before the first landing on the moon in 1969, there were many well-educated scoffers about space travel. If we can't get to the moon, they thought, then manned trips to other planets in the solar system, and certainly beyond, would be impossible. Here is a typical negative statement about travel to the moon from Lee DeForest, the father of modern electronics: "To place a man in a multi-stage rocket and project him into the controlling gravitational field of the moon, where the passengers can make scientific observations, perhaps land alive, and then return to Earth; all that constitutes a wild dream worthy of Jules Verne. I am bold enough to say that such a man-made moon voyage will never occur, regardless of all future scientific advances." (February 25, 1957, *St. Louis Post Dispatch*.) It took only 12 years to accomplish the impossible. The Astronomer Royal of the UK was also quoted around that time as saying space travel was "utter bilge."

An important poll was taken by Industrial Research and Development Magazine back in 1971, and repeated again in 1979. This is a controlled-circulation monthly publication going to about 100,000 people involved in research and development activities, and therefore having a higher level of education than the general public. As a matter of fact, 40 percent had BS degrees, 25 percent had Masters degrees, and 23 percent had a

Table 3 (R & D Mag.)

Question 1. Do you believe that UFOs exist?

	1971	1979
Definitely	20 percent	27 percent
Probably	34	34
Undecided	15	12
Probably Not	23	20
Definitely Not	8	8

Question 6. If you consider the possibility, what is their origin?

	1971	1979
USA	5 percent	2 percent
Communist Nations	1	less than 1
Outer Space	32	44
Natural Phenomena	27	28
Undecided	35	26

Percentage Definitely or Probably in Q I versus age (1979 only)

Age	% of Respondents	Def. or Prob.
Under 26	4	82
26–35	28	70
36–45	28	59
46–55	25	57
56–65	13	48
Over 65	1	35

PhD. They have a reader-reply-card poll in every issue about any of a wide variety of topics. Note in Table 3 on page 209 the favorable response in both polls, again with believers outnumbering nonbelievers. I find this consistent with the enthusiastic response I receive from lectures to R&D people. It was also found that perhaps 8 to 12 percent of the respondents have had sightings.

More or less similar polls have been conducted by other professional groups. Dr. Peter Sturrock, now a retired Stanford University astrophysicist, polled the membership of the American Astronomical Society. Unfortunately, he used different questions than those used by Gallup or R&D, so direct comparisons cannot be made. He had also, in 1973, surveyed the members of the San Francisco chapter of the American Institute of Aeronautics and Astronautics. An important (and unsurprising) result of Sturrock's survey was the fact that the greater the amount of time one spent on reading UFO-related material, the more likely one is to accept their reality. Sturrock found that there had indeed been sightings (more than 5 percent), but almost none of the respondents would allow their names to be used. A wide diversity of opinions was expressed.

Gert Herb conducted a survey of amateur astronomers who, as a rule, spend more time at night outside looking at the sky than do professionals who rarely look through scopes, but program instruments to examine and photograph a particular preprogrammed location in the sky. He had responses from 1,805 members of the American Astronomical League. Of the respondents, 23.9 percent claimed to have observed "an object which resisted [their] most exhaustive efforts at identification"; 8.9 percent had seen a High Strangeness Object. Only 6 percent were skeptical about UFOs.

Strangely, despite the facts, a common claim by debunkers is that neither professional nor amateur astronomers ever see UFOs! Dr. David Morrison, senior scientist of NASA's prestigious Astrobiology Institute at Ames Laboratory near San Francisco, made such a ridiculous claim in eSkeptic, a blog magazine published by *SKEPTIC* magazine publisher Dr. Michael Shermer, in November, 2007. There is no reference to any of these sources, of course. Shermer and I clashed on a *Larry King* show on July 13, 2007, and again in a three-hour debate (just the two of us) on George Noory's *Coast to Coast* radio program on August 1, 2007. Noory polled his audience at the end; 80 percent thought I won the debate. The reason was obvious: Shermer had apparently not done any homework about the subject, ever. He gave no references, made false claims, and so on. In the 19 days between the two programs I dug out two of his books from the University of New Brunswick Library and was able to use his words to refute his own arguments. He hadn't bothered to get any data or to read my books. Some psychologist ought to do a PhD thesis on resistance to UFO reality by some professionals. Shermer's explanation in *Why Smart People Believe Weird Things* of why sensible people believe strange things certainly applies to those, such as himself, who claim that there is nothing to UFOs. On page 283 he writes, "Smart people believe weird things because they are skilled at defending beliefs they arrived at for non-smart reasons." He gives a second reason, which I find equally important for the well educated debunkers, on page 299: "The Confirmation Bias, or the tendency to seek or interpret evidence favorable to already existing beliefs and to ignore or reinterpret evidence unfavorable to already existing beliefs." This is a much more sophisticated way of giving one of my major rules for debunkers: "Don't bother me with the facts; my mind is made up." Shermer continued to express his irrational negativity in appearances in January 2008, attacking the sightings in Stephenville, Texas, on *Larry King* and elsewhere.

Some people actually think that astronomy professors use their telescopes to look around the skies and would surely see UFOs. However, a small telescope sees only a very tiny region of the sky. Rarely are airplanes seen, because, not only is the field of view very small, but also a plane or UFO would pass through it almost instantaneously.

An important poll had been conducted in 1991 and 1998 by the Roper Organization to try to determine not only people's views, but also some indication as to how many Americans may have been abducted by alien visitors. A number of questions were asked that individually didn't mean too much. It was thought that if there was a yes answer to four out of five of the questions, there was a great likelihood that the respondent had had an abduction experience. The poll has been taken several times, and seems to indicate that perhaps 1 to 2 percent of the public have been abducted. That is well over a million persons. Much newspaper coverage has unfortunately implied that that number of people had claimed to be abducted, which is not the case. The statistics, when one is dealing with a small subset of 10 to 15 people of the 1,000 polled, are poor. In addition, what does one do about false positives? In all medical testing one typically finds initial test results suggesting that a certain condition might be present, when subsequent, more sophisticated tests indicate the initial diagnosis was in error. There may also be false negatives: people who, upon later testing, do turn out to have the condition being evaluated. As it turned out, about 7 percent of respondents in both polls indicated they had seen a UFO. Someday it might be possible to test a large number of "certified abductees" and a control population to try to evaluate the test results. The important point is that some significant number of Americans have apparently been abducted. If, as noted previously, people are reluctant to report a common garden-variety UFO sighting, they would be much less likely to report an abduction, especially if the memory is suppressed, as was the case in the abduction of Betty and Barney Hill (described in *Captured! The Betty and Barney Hill UFO Experience* by myself and Kathleen Marden, Betty's niece).

Unsophisticated Polls

Aside from the large-scale, sophisticated polls, many more have been conducted involving people responding to a TV or radio show. Here are some examples: On April 28, 1974, The San Diego TV station KFMB asked its listeners to respond with a yes or no to this question: "Do you believe that UFOs have brought intelligent visitors to Earth from Outer Space?" The question was asked in conjunction with a debate about UFOs between myself and Dr. Elia Schneor, a former member of the National Academy of Sciences Committee on Extraterrestrial Life. A total of 361 people (75 percent) said yes, and only 116 (25 percent) said no. TV Ontario, an educational TV network, had a debate between myself (on the pro side) and Dr. Robert F. Garrison, a University of Toronto astronomer (on the con side). The discussion question on the February 1983 program *Speaking Out* was, "Do you believe that some UFOs are extraterrestrial spacecraft?" The tally was recorded electronically from calls placed to one number for yes and another number for no. Of the 1,244 votes recorded, 908 (74 percent) were yes, with only 336 (26 percent) being no. I presume the average educational attainment of the viewers is higher than for the general public, as the vote matches that of the 1978 Gallup poll for those with a college background.

On March 14, 1988, a UFO debunker, the late Philip Klass, and I, appeared on a live, widely distributed TV program called *People Are Talking* in Secaucus, New Jersey. A telephone poll was conducted using the Gallup poll question (real or imaginary), without the "unsure" category. Fully 83 percent of the callers said UFOs are real.

I also found friendly audiences in England. In October 1995 I did a debate at Oxford University Debating Union. The debate concerned the statement, "This house believes that intelligent alien life has visited planet Earth." My teammate on the pro side was barrister (attorney) Harry Harris. In opposition was English author Peter Brookesmith and a couple of students. I used slides of data. Peter used quotes from tabloids. About a month later he called to buy copies of some of the reports I distribute—a little late. A vote was taken of debate union members: 60 percent said my team won. This was particularly satisfying, as I did a total of 41 interviews while giving a number of lectures during that visit to England. None of the journalists were well informed at all. The debate was actually covered by a reporter for the *Fortean Times* (named after Charles Fort, who was an early collector of various anomalies). His article wasn't used, apparently because my team had won the debate!

On June 27, 1997, the ITV TV network in the UK sponsored a much less formal debate with a live studio audience and a nationwide TV audience. My team included two top English ufologists, Nick Pope and Tim Good. The other team had three PhDs: a physicist, an astronomer, and a psychologist. None of them had done any homework. The audience called in their votes in response to this question: "Are aliens visiting Earth?" My team got 92,000 of the 100,000 votes. That is a powerful affirmation. The live audience voted before the debate. Only 73 percent said yes.

None of these polls could be considered scientific, and all involved exposure by the respondents to comments by myself and by nonbelievers. But they do help people understand my response when well-meaning reporters suggest I must get a hard time for coming on so strongly. I don't, as demonstrated by the fact that in 40 years of lecturing to more than 700 audiences, I have only had 11 hecklers, two of whom were drunk. I am sure I would have had at least as many if I was talking about sports, religion, or politics.

It comes as a surprise to many people, but several public opinion polls were also taken for the University of Colorado Study of UFOs as reported in the Condon report. There is a detailed chapter (pages 209 to 243) with a total of 21 tables of data. The 1966 Gallup poll results were reviewed, and a variety of polls taken in 1968 of adults, teenagers, UFO observers, college students, those taking courses on UFO, and so on. These again indicated that the greater the education, the more likely one is to be a believer, and that more than 60 percent of the respondents felt that the government was not revealing all it knows. Dr. Condon did note the positive effect of education on attitudes in his summary, but added (unsurprisingly, in light of his many unsubstantiated negative comments about UFOs): "Perhaps this result says something about how the school system trains students in critical thinking." I would say his comment reflects both his bias and his ignorance of the subject.

Over and over again polls have shown that a substantial majority believe the government hasn't told us all it knows about UFOs. And yet over and over again I hear derogatory comments from noisy negativists about supposed conspiracy theorists. Having worked under security for 14 years, I have never thought that keeping classified materials classified constituted a conspiracy. It is following regulations established under law. No, we are not guaranteed access to *any* classified materials, much less to them all. Rule number one for security is that one can't tell one's friends without telling one's enemies. There are national security considerations for all countries: The first country to duplicate saucer technology may well rule the world. Flying saucers can fly circles around anything we earthlings can fly. We certainly don't want anybody else to know what we have learned from monitoring UFO flights and from analysis of wreckage. We also would like to try to determine what other countries have learned. Those who scoff at the notion of a cover-up haven't been able to show what is under the white-out on 156 formerly TOP SECRET ULTRA pages of old UFO information from the NSA, or the many heavily blacked-out pages from the CIA. People looking at these documents have sometimes asked me if that was legal. Yes, it is legal. Frustrating? Yes. But the documents provide proof that material is being withheld.

As an indication of how much things have changed in 60 years, here are the results of the August 1947 Gallup poll question, "What do you think these saucers are?"

No answer/don't know:	33 percent
Imagination, optical illusions, mirages:	29 percent
Hoax:	10 percent
U.S. secret weapon, part of atomic bomb:	15 percent
Weather forecasting devices:	3 percent
Russian secret weapon:	1 percent
Searchlights on airplanes:	2 percent
Other:	9 percent
Total (some chose more than 1):	102 percent

Notice that "spaceships from other planets" wasn't even a category on the list! Also notice that, although the Germans had used V-1 and V-2 rockets to bomb England, not many thought flying saucers were Russian rockets, despite the fact that the cold war was rapidly heating up in 1947. The weather balloon explanation for Roswell on July 9, and mention of tests of weather balloons supposedly explaining away UFOs in general, don't seem to have had much influence on the survey results. Incidentally, there was a high awareness score for "Have you ever heard about Flying Saucers?" Many may not be aware that there was a huge amount of newspaper coverage of flying saucers (or flying disks) in July 1947, especially during the July 4 weekend before the July 8 Roswell coverage. The phony weather balloon explanation for Roswell on July 8 and 9 didn't seem to have convinced too many people.

The reality of flying saucers as alien visitors is not determined by public opinion polls. However, one can understand why there has been so much disinformation and misinformation put out by people such as Colonel Weaver in his viciously inaccurate *Roswell Report: Fact vs. Fiction in the New Mexico Desert*. As long as the press emphasizes the nasty, noisy negativism of the debunkers, many scientists, journalists, politicians, and retired military people will be reluctant to speak out for fear of ridicule.

It would certainly appear to be past time to lift the laughter curtain that gets in the way of full disclosure by individuals, and inhibits full investigation by scientists and journalists. If you are ready to speak out, please contact me at fsphys@rogers.com .My toll-free number is on my Website, *www.stantonfriedman.com*.

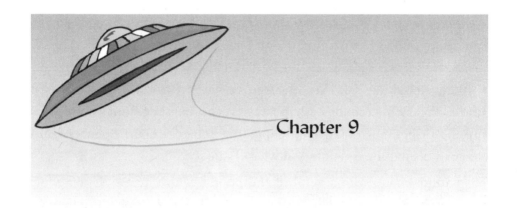

Chapter 9

Update on Crashed
Saucers at Roswell

It is surprising to me that the recovery of crashed saucers in southeastern New Mexico in July 1947 is still a major bone of contention in 2008. I began the civilian investigation of the so-called Roswell Incident back in the early 1970s, having first heard about it from a woman named Lydia Sleppy, who had been working at a radio station in Albuquerque. I was talking to her with an associate, the late Bobbi Ann Slate Gironda, with whom I had been working on some UFO magazine articles. She was a fine writer. I, as a scientist, had to make things clear enough that she could understand them and write them in popular language. We had spoken with Sleppy's son, a California forest ranger, who had had an excellent recent sighting. He suggested we talk to his mother, who had had a good sighting in the Albuquerque area many years earlier. Her sighting was an interesting one, and she mentioned that years ago her station had received a call from their Roswell, New Mexico, affiliate about a crashed saucer. She was a good typist, though not a journalist, and was asked to type the story on the news wire. The Roswell source said that a saucer had crashed and was being shipped to Wright Field in Ohio. As she typed the story for the Associated Press wire, a bell went off. A message said, "Do not continue this transmission, FBI." She checked with the Roswell source and was told to follow instructions. I had heard several earlier stories about sup-posed crashes, such as from a character named Robert Spencer Carr, but had been quite unimpressed when I checked up on it.

I followed up with several of the people whose names Lydia could remember. But I could only go so far—people either couldn't remember or couldn't be found. So I filed Lydia's story. I could find no reason not to believe what she said. Thus, I was ready when, entirely by accident, I again heard about a Roswell crashed saucer story in 1978. I was at a TV station in Baton Rouge, Louisiana, scheduled to do three different inter-views to promote my lecture that evening at Louisiana State University. The station manager knew the woman who had brought me to the sta-tion. The first two interviews went off without a hitch; the third reporter was nowhere to be found (there were no cell phones back then). The station manager, Johnny Allen, was giving me coffee, looking at his watch, and frankly was embarrassed. He knew I had other things to do. Com-pletely out of the blue, he suddenly said, "The guy you really ought to talk to is Jesse Marcel. He handled wreckage of one of those saucers you are interested in when he was in the military." I was shocked. I thought, my lecture title was "Flying Saucers ARE Real," so presumably he felt safe talking to me. It was clear he wasn't joking. There was no one else around, so I asked for more information. "Jesse and I are old ham radio buddies," he said. "He lives over in Houma. Great guy. You ought to talk to him." I had no idea where Houma was (though I have been there since, to interview Marcel). We talked a bit more, and Allen spoke very highly of Marcel. Finally the reporter showed up. I did the interview and moved on, and had a great response that night at LSU. I found out much later that all Allen had really known was what was in a New Orleans newspaper article about the crash. It had mentioned Jesse having been from Houma. Years later, when Allen asked Marcel about it, he was told: "I can't say anything about that."

The next day, from the Baton Rouge airport, I called information in Houma, and then talked to Marcel. I didn't have a tape recorder with me, and, of course, I had no idea that 30 years later I would still be working on the case. He gave me a rundown on the event: He was the intelligence officer of the 509th Bomb Group based at Roswell, and on that Sunday he was the duty officer when the sheriff called to say that a local rancher had come in with some strange wreckage. There was an agreement between the base, then known as Roswell Army Air Field (RAAF), and the sheriff, that he would call them if anything happened that might be related to the base (it could be a drunken airman, an airplane crash, or the like). The sheriff said the material was very strange. Marcel talked to the base commander, Colonel Blanchard, who instructed him to check it out at the sheriff's office a few miles north of the base. Marcel did so, and reported to the colonel that the rancher said there was a lot of this very strange stuff in small pieces out at the sheep ranch he managed. Marcel said he couldn't identify any of the stuff; there was nothing conventional about it.

Colonel Blanchard told Marcel to follow the rancher to the ranch, and take along one of the Counter Intelligence Corps guys, Sheridan W. "Cav" Cavitt. The colonel was concerned about who might be spying on the 509th, which was the most elite military unit in the world, having dropped two atomic bombs on Japan in August 1945 to end WWII. They were involved in 1946 with the explosion of two more nuclear weapons at a test series, Operation Crossroads, in the Pacific, before being relocated to Roswell. A great deal of other classified work was also going on in New Mexico. There was much more to the story about the trip to the ranch: a subsequent trip to Fort Worth with some of the wreckage, an order there from Colonel Blanchard's boss, General Roger Ramey in Ft. Worth, for Marcel to say nothing while the general explained it away as a weather balloon. But Marcel didn't have an exact date, and I knew that the summer of 1947, after Kenneth Arnold's sighting on June 24, was full of UFO sightings. Remember, as I found out later, that Marcel was mentioned by name in a lot of evening papers on July 8, 1947. That he was involved could not possibly be denied.

Major Jesse Marcel with substitute balloon wreckage for Roswell wreckage, Fort Worth. Courtesy of the University of Texas archives.

A few months later at a lecture in Bemidji, Minnesota, at the state college, I heard from Vern and Jean Maltais another story about a crashed saucer in New Mexico, as observed by a Soil Conservation Service field operator, their friend Barney Barnett. I shared the story with Bill Moore, whom I saw the next day in Minnesota. Again there was not a specific date associated with the crash. Soon he had another story about a crashed saucer in New Mexico in the late 1940s. It had been reported in the *Flying Saucer Review*, an English journal still being published. An English actor named Hughie Green had been driving from Los Angeles to Philadelphia and heard a story on the radio about a crashed saucer in New Mexico. He expected a big fuss in Philadelphia, but there was none. He could recall the date as being early in July 1947, as that wasn't a trip he made often. I did talk to him in England later on, and Moore went to the University of Minnesota Library periodicals department and found the story. This gave us more names of people, and because of the date of the first articles, July 8, 1947, a way to find any other stories there might have been in other papers. It also gave us a chance to verify what I had heard from Lydia Sleppy and from Marcel.

Bill Moore and I played detectives for the next few years, spending a lot of money on phone calls and travel in those pre-Internet days to track down people mentioned in the many newspaper accounts we discovered. By 1980 we had found 62 people who had a connection to the crash. The first book on the subject, *The Roswell Incident*, was published in 1980 by Moore and Charles Berlitz, of Bermuda Triangle fame. Moore and I did 90 percent of the research; Berlitz did most of the writing. (I got a percentage of Moore's royalties.) By 1986, our total was 92 people, and we had presented a number of papers at MUFON symposia. As I will detail in Chapter 10, I convinced the *Unsolved Mysteries* NBC TV program to do a segment on Roswell, which brought in another batch of witnesses. I coauthored the book *Crash at Corona: The Definitive Study of the Roswell Incident* in 1992, with a second edition in 1997, with Donald Berliner, an aviation writer who has been active in ufology since the 1950s. Moore had talked to Barnett's boss and found again that the date of that crash was early July 1947.

I have gone through these details so that the reader will know the falsity of a host of charges by Roswell debunkers. For example, some have portrayed the witnesses as coming forth for fame and fortune. They didn't—we had to find them; sometimes I got lucky. For example, I called the *Roswell Daily Record* and asked for the 1947 editor. He was long gone. I told the receptionist I had a story about the base public information officer, Walter Haut. I was shocked to find that his wife worked at the newspaper, and that he was still in Roswell after more than 30 years! He also had a base yearbook for 1947, and was most helpful. I happened to call Information looking for anyone who might be related to the rancher, Mac Brazel. That got me his son William, who had just had a phone installed less than two weeks earlier.

The author holding the July 8, 1947 Los Angeles Herald Express *front-page Roswell story. Courtesy of the author.*

People told us their stories. There were a host of newspaper stories in evening papers on July 8, 1947, from Chicago west. Because of the time zones, papers out west had had more time to check for more information with people in Roswell. This was front-page headline material. The original press release had gone out from Haut, then the base public information officer, just after noon, New Mexico time—too late for the East Coast papers, and for all the morning papers. By the time of the final edition of the *Los Angeles Herald Express*, General Roger Ramey, head of the 8th Air Force in Fort Worth, Texas, of which the 509th was a vital part, had issued a new press release explaining away the flying saucer (also called a "flying disk") as simply a radar reflector/weather balloon combination. Pictures taken in his office were flashed around the world. They indeed had balloon wreckage that had replaced the material actually brought to Fort Worth by Major Marcel.

At least four pictures were taken in the office; Marcel was in one. General Ramey and Colonel Thomas Jefferson DuBose, his chief of staff, were in others. A meteorologist named Irving Newton was in another, saying that what was shown was just a weather balloon/radar reflector combination.

Despite all the research that had been done before the TV cameras came into play, the noisy negativists are still lying through their teeth about what actually happened and how the story came out. On January 9, 2008, Dr. Joe Nickel, the paid "scientific" investigator for the group formerly known as the Committee for the Scientific Investigation of Claims of the Paranormal, now renamed the Committee for Skeptical Inquiry, on *Coast to Coast* radio, made the outrageous claim that the Roswell story was a nothing-story about a rancher finding sticks and paper and bringing them into Roswell. "If only people would look at the original story, they would know it was a big deal made up later by others," he said. His "original story" was published on July 9, after the rancher had been brought back into town by the U.S. Army Air Force and given a new story to tell. If Nickell, whose three degrees are all in English, had done any research at all, he would have known that. This same lie using the cover-up story has been told over and over again. It had a new date for the recovery of the wreckage: mid-June. The real, original, July 8 stories all said "found last week."

General Roger Ramey, 8th Air Force commander, and Colonel T.J. DuBose, July 8, 1947, with substituted Roswell wreckage. Courtesy of the University of Texas archives.

I suppose I should appreciate the fact that, 10 years earlier, Nickell had made an even more outrageous claim to a TV reporter in Los Angeles while I was also being interviewed in Roswell. We couldn't see each other, but could hear over the earphones. Nickell claimed that the story had been made up by "the public information officer" to get attention. He didn't even know Haut's name! He also didn't seem to understand how absurd his claim was, as the 509th was such an important group. Haut, whom I had known for almost 20 years by that time, was a prominent citizen in Roswell, had flown as a bombardier on more than 20 missions over Japan, and had been chosen, because of his skills, to drop the instrument package during one of the two 1946 Crossroads nuclear weapon tests. Nickell said nothing on *Coast to Coast* about Major Marcel, Haut, the sons of rancher Mac Brazel and Major Marcel, retired General Thomas Jefferson Dubose (whom I had tracked down years earlier), or a host of other firsthand witnesses. He didn't even seem to know that Brazel *operated* the Foster ranch, but didn't own it. Witness Dubose had told me face to face that he had taken the call from General Ramey's boss (General McMullen in Washington, D.C.) ordering the real story to be covered up. DuBose, as had Marcel, had appeared in pictures on July 8, 1947. This had all been published, of course. Nickell followed one of the major rules for UFO debunkers: "What the public doesn't know, I won't tell them."

Nickell also claimed that he had participated in a Discovery channel "documentary" in which it was shown that the exploded simulated balloon train that was supposed to match the Mogul balloon explanation (posited in 1994) matched it well. Everyone else who participated said that it showed the balloon wreckage produced could *not possibly* match what the witnesses described. Even then the simulated debris field didn't match what Major Marcel had said to me on the phone, and on film for *UFOs Are Real*. He said there was a huge area, more than half a mile long and hundreds of feet wide, strewn with small pieces of very lightweight materials, including a foil-like material, and I-beams. There was nothing conventional about the wreckage, as one would expect from an airplane, or a silly balloon, or even the vaunted Mogul balloon train. The debunkers insist on totally ignoring the firsthand testimony of those who were involved, including, for example, Jesse Marcel, Junior, now a medical doctor, flight surgeon, and helicopter pilot, who recently returned from a year as a colonel in the reserves in Iraq. That stint included 225 combat hours as a pilot. And Nickel wants to keep him and his father out of the story, despite his having *held* pieces of the wreckage at his home, brought back from an overnight stint at the crash site by his father in 1947!

The author with retired General Thomas Jefferson DuBose.
Courtesy of the author.

Nickell and other debunkers can't bring themselves to admit that if all there had been was a weather balloon, Brazel would have brought it to town, and there would have been no need for Marcel and Cavitt to go all the way out to the ranch—a rough trip over country roads with the last leg more than 10 miles cross-country. In a laughable statement by Cavitt to Colonel Weaver, author of the Air Force's monstrous 1994 report, Cavitt had stated that all there was was a balloon that would easily fit into one vehicle and covered an area 20 feet square! This is despite the fact that the cover-up story on July 9 (Nickell's "original report") noted that the wreckage had covered an area 200 yards in diameter. Mogul had 20-plus balloons, at 20-foot intervals, sono-buoys, radar reflectors, and so on—that would hardly fit easily in one vehicle, as claimed by Cavitt. The same article also noted that the rancher had previously recovered weather balloons, and was "sure what I found was not any weather observation balloon." The comment was left out of Colonel Weaver's huge report. Why start telling the facts when lies will do?

Nickell and CSICOP have pretty much been given a free ride by the press and the scientific community. (He had even explained the so-called Flatwoods monster seen by a number of witnesses in Flatwoods, West Virginia, on September 12, 1952, as just a 6-foot-tall owl seen after a meteor came down! A number of witnesses had actually seen the so-called meteor make a slow turn around the town and come down slowly on a hill. There was no crater, no shock wave, and no meteor. Nickell visited Flatwoods, but didn't talk to the major witnesses, and didn't visit the actual site. I have done both, and again was appalled at his pseudoscience. (This is discussed in more detail in *Shoot Them Down.*) One would never know, from listening to him, about all the other first-hand Roswell witnesses who had been interviewed throughout the years by serious investigators, as recorded, for example, on the 105-minute video *Recollections of Roswell*, with testimony from 27 firsthand witnesses, most of whom have since passed away. In the business world, one would have to say he has been guilty of fraudulent misrepresentation. The people who made the 2005 Peter Jennings ABC TV mockumentary about UFOs had a copy of that video, but basically ignored the data in it. And yes, for those who saw the program, I strongly resent my being called a promoter twice, my professional credentials being ignored, and the use of only 20 seconds of an hour-long interview.

Duke Gildenberg and Dr. Charles Moore, Roswell balloon expert debunkers. Courtesy of the U.S. government.

In 2007 two more books were published about Roswell. One was by Colonel Jesse Marcel, Jr., MD: *The Roswell Legacy.* This book presents his personal insights into the lives of his parents, and the details of the incident. It includes a review of his meeting with Dr. Charles Moore, and Moore's attempt to convince Marcel that the symbols he saw on a light-weight I-beam were just on toymaker tape used to hold the supposed radar-reflecting kite together. The attempt was not successful. (Funny how the Air Force never produced any photos of that tape...) I wrote the fore-word for the book.

The second book was *Witness to Roswell*, by Tom Carey and Don Schmitt, who have been researching Roswell for many years. They have found some new witnesses and evidence of there having been another UFO crash much closer to Roswell, discovered while Jesse Marcel Sr. was off to the Foster ranch crash site. Of most importance is an affidavit signed by Walter Haut well before his death, but published for the first time in this book. The authors make the claim that, contrary to all his previous statements about having seen nothing, Haut had in fact been shown a body and wreckage. In addition, they claim that General Ramey and Colonel DuBose had actually come over from Fort Worth and had attended the morning meeting at the base on July 8, at which Jesse Marcel had been instructed by Colonel Blanchard to take wreckage to Ft. Worth to General Ramey. I certainly don't feel that Haut was intentionally lying about this, but I would like some evidence that Ramey and Dubose had made that quick trip. We know they were back in Ft. Worth with Marcel later that day, because of the pictures taken in Ramey's office. (Effort is being made to find flight logs.) The statement from Haut would indicate that Marcel also saw a body. There is some indication that Haut had been having some memory problems—he had certainly been interviewed many times. Hopefully, new evidence will be found to sort out this new information. Neither DuBose nor Marcel had told me or Jesse Jr. about that trip of Ramey and DuBose's.

I am absolutely sure that there are still people who are alive who were connected with the Roswell Incident, even though it was more than 60 years ago. A lot of men were used to go over the Foster ranch site to make sure not a scrap of the strange stuff was left behind. (Many WWII veterans were in the habit of taking souvenirs from war zones.) Apparently, Roswell pilot Pappy Henderson had kept a small piece. The descriptions from the Marcels and the Brazels indicate many small pieces. I feel certain that some are still in bureau drawers. The problem is that many veterans would have been afraid to speak out for fear of reprisal or possible loss of medical benefits, and fear of possible laughter from anyone they tried to tell. (They or their families are welcome to call my toll-free number: (877) 457-0232. I won't use witness names without permission.) How would you feel if you had seen an alien body, and your government is saying that all the stories are due to crash-test dummies dropped in New Mexico—after 1953? Many in the press let the liars get away with it. As a scientist, I am angry about such intentional deception.

Crash-test dummy Sierra Sam in the middle, Madson, in charge of the progam, on the right. 1953. Courtesy of the U.S. government.

Dr. Park Deception

A student had sent me a copy of an article about UFOs written by a well-known physicist, Dr. Robert L. Park. The article is entitled "An Alien

Spaceship Did Not Crash in Roswell." In common with UFO debunkers and propagandists (sometimes there isn't much difference), he makes sure he lets us know how smart he is compared to an average Joe. On the way to Roswell in 1954 as an Air Force officer, he experienced two sightings, which he easily identified. Park claims that Roswell at the time was the hub of many speculations about the UFO sightings that seemed to make the news almost daily (I very seriously doubt this). He then does some amateur psychology about people knowing what saucers are supposed to look like and shaping observations to fit their preconceptions.

Park further makes this extraordinary claim: "The current fascination with aliens can be traced back to the strange events that took place near Roswell, New Mexico, in the summer of 1947." This is completely absurd, as there were only two mentions of Roswell—inaccurate and less than a page in Frank Edward's 1966 *Flying Saucers: Serious Business*, and a fast, just-as-inaccurate, one-paragraph mention in Ted Bloecher's *Report on the UFO Wave of 1947*—between 1947 and the publication of *The Roswell Incident* in 1980. Aliens certainly weren't mentioned in connection with Roswell until then either. Park says, "On June 14, 1947, William Brazel, the foreman of the Foster ranch, 75 miles northwest of Roswell, spotted a large area of wreckage about seven miles from the ranch house. The debris included neoprene strips, tape, metal foil, cardboard, and sticks." This is a commonly repeated lie about the event. It appeared in the front-page July 9 article in the *Roswell Daily Record*, headlined "Harassed Rancher Who Located 'Saucer' Sorry He Told About It." Brazel had been brought back to town and fed a new, false story. The article also includes the comment that the wreckage covered an area 200 yards in diameter. Park, similar to Nickell, seems to be unaware of the fact that the July 8 articles on the front pages of evening papers, from Chicago west, noted that the wreckage was found "last week"—hardly June 14. Park says, "Weeks later he heard about reports of flying saucers. The next day he drove to the little town of Corona to sell wool, and while there he whispered, kind of confidential-like, to the Lincoln County sheriff, George Wilcox, that he might have found pieces of one of the those flying discs people were talking about." More slices of baloney. The rancher, according to witness testimony, found the wreckage about July 2 or 3, and went into Corona to do his usual Saturday shopping on July 5. When there he heard about flying disks at the general store, and also that rewards were being offered. Brazel didn't have electricity or get a newspaper. The people there suggested he go to the sheriff's office—which is in Roswell, not in Corona, and in Chavez County. He did so on Sunday, July 6.

Wilcox called the local base and talked to Major Jesse Marcel. He checked out the small amount of material Brazel had brought in, found it was very unusual indeed, and certainly not a weather balloon. The article notes that Brazel had previously found balloons and collected small rewards for their return. Marcel was then instructed by base commander Colonel Blanchard to take a counterintelligence officer (Sheridan Cavitt) with him and check out the large debris field observed by the rancher. The officers followed him out (the ranch was in the middle of nowhere), had a can of beans, stayed overnight in their sleeping bags, and viewed the debris field on Monday morning. They then collected some more of the debris, leaving most of it behind, and came back the long way to Roswell. Marcel stopped at home and showed some wreckage to his wife and son.

The next morning, Blanchard, after reviewing the wreckage, ordered Marcel to have one of the B-29s fly him and the wreckage to Wright-Patterson AFB with a stop at the 8th AF headquarters in Fort Worth, which is on the way. He also ordered Walter Haut to issue the infamous press release. Of course, Blanchard and Marcel were quite familiar with weather balloons from their air service in the Pacific during WWII. The 509th at Roswell was, after all, the most elite military group in the world. Marcel was also familiar with foil and paper radar reflectors from a course he had recently taken. Before he arrived in Ft. Worth, Colonel Thomas Jefferson DuBose (chief of staff to General Ramey, Blanchard's boss),

Harassed Rancher who Located 'Saucer' Sorry He Told About It

W. W. Brazel, 48, Lincoln county rancher living 30 miles south east of Corona, today told his story of finding what the army at first described as a flying disk, but the publicity which attended his find caused him to add that if he ever found anything else short of a bomb he sure wasn't going to say anything about it.

Brazel was brought here late yesterday by W. E. Whitmore, of radio station KGFL, had his picture taken and gave an interview to the Record and Jason Kellahin, sent here from the Albuquerque bureau of the Associated Press to cover the story. The picture he posed for was sent out over AP telephoto wire sending machine specially set up in the Record office by R. D. Adair, AP wire chief sent here from Albuquerque for the sole purpose of getting out his picture and that of sheriff George Wilcox, to whom Brazel originally gave the information of his find.

Brazel related that on June 14 he and an 8-year old son, Vernon were about 7 or 8 miles from the ranch house of the J. B. Foster ranch, which he operates, when they came upon a large area of bright wreckage made up on rubber strips, tinfoil, a rather tough paper and sticks.

At the time Brazel was in a hurry to get his round made and he did not pay much attention to it. But he did remark about what he had seen and on July 4 he, his wife, Vernon and a daughter Betty, age 14, went back to the spot and gathered up quite a bit of the debris.

The next day he first heard about the flying disks, and he wondered if what he had found might be the remnants of one of these.

Monday he came to town to sell some wool and while here he went to see sheriff George Wilcox and "whispered kinda confidential like" that he might have found a flying disk.

Wilcox got in touch with the Roswell Army Air Field and Maj. Jesse A. Marcel and a man in plain clothes accompanied him home, where they picked up the rest of the pieces of the "disk" and went to his home to try to reconstruct it.

According to Brazel they simply could not reconstruct it at all. They tried to make a kite out of it, but could not do that and could not find any way to put it back together so that it would fit.

Then Major Marcel brought it to Roswell and that was the last he heard of it until the story broke that he had found a flying disk.

Brazel said that he did not see it fall from the sky and did not see it before it was torn up, so he did not know the size or shape it might have been, but he thought it might have been about as large as a table top. The balloon which held it up, if that was how it worked, must have been about 12 feet long, he felt, measuring the distance by the size of the room in which he sat. The rubber was smoky gray in color and scattered over an area about 200 yards in diameter.

When the debris was gathered up the tinfoil, paper, tape, and sticks made a bundle about three feet long and 7 or 8 inches thick, while the rubber made a bundle about 18 or 20 inches long and about 8 inches thick. In all, he estimated, the entire lot would have weighed maybe five pounds.

There was no sign of any metal in the area which might have been used for an engine and no sign of any propellers of any kind, although at least one paper fin had been glued onto some of the tinfoil.

There were no words to be found anywhere on the instrument, although there were letters on some of the parts. Considerable scotch tape and some tape with flowers printed upon it had been used in the construction.

No strings or wire were to be found but there were some eyelets in the paper to indicate that some sort of attachment may have been used.

Brazel said that he had previously found two weather observation balloons on the ranch, but that what he found this time did not in any way resemble either of these.

"I am sure what I found was not any weather observation balloon," he said. "But if I find anything else, besides a bomb they are going to have a hard time getting me to say anything about it."

Roswell Daily Record Army Air Force false cover-up Roswell story, July 9, 1947. Courtesy of the Roswell Daily Record.

took a call from General Ramey's boss in D.C., General Clements McMullen, instructing Ramey to send the wreckage to D.C. with one of his couriers, to get the press off their backs in any way possible, and never to talk about it again. When Marcel arrived, General Ramey instructed him not to say anything. Pictures were taken with phony wreckage, and the cover story went out from Ft. Worth—not Roswell—within hours. Blanchard went on to be a four-star general and vice chief of staff of the Air Force.

None of these experienced officers could recognize a standard, run-of-the-mill weather balloon??

Dr. Park seems blissfully unaware. How do I know my version is more accurate? Because I got it firsthand from Major Marcel, from his son, Dr. Jesse Marcel, Jr., from retired General DuBose, from Brazel's son, from Brazel's neighbors, from Blanchard's family, and many more people, as well as from contemporary news coverage.

Here is another silly quote from Park: "The sheriff reported the matter to the nearby base. The army sent an intelligence officer, Major Jesse Marcel, to check out the report. Marcel thought the debris looked like pieces of a weather balloon or radar reflector; in any event, all of it fit easily in to the trunk of his car...." More silly nonsense. Marcel had stayed overnight on the ranch, had observed a debris field more than half a mile long and hundreds of yards across. He noted to me in our first conversation (and later on camera) that there was nothing conventional about the wreckage: no wires, vacuum tubes, rivets, or propellers. He and his son both noted this. There were I-beams that couldn't be broken, burned, or bent, that had strange symbols on them; foil-like material that was a memory metal. He furthermore made clear that although he and Cavitt brought back what they could in their cars, most of the debris was left out there. If a trunk load had been all there was, the rancher would have brought it in and there would have been no need for the officers' trip to the ranch.

Park goes on: "By 1978, 30 years after Brazel spotted wreckage on his ranch, actual alien bodies had begun to show up in accounts of the crash." Really? I wonder where these accounts appeared. I first heard stories about bodies at the Barney Barnett crash site in 1978. The first mention of Roswell-related bodies came from mortician Glenn Dennis to me in 1989 in Lincoln, New Mexico, on Billy the Kid day. Park says, "Major Marcel's story about loading sticks, cardboard, and metal foil into the trunk of his car [there never was such a story] mutated into the saga of a major military operation which allegedly recovered an entire alien spaceship." In truth, it was all small, strange pieces. Hardly a spaceship. Most of it was left behind.

Under the heading "A Full-Scale Myth," Park has the gall to lie: "Like a giant vacuum cleaner the story had sucked in and mingled together snippets from reports of unrelated plane crashes [Where? With whom?] and high-altitude parachute experiments involving anthropomorphic dummies, even though some of these events took places years later and miles away. And with years' worth of imaginative energy to drive their basic beliefs, various UFO 'investigators' managed to stitch those myths into a full-scale myth of an encounter that has been covered up by the government."

Does physicist Park have any idea of the stupidity of what he is saying? It was USAF Colonel Weaver and Captain MacAndrew in the two ridiculous USAF volumes of *The Roswell Report* who introduced the crazy notion of crash-test dummies to explain the bodies (even though none of the dummies were dropped until 1953 and later, and were 6 feet tall and weighed 175 pounds). It was the USAF that introduced high-altitude parachute jumper/balloon pilot Joseph Kittinger as the redhead reported at the base in July 1947, but who wasn't actually there until 1959. The supposed UFO investigators in question were two Air Force officers lying through their teeth. We serious investigators had done firsthand homework, unlike Dr. Park, who had done none.

Park then buys into the Mogul balloon explanation hook, line, and sinker, as espoused by Colonel Weaver in *The Roswell Report: Fact vs. Fiction in the New Mexico Desert* (1995). He claims Mogul was still classified. This is false. He touts Dr. Charles Moore's Flight 4, although Dr. David Rudiak's careful work indicates it wasn't even flown, and couldn't, because of the weather, have made it to the ranch. Park says, "The debris found on the Foster ranch closely matched the materials used in the balloon trains." Yet another lie, if one notes the reports from such witnesses as Major Marcel, his son, Brazel's son, neighbor Loretta Proctor, radio station manager Judd Roberts, and more. There was also the absence of any string (20-plus balloons were tied 20 feet apart by string), no mention of sono-buoys, radio transmitters, or the like. Park is trying to make a sow's ear into a silk purse. He then talks about *Vol. 2: Case Closed* as a massive report that collected every scrap of information dealing with the Roswell Incident report published in 1997. Funny, *Case Closed* was much smaller than Vol. 1, which was the Mogul explanation published in 1995.

Park then buys into the CIA lies about many UFO reports in the 1950s being the result of observations of super-secret U-2 aircraft, and later the SR-71. The CIA was glad to deceive all by accepting those reports. Park provides no backup for this baseless claim, which Dr. Bruce Maccabee has demonstrated was clearly false: The number of UFO sightings did *not* increase when they started flying. Park's last line is more true than he intended: "Concealment is the soil in which pseudoscience flourishes." I fully agree that organized anti-ufology is indeed a pseudoscience, concealing and ignoring facts and data and doing its research by proclamation.. His motto is, "Don't bother me with the facts; my mind is made up." It is of interest that Park doesn't reference my book *Crash at Corona: The Definitive Study of the Roswell Incident*, although I am a member of the American Physical Society, with which he had been closely associated. He doesn't mention Weaver's report or the Randle and Schmitt books. He does mention the debunker books by Klass, Korff, Schaefer, and Peebles. This, indeed, is pseudoscience. (One can read more of his pseudoscience in *Voodoo Science: The Road From Foolishness to Fraud*. His totally biased and ignorant comments are also noted in a January 18, 2008 *Newsweek* science story.)

James T. Westwood

There was another seemingly scholarly attack on Roswell in November 2004, by James T. Westwood of Military Science and Defense Analytics. He claims to have shown, using "historiographical" methods, and primary historical resources, that a UFO did not crash, and thus was not recovered in New Mexico in July 1947. His subject is "Proving a Negative: The Ruse That Was Roswell." His three sources are *Truman in the White House: The Diary of Eben Ayers* (edited by R.H. Ferrell, U. of Missouri Press, 1991), *The Forrestal Diaries* (Walter Millis, Viking Press, 1951), and a small diary kept by Truman himself, not found until 2003. (The lost diary can be found at *www.trumanlibrary.org/diary/transcript.htm*.)

Westwood also places great trust in an unnamed source, who claims to have been engaged in military duties in Forrestal's office until mid-September 1947, and says that "there never occurred in his keeping any printed or voiced material, data, or other information whatsoever concerning the crash recovery of a spaceship from a distant planet." No reason is given for thinking he would have been aware of everything, no matter how classified, that happened in the office. Westwood hadn't checked the Web, or he would have noted that Truman's journal about his decision to use the atomic bomb "was kept even from Eben Ayers, who had been directed to prepare an account of the atomic bomb decision during the Potsdam Conference" (see *www.he.net/ douglong/ guide3.htm*). Ayers was a press secretary. Would he be expected to have access to everything? Hardly likely.

The first problem with Westwood's conclusions is that the three written sources are all unclassified. Certainly one wouldn't expect to find TOP

SECRET or TOP SECRET CODE WORD material in them. Some have said that, surely, all the material from 1947 has been declassified! Nonsense. The Eisenhower Library told me in 2003 that they still have about 300,000 pages of classified material. Westwood himself notes that the Forrestal material had been carefully reviewed before being released in 1951.

The second problem is this: Why should we expect any of the sources to cover *everything* that happened during that time period? I did an article in 2003 about the Truman diary, which only contained 42 handwritten entries. The first 160 pages contain member listings and advertisements from the Real Estate Board of New York, which had given him the diary. It was not classified. The July 2003 press release about the diary notes that Truman was an erratic diarist. Indeed. There are no entries between January 16 and March 2, between March 31 and June 27, between October 1 and November 17, and between November 17 and December 13. Would Westwood have us believe that Truman did nothing during these periods? In actuality, 1947 was a very busy year, what with the Marshall Plan, the growing cold war with the Soviet Union, the formulation of the Defense Department, the conversion of the Central Intelligence Group into the CIA, the establishment of the U.S. Air Force, separate from the Army Air Force, the establishment of the National Security Council, and so on and so forth.

According to George Elsey, with whom I had several phone conversations, and who worked for Truman the entire time he was in the White House (April 1945 until January 1953), Truman was very security conscious. (Elsey walked in once when Truman was chewing out a senator for being careless about security.) The diary entries seemed to be brief, mostly personal notes.

Westwood says nothing about having visited the Truman Library in Independence, Missouri, or the Firestone Library at Princeton University, where the Forrestal papers are housed. Having spent time at both, I can attest to the fact that there are huge paper collections, including daily calendars in which are mentioned various meetings. Frequently the entries give no clue as to the subject of discussion.

Westwood says nothing at all about the eyewitness testimony of people who were directly involved in the Roswell crash, such as Major Marcel, his son (now Dr.) Jesse Marcel, or retired General Thomas DuBose. He makes no mention of the rancher, Mac Brazel, or his son Bill, or neighbor Loretta Proctor. He doesn't mention the contemporary newspaper coverage in front-page stories in evening papers from Chicago west on July 8, 1947. I am surprised he doesn't try to use absence of an article about Roswell in the *New York Times* on July 8 as evidence for the absence of the crash. (The press release had gone out too late to make the *NYT*.) Westwood can't be bothered to reference the books that note the testimony and results of serious investigations, such as Don Berliner's and my *Crash at Corona: The Definitive Study of the Roswell Incident*.

Westwood's finding is, "The three diaries make no mention, direct or by innuendo, of such a bizarre, sensational, and unlikely event as an ET 'hardware' crash and recovery in July 1947, sensational books by such authors as Randle, Friedman, Moore, Berlitz, and others since 1980—to the contrary. All of the diaries are frank.... Ayers spoke with the president almost every day...." Surely Westwood is well aware of the need not only for high-level security clearances, but also a need-to-know for the information for the person involved. One might hope he would provide evidence that people with such clearances and need-to-know would discuss highly classified matters in unclassified entries, books, and comments. Often, most people in a particular group would have a clearance, but no need-to-know, for particular TOP SECRET CODE WORD information.

President Truman became vice president in January 1945. He was not informed about the very expensive Manhattan Project to develop nuclear weapons until well after becoming president (upon the death of

President Roosevelt) in April 1945. He hadn't had a need-to-know. President Eisenhower, in his book *Mandate for Change*, describes a meeting that he, as president elect, had with President Truman at the White House on November 18, 1952, two weeks after the election and two months before his inauguration. Ike makes no mention of the fact that he and his advisors went directly to the Pentagon from the White House for a briefing on high-level national security matters. We know the meeting happened, not only because of an article in the *New York Times*, but also because of desk calendar entries from others who were there, such as Army Chief of Staff Collins and USAF Vice-Chief of Staff (and Majestic 12 member) General Nathan Twining. The entries, of course, give no classified information as to what was discussed. That Ike didn't mention it certainly doesn't mean that it didn't happen. November 18, 1952, is the date of the Eisenhower Briefing Document describing Operation Majestic 12.

Westwood can't be bothered to tell the reader why he considers the crash and recovery of ET hardware "bizarre, sensational, or unlikely." There were 2,000 sightings of flying saucers during the summer of 1947; why would it be surprising if some of them crashed? Plenty of our aircraft have crashed. The first clue that the U.S. government had that the Germans were developing rockets during the early years of WWII came from analysis of a piece of "bizarre" wreckage from a German test rocket that had crashed or exploded in Sweden.

Westwood chastens those of us who have written in-depth investigations of the Roswell Incident: "None of the eminent ufologists that have written and spoken at insufferable length about the Roswell UFO event have ever mentioned yet the Ayers and Forrestal diaries and what they do not reveal." This is true...and truly absurd. There are literally millions of pages at the Truman and Eisenhower Libraries and a multitude of other archives that say nothing about Roswell. Gold ore is worth mining if there is an ounce of gold in a ton of ore. Only one of hundreds of naturally occurring isotopes is fissionable. Should we say there is no gold in them thar hills or that no isotopes are fissionable? It is the evidence we have that matters, not that which we don't have.

Westwood brags that even the Air Force reports on Roswell didn't take note of his "sources," but makes the claim that "they do make much use of historical research and historiographical methods." Quite frankly, both government reports are loaded with false and misleading statements—lies—and are easily shown to be splendid examples of propaganda such as described in a paper by William Broad, "The Roswell Incident, the USAF, and the New York Times." Remember that the USAF "Case Closed" report tried to explain reports of small bodies noted in connection with New Mexico crashes as crash-test dummies. This isn't research. It is baloney.

Most scientists I know say that one shouldn't try to prove a negative. Westwood brags about doing so, and complains that others don't. If this represents historiographical research, then I want no part of it. I don't feel my many visits to 20 archives and discussions with many dozens of witnesses have been in vain. My goal has always been to find out what did happen, not to determine what didn't.

One thing I can be sure of is that there will continue to be attacks on the Roswell Incident by people unwilling to do their homework.

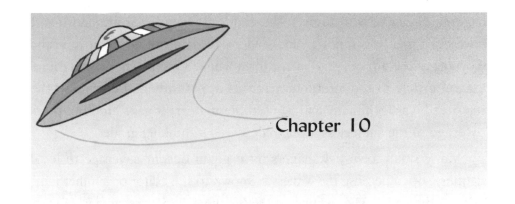

Chapter 10

The Press and Flying Saucers

Dr. Herbert J. Strentz, in his 1970 PhD thesis, "A Survey of Press Coverage of UFOs, 1947-1966" at the Northwestern University Medill School of Journalism, had some very strong comments to make about press coverage of UFOs: "The high degree of ridicule present in the UFO phenomenon was reflected in the press coverage.... The coverage has been marked by superficiality, redundancy, silliness, careless reporting, and lack of relevant information. The lack of relevant information was also attributable to the reluctance of the press to ferret out information about the phenomenon and those involved in it." He actually looked at tens of thousands of press clippings—not a joyful experience.

There has been some improvement in the 38 years since then, but not nearly enough. As I noted in Chapter 8 on opinion polls, there has been a good deal of misleading coverage. I should stress that I personally have had overwhelmingly decent coverage, about which, taken as a whole, I can't complain. The newspaper coverage of me and my views as expressed in lectures has also, with some few exceptions, been accurate and fair. I have been met by a reporter and student-activities representative in the morning at the airport in a college town where I was to speak, and found a good article in the afternoon paper. I apparently had convinced the reporter I was legitimate, and he used the material I gave him. But press coverage of the subject as a whole deserves a flunking grade.

Many small-town newspapers have given decent coverage to local sightings, often because the witness is known to the editor or another journalist at the paper. The sightings in the Stephenville, Texas, area in January 2008 received straight coverage in the local paper, which in turn encouraged others to come forth. The real problems come with regard to coverage by such nationally reputed newspapers as the *Washington Post* and the *New York Times*. So-called television documentaries have been a mixed bag, with some outstanding shows and some real duds. I would say that most people don't understand how most TV documentaries, say, on the History Channel or the Learning Channel, are made. Generally it is not the channel that makes the documentary. Usually an independent producer comes up with an idea, writes a summary and proposal, approaches a network for funding, and, if lucky, gets both the approval and the funding. Often this means bringing in individuals who are interviewed and then sent home. Rarely are many of the interviewees brought together. Then the producer and his editor do a cut-and-paste job. I have, for example, appeared in the same portion of a show with Robert Lazar, whom I believe is a fraud (not a scientist), and has not told the truth about his background or his experiences at Area 51 and Los Alamos. The viewer would have no way of knowing that he is lying about himself and his "research." Neither of us was there when the other was interviewed. Contrary to what many people seem to feel, accuracy and truth are not the primary concerns of the sponsoring channels or networks. Ratings are.

One example of an excellent job is a show done by *Unsolved Mysteries* in 1989 about the Roswell Incident. The show had previously done a good job on UFO sightings around Gulf Breeze, Florida. One of the scientists featured in that show was an old friend of mine, and one of the top ufologists in the world, Dr. Bruce Maccabee, an optical physicist. I called Maccabee and asked for the name and number of his contact person on the show, produced by Cosgrove-Meurer for NBC. I called his contact and left messages twice, with no call back. The third time I managed to reach her. Turns out she somehow confused Ray Stanford, who had been obstructive about the Gulf Breeze show, with Stanton Friedman. I guess Stanton and Stanford sound similar... Anyway, I pitched the idea that *Unsolved Mysteries* should do a show about Roswell, and during a visit to Southern California had detailed discussions with the people at CM. They wanted some new people, and, besides a small consulting fee, agreed to cover some research costs.

A primary effort was to obtain back-up information on a story that long-time researcher Leonard Stringfield had published in the MUFON journal about Sappho Henderson. She had told him that her husband, Pappy Henderson, had been a pilot at the base in Roswell in 1947, and had told her in 1980, after seeing an article in a tabloid about Roswell, that he had flown some of the wreckage from Roswell and had seen at least one body. He presumed that because the story was in a newspaper, it was no longer classified. He died in 1986. I was concerned because there were some other claims I knew to be false in the article. Stringfield refused to tell me how to reach Sappho or to have her call me collect. I stressed the need for finding back-up witnesses besides Pappy's wife. Stringfield wouldn't cooperate because he was "protecting" Sappho. I played detective, with calls to the Roswell Library and the reference librarian. She looked up listings in old city directories for the Hendersons and then names and numbers of those who lived nearby at the time when they left. Then she found those who were still there when I called. They referred me to others who knew the Hendersons well, and I finally obtained an obituary from the *Roswell Daily Record* (people there, perhaps not surprisingly, have always been helpful),

Sappho Henderson, wife of Roswell pilot Pappy Henderson, who handled wreckage and saw a body. Courtesy of the author.

after, with much effort, finding a date of death for Pappy in California. The obituary gave the names of survivors, including of his married daughter who lived in Hawaii. Obviously, one has trouble finding a married woman if you don't know the name of her husband. I eventually found her, and she was most cooperative, giving me her mother's number in California. I had been only 20 miles away a few weeks earlier. Sappho gave me contact information for five different friends of Pappy's to whom he might have spoken about the Roswell Incident. One was Pappy's WWII bombardier, Vere

McCarty, who had been a pallbearer at Pappy's funeral. Pappy had indeed told him the story at their last WWII military group reunion. McCarty wrote me a letter telling the story.

The producers at CM were favorably impressed, and used Sappho on the show. Stringfield had, for reasons unknown, even tried to keep her from appearing. He just didn't understand that she wanted to validate Pappy's experience. She understood that her word really wasn't enough. As a matter of fact, after the show appeared on NBC, in September 1989, as seen by 28 million people, she was called by another old buddy of Pappy's, John Kromschroeder, a dentist, to whom he had very quietly told the story and even provided a piece of wreckage, which was taken back right away, and now nowhere to be found.

Cosgrove-Meurer sent a producer out to talk to each person they were planning to bring on, to pick their brains. He actually visited me in Fredericton. All of us were then brought to Roswell, where we were interviewed by the producer. The show was extremely well done. When repeated in early 1990, it was seen by 30 million people. There were some minor mistakes, but overall the show was quite accurate. Because they were trying to present the facts, they did not bring on a debunker, who, knowing almost nothing, would just have ranted that it was all baloney. In contrast, the February 24, 2005, ABC mockumentary, hosted by Peter Jennings, was only seen by 11.6 million people. It, and many guest shows such as *Larry King*, seems to think it has to have debunkers—no matter how little investigation they have done.

A number of my experiences with TV crews have been bad. One of the worst was a UPN network show about the supposed permanent alien abduction of the MacPherson family in Minnesota. Supposedly they had disappeared, but left behind a videotape of the aliens who abducted them. I was called by a production company in Hollywood asking me to fly to California to be interviewed about UFO abductions. (As with most TV shows, I wasn't to be paid for my time, though Fredericton is four time zones ahead of California. I would be able to see my daughter, who lives in the L.A. area, I would get frequent flyer points, and my expenses would be covered, so I agreed.) Supposedly the network was in a hurry to fix up a partially completed show for Dick Clark Productions. I figured that if one can't trust Dick Clark, who can one trust? I was wrong.

The studio in Burbank was an old converted house. The woman who asked the questions had obviously done her homework, and asked sensible questions. They must have liked my answers, because they even used some things I said in the commercials for the show, and included a number of my comments in the show. They hadn't shown me the supposed video that had been shot by the family that had "disappeared," and hadn't asked me about it. Viewers were definitely given the impression that I had seen the footage and was favorably impressed by it. The screen would show an electromagnetic effect, and then me talking about such effects. It was skillfully done and totally misleading. I was quite angry when I saw it, because the producers even had at the end of the show the names of the actors who played Alien 1, Alien 2, and Alien 3. One poll indicated that half the people who saw the program thought it was factual!

However, I was severely criticized by many ufologists. Kevin Randle had even complained that I should have known better than to deal with any program with which Robert Kiviat had been involved. I certainly agreed that I wouldn't have done another program for Kiviat, who had been heavily involved in another misleading and sensational show, by Fox Network, about the so-called alien autopsy footage. I was in that one too. However, Kiviat had had nothing to do with the UPN show. I finally managed to get on the late-night *Coast to Coast* radio program with Art Bell to explain what had happened. I should stress that no one complained about what I had actually said, only about the misleading picture presented. I asked several people if they would have preferred having somebody on who knew less about the subject. The answer was no. I was also asked why I didn't sue. My answer was that suing for libel or some such in the United States is difficult, but does enrich lawyers. (The laws in England are much more inclined to protect reputations than in the United States. I did win an out-of-court settlement with an English researcher and the *Manchester Evening News* for libelous statements she had made that had been printed. The reputation of a "public figure" in the United States is not nearly as well protected.)

While on *Coast to Coast*, I pointed out that *Nightline* with Ted Koppel had me appear with Philip Klass on June 24, 1987, the 40th anniversary of Kenneth Arnold's famous sighting of nine flying discs near Mt. Rainier. I was in Washington, D.C., for the 1987 MUFON Symposium, where the focus was supposed to be on the cover-up. The start of the discussion was somewhat delayed by the fact that Jackie Gleason had died earlier in the day, and a tribute was expressed. When we went to go in the studio, I had several blacked-out NSA documents with me to prove the cover-up. I was not allowed to bring them in. I argued—to no effect. There was proof! Then they told each of us, sitting about two feet apart, not to look at each other, but only "look at your camera." Strange way to discuss a topic. It also turns out that we never met Koppel, and did not see him on a monitor. We heard him through ear plugs, so were denied all the nonverbal input one normally has, such as a raised eyebrow, a smirk, and the like. People at the MUFON conference the next day asked how it went. I had to admit I had no idea because I had no clue as to what they actually saw from the three cameras. When I finally saw the tape my wife had made, I was reasonably pleased.

Another experience with Klass was at a Detroit TV studio. I had just come back from Europe. We were told on a PBS show that we couldn't bring anything in. As soon as we were in the studio, Klass pulled out a grossly misleading clipping from his pocket! One of the usual debunking ploys is to raise irrelevant questions to avoid discussing the solid stuff. Again with Klass in Hamilton, Ontario, he suddenly brought up the stupid question as to why I hadn't applied for the Cutty Sark Scotch $1 million award for any evidence of flying saucers. I had to waste time pointing out the terms of the award, which included providing either a saucer or a piece of a saucer certified by the National Academy of Sciences as being of ET origin. Of course, I had never claimed to have such evidence. Furthermore, such evidence would be worth far more than a million dollars, and the U.S. and other governments would have a strong interest in preventing it from being turned over to Cutty Sark.

I am not a conspiracy theorist, as I can certainly prove, as noted in Chapter 4, that agencies such as the NSA, the CIA, and the Air Force have been covering up UFO information. I don't know why the *Washington Post* and the *New York Times* have been not only negative, but also guilty of poor journalism. My best suggestion is that both have been suffering (along with others) from the David Susskind Syndrome, a medical condition I derived from my interactions with TV talk show host David Susskind. I was living in Southern California after there had been a major wave of sightings in the 1970s. His people told me they were planning a show on UFOs. They wanted a good abduction case, so I put them in touch with Betty Hill and John Fuller, author of the book *The Interrupted Journey*. They wanted a good skeptic. I noted that there really weren't any, but referred them to the late Philip Klass. They wanted a good, recent case. I suggested the Colonel Larry Coyne helicopter case that had happened not long before. They wanted me to send them much material, which I did. Then they brought all the actors in this talk show together in New York. The set was quite tense and uncomfortable, in contrast to a show I had done not long before in Toronto with Norm Perry of the Canadian Television Network. Between taping segments, Susskind said, "I read the *New York Times* and haven't seen anything in it to convince me these things are real." I am sure he hadn't. I have come to delineate the Susskind Syndrome this way: Susskind and everyone else would acknowledge that, if aliens were visiting Earth, and the government was covering it up, it would be a big and important story. But because he and other bright but clueless intellectuals such as Dr. Carl Sagan and Dr. Isaac Asimov take great pride in knowing about the important stories, and haven't known anything about flying saucers, then they must not be real. Anyone who thinks they are must not be very bright, and doesn't understand that such secrets couldn't possibly be kept from such smart people as Susskind, et al. Right?

Absolutely wrong. Journalists for the *New York Times* and the *Washington Post* seem to think the same way. After all, the *Times* had broken the Daniel Ellsberg Pentagon Papers story about Vietnam. The *Post* had broken the story of the political Watergate. They earned their stripes by really digging in, so why bother with saucers? Of course, there is the additional difficulty of having to admit they had neglected such an important story for all these years. Most of us don't like to admit we have made a mistake. Better to keep the status quo. Perhaps I should add, having grown up in Linden, New Jersey, 18 miles from New York City, that especially back in the 1940s and '50s, Easterners were convinced that the East Coast was the center of the universe—art, science, politics, sports— a sort of holier-than-thou attitude. (New York City was the most populous city in the United States; New York was then the most populous state.)

Here are some stories that weren't covered properly:

- Roswell, July 9, 1947. How could anyone accept the notion that the commander (Colonel William Blanchard) and the intelligence officer (Major Jesse Marcel) of the 509th Bomb Group, the only atomic bombing group in the world, could not immediately recognize a weather balloon? In case the reader has seen all those TV dramatizations of Roswell showing a huge polyethylene teardrop-shaped balloon, forget it. The mystical Mogul involved standard round neoprene weather balloons then flown every day all around the world. They turned to dust when out in the sun for a week or two.

🪐 How could the press blindly accept the temperature inversion explanation for the multiple aircraft and multiple radar observations of flying saucers over Washington, D.C., in the summer of 1952? How could they blindly accept these claims of USAF General Samford?

🪐 Why did neither the *Post* nor the *Times* carry the official Air Force statement that interceptor pilots had been ordered to shoot them (UFOs) down if the saucers don't land when instructed to do so? The story did appear in other papers. Why did neither carry Major General Roger Ramey's statement that pilots had already been scrambled to chase UFOs 300 times that summer? It was in other papers.

🪐 How could any legitimate journalist not ask for the title, the authors, and the name of the organization that put together *Project Blue Book Special Report No. 14* in 1955, and not even ask for the basis for the absurd 3 percent UNKNOWN figure given out by the secretary of the Air Force?

🪐 How could they so blindly accept the unsubstantiated and totally misleading claims of Dr. Edward Condon in the summary of his study when the Final Report of the University of Colorado was published in 1969? Others provided room for fact corrections. The *Pittsburgh Post Gazette* gave fine coverage to the comments by and colleagues and myself issued on behalf of the UFO Research Institute of Pittsburgh at the time. I had actually been given my first copy of the Condon report, just before the official release, by KDKA Pittsburgh, on the condition that I appear on the KDKA *Contact* radio show to discuss it. No one warned me that it was 965 pages long! Our group, which contained a number of professional people from Westinghouse and other professional groups, had earned the press's trust.

✒ We didn't believe in being apologist ufologists or closet ufologists as so many people still think is necessary. All that approach does is reinforce the false notion that there is nothing to the reports of flying saucers—the idea being that if there was some solid evidence, people who are heavily involved would come on strong. Most are reluctant to do so, just as so many witnesses are reluctant to come forward. Fear of ridicule is the reason. My own experience would say the fear is unjustified, if one comes equipped with facts and data.

✒ How is it that they didn't question the USAF about its carefully crafted and totally misleading statements when Project Blue Book was closed in late 1969? There was this statement, still being promoted by the USAF, almost 40 years later, in response to any queries: "1. No UFO reported, investigated, and evaluated by the Air Force has ever given any indication of a threat to our national security. 2. There has been no evidence submitted to, or discovered by, the Air Force that sightings categorized as 'unidentified' represent technological developments or principles beyond the range of present-day scientific knowledge," and 3. There has been no evidence indicating that sightings categorized as 'unidentified' are extraterrestrial vehicles." If one of the three functions of reporting, investigating, or evaluating was performed by some other agency than the Air Force, the statement would be true, but meaningless. Who could the other agency be? Try Operation Majestic 12, by whatever its new name is now that the program has been openly discussed, or the CIA, or DIA, or NSA, or NRO, or Office of Naval Intelligence, and so on.

✒ There's no evidence of technology beyond our knowledge? As is noted in Chapter 2, fission and fusion propulsion are not beyond our knowledge; we just haven't been building and using such systems.

✒ Not a threat to security? Is that the right question? Penguins in Antarctica aren't a threat to our security either, but they surely are real. If UFOs weren't a threat, why were pilots ordered to shoot them down in 1952? Real journalists, if they did their homework, would understand this.

Here is another situation that illustrates the failure of the *Times* to do its job. The *New York Times* of September 18, 1994, gave front-page coverage (above the fold), and more on the second page, when the USAF released its totally misleading volume *The Roswell Report: Fact vs. Fiction in the New Mexico Desert*. The Air Force provided the fiction. The article was written by Pulitzer Prize–winner William Broad, who bought the grossly misleading and false Mogul balloon story hook, line, and sinker. There were still a number of Roswell witnesses alive; he didn't talk to any of them, but talked to some Mogul balloon people who quite obviously knew nothing about Roswell. Naturally he used such pejorative labels as "flying saucer fans," "devotees," and "cultists." He mentioned some Roswell books, but not mine (*Crash at Corona*) by myself and aviation science writer Don Berliner. It is the only one by a scientist. He talked to a number of balloon experts, and mentions Walter Haut as the president of the Roswell UFO museum, but says nothing about his having been the public information officer who issued the press release of July 8, 1947. He says nothing about the 509th being the most elite military group in the world in 1947, or about Major Jesse Marcel having been the intelligence officer for the group. There were still plenty of firsthand witnesses alive; he talked to none. The story was unfortunately picked up by many other newspapers. The *Post* has talked about the Majestic 12 documents, but wouldn't correct the many false claims that I pointed out to their ombudsman.

There are many other examples of irresponsible journalism about UFOs. The most recent one is a "Science" article in *Newsweek*, on January 18, 2008, called "Demons in the Dark: How Scientists Talk About UFO

Sightings" (a *Newsweek* Web Exclusive to be found at *www.newsweek.com/id/96014*). The author, Dr. Charles Euchner, is a lecturer in English at Yale University who is completing a book about suicide at the Golden Gate Bridge. I can't see any relevance to his background or the views he discusses from professional debunkers (all have PhDs) Michael Shermer (editor of *Skeptic*), Robert Park (professor of physics at the University of Maryland), and Michael Persinger (a behavioral neuroscientist at Laurentian University). Their past writings, such as Park's *Voodoo Science: The Road From Foolishness to Fraud* (discussed in Chapter 9) and Shermer's *Why Smart People Believe Weird Things*, clearly demonstrate that they are almost completely ignorant of scientific publications about flying saucers. The starting point of the article is the Stephenville, Texas, sightings of January 2008. It is followed by nonsensical amateur psychology explanations, and no mention of the MUFON investigators or the actual statements made by the witnesses. The idea of intergalactic travel is thrown in for no good reason, as is Shermer's thinking he saw a UFO when he was overtired many years ago. Maybe the fact that *Newsweek* is connected with the *Washington Post* is relevant. I am accustomed to poor coverage of UFOs, but it always worries me that many other topics must be covered just as badly. Shermer tried his "residue" theory about UFO sightings in general, and at Stephenville, on *Larry King* in mid-January 2008. He tried to make the point that when one is trying to explain things there is always a residue of perhaps 5 percent that can't be explained. He tried that on me during our debate on *Coast to Coast* on August 1, 2007. I pointed out that it was totally false and noted the 21.5 percent of *Project Blue Book Special Report No. 14*, the 30 percent of the University of Colorado Study, the 16 percent of the UFO Evidence, and so on. Frankly, Dr. Charles Euchner owes the readers of *Newsweek* an apology for such unscientific claptrap.

Several TV documentary series about UFOs are supposedly in the works. I have my fingers crossed that good sense will prevail, but cannot be optimistic about the outcome.

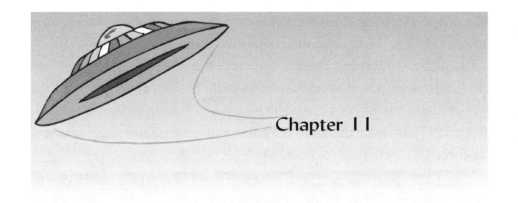

Chapter 11

The Operation Majestic 12 Documents

An excellent way to start an argument among ufologists is to bring up the topic of Majestic 12 (MJ-12 or MAJIC 12). I have been researching the subject since first hearing about the MJ-12 documents in December 1984, from William Moore and Jaime Shandera. We had worked closely together prior to that on Roswell and related topics. It should be no surprise that the various highly classified Operation Majestic 12 documents have been attacked since their existence was first made public in 1987. Equally unsurprising is the fact that a number of fraudulent MJ-12 documents have been released as well. Clearly, if the original documents—the Eisenhower Briefing Document (EBD) of November 18, 1952, the Truman-Forrestal memo (TFM) of September 24, 1947 (page 8 of the EBD), and the Cutler-Twining memo (CTM) of July 14, 1954 (found in July 1985, in Box 189 of Entry 267 of Record Group 341 at the National Archives by Jaime Shandera and William Moore)—are genuine, then the consequences are enormous. Aliens are visiting Earth, the government has recovered at least one crashed saucer and several alien bodies, and a significant group of outstanding American scientists and military leaders has collected, reviewed, evaluated, and kept secret all kinds of information about the visitors. Man is *not* alone, and the government has covered up the biggest story of the millennium (at least since 1947). In short, these are the most important classified government documents ever leaked to the public

Just 10 years after the 1984 receipt of a roll of exposed 35mm film by Jaime Shandera at his Burbank, California, home, and his efforts with William Moore and myself to evaluate them, a new roll of film showed up in the mailbox of aviation and science writer (and long-time ufologist) Don Berliner. (Berliner and I had earlier worked together on *Crash at Corona*.) The roll of film contained many pages of SOM 1-01: Majestic 12 Group SPECIAL OPERATIONS MANUAL: "Extraterrestrial Entities and Technology, Recovery and Disposal." Meanwhile Tim Cooper, a researcher in Big Bear Lake, California, began receiving loads of supposedly related MJ-12 documents. There would appear to be no connection between the original three documents and the SOM 1.01 (mailed from Wisconsin rather than Albuquerque, N.M.), or the mass of Tim Cooper documents that were usually in the form of Xerox copies, often only legible with difficulty, and received by him through the mail.

The Debunkers

There seem to be several distinct groups attacking the documents:

A. Those who believe (despite all the evidence to the contrary) that no alien spacecraft have ever visited Earth. Therefore, any documents saying that they have, must be false. No need to do a detailed investigation, to spend time in archives, research the people involved, or the like. They must be fraudulent!

B. Those who are convinced that some UFOs are indeed alien spacecraft, but that no saucer crashed near Roswell because they haven't found any other classified documents indicating any have. Karl Pflock, in his book *Roswell: Inconvenient Facts and the Will to Believe*, epitomizes this approach. If no saucer crashed at Roswell, then the documents saying it did must be fake.

C. Former military people who are convinced that the documents must be false because the style, format, details, and so on, do not match what they would have expected, based on their military service from the 1960s onward. This ignores the many changes in office procedures (copy machines, word processors), and the fact that the White House is a civilian organization—not a military one.

D. Armchair theorists who think they can make judgments without doing any homework at all.

In much of the discussion, one finds the use of the four basic rules for debunking of any controversial idea, which I detailed previously. Another important rule for some of the attackers is that absence of evidence is evidence for absence. Karl Pflock and others cite numerous documents, mostly only classified SECRET, that say nothing about Roswell or Majestic 12. This, of course, neglects the fact that there are still numerous documents from the Truman and Eisenhower eras (1945–1961) that are still classified, that we rarely see documents that have classification stamps of TOP SECRET CODE WORD. I was told in November 2003 by an archivist at the Ike Library that they still have about 300,000 pages of classified documents. We know that the NSA classified 156 UFO documents (found in response to a judge's directive) as TOP SECRET UMBRA when they finally released a highly expurgated version—about two lines per page are not covered with white-out. Supposedly the redacted information is about sources and methods. Why would it be filed under UFOs if only 5 percent is about UFOs?

In addition, as a result of my spending a lot of time at 20 different document archives from coast to coast, I can say that almost never does one find TOP SECRET CODE WORD documents about anything. The best documents for comparison with the EBD would be the four National Security Briefings for president-elect Eisenhower presented by Director of Central Intelligence Walter B. Smith in the time period between Ike's election on November 4, 1952, and January 9, 1953, when Smith informed President Truman of his security briefings for Ike before and after the election. Unfortunately, despite my FOIA request to the CIA and a subsequent appeal to their response ("We have nothing in response to your request," even though I gave the dates and times of two of the briefings), we have no such documents for comparison.

Academics have found it necessary to jump into the fray, often without benefit of any research. For example, Carl Sagan said in *The Demon Haunted World*, "The Air Force says the documents are bogus.... And UFO expert Philip J. Klass and others find lexicographic inconsistencies that suggest the whole thing is a hoax." He seemed to be totally unaware of the fact that Klass had paid me $1,000 for providing more than 14 documents done in exactly the same Pica typeface as the Cutler-Twining memo. Klass, on the basis of nine Elite typeface documents (obtained by him via mail; he had never been to the Ike Library) of the 250,000 pages of NSC material at the Ike Library, had insisted the CTM should have been done in Elite type! Some lexicographic research! (Our correspondence and a copy of his check to me are in my *Final Report on Operation Majestic 12*.) It is interesting that he had told many people of his challenge to me to find any other legitimate examples of the use of the same style and size Pica type as used in the memo, but told nobody about paying me. He had offered me

A-9

Notes by S.T. Friedman: This document was found after a few days of searching in the just declassified boxes of Record Group 341 in Mid 1985 by Jaime Shandera and William Moore. Stanton Friedman had discovered during a visit to the National Archives in March 1985 that the RG was in the process of being classification reviewed. Post cards were received hinting that checking the file would be a good idea. This memo clearly has nothing to do with anything else in Box 189 where it was found. Most likely it was planted there during the classification review which involved many teams of 4 each working for a few weeks in a location where they were able to bring in notes, files, brief cases etc.The item in its original form is a carbon on Dictation Onion Skin by Fox Paper. It is discolored around the edges. My best bet for the actual author is James S. Lay who was Exec. Sec of NSC and worked very very closely with Cutler and met "off the Record" with Ike at the WH on July 14, 1954. The mark through the classification is red.

July 14, 1954

TOP SECRET RESTRICTED SECURITY INFORMATION

MEMORANDUM FOR GENERAL TWINING

SUBJECT: NSC/MJ-12 Special Studies Project

The President has decided that the MJ-12 SSP briefing should take place during the already scheduled White House meeting of July 16, rather than following it as previously intended. More precise arrangements will be explained to you upon arrival. Please alter your plans accordingly.

Your concurrence in the above change of arrangements is assumed.

Note that the last sentence is almost identical to the wording of another TS Cutler-Twining memo found at the Library of Congress in the Twining papers.

ROBERT CUTLER
Special Assistant
to the President

Note that there is no signature and no /s/

Authority MND 857013
by S b 5TH NARA date 1/12/87

COPY

from
E NATIONAL ARCHIVES
ord Group No.. RG 341, Records of the Headquarters United
States Air Force

The Cutler-Twining memo.
Courtesy of the U.S. government.

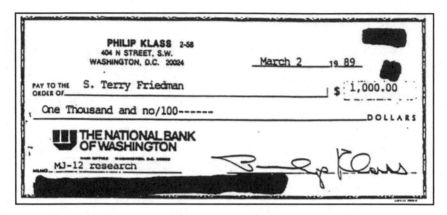

Payment to the author from Klass, proving Klass mistaken.
Courtesy of the author.

$100 for each, unfortunately setting a maximum of 10. He got upset with me for having published our correspondence and a copy of the check, and threatened to sue me. I pointed out that I had Xeroxed the check, and the bank had cashed it, and I could do what I wanted with the Xerox.

Dr. Robert Alan Goldberg, in the Roswell chapter of his book *Enemies Within*, stated, "Evidence of malfeasance was plentiful. Critics noted that the date format did not conform to governmental style, the papers carried no top-secret registration number, military titles were improperly noted, and signatures appeared to be grafted on to the document. Anachronistic usages like *media* and *impacted* further betrayed the find." This is an excellent example of research by proclamation. Goldberg is a professor of history at the University of Utah. Anyone spending much time at the Truman and Eisenhower archives would find many different date formats in old, classified, limited-distribution documents. In my *Final Report*, I published three brief cover memos from CIA Director Allen Dulles to White House Staff Secretary Colonel Andrew Goodpaster, done within a 10-day period, using these three date formats: "12 November 1956," "November 20, 1956," and "NOV 22 1956" (a rubber stamp). I even noted one file folder that used seven different date formats, and found examples of both Roscoe Hillenkoetter and W.B. Smith (DCIs and MJ-12 members) using the day, month, year format of the EBD. Goldberg didn't bother to check the Oxford Dictionary—both *media* and *impacted* were in use at the time. I will discuss military titles in a moment.

Top Secret Control Numbers

The old military guys have persistently attacked the fact that the EBD, the TF, and the CT items all lacked a TOP SECRET control number. They vociferously insisted that *all* TOP SECRET documents must have a TOP SECRET control number. With the help of archivists at the Marshall Archives and the Eisenhower Library, I was able to prove this was a totally false claim. I should note that there is a big difference between a 20-page TOP SECRET document of which 20 copies have been made, and one copy of an eyes-only document. The former requires a control number. Many of the latter do not.

Top Secret Restricted

Many people, including those in the U.S. government, have made a big thing about the typed security marking on the brief CT memo: TOP SECRET RESTRICTED, above a line saying "Security Information." Their point is that, supposedly, this designation was never used, and doesn't make sense, because TOP SECRET is the highest category and RESTRICTED is the lowest.

This uncertainty was removed when the General Accounting Office, in its pursuit of many archives for Roswell-related material, made the following statement on page 80 of their 400-plus-page report on their Roswell investigation: "Dec. 7, 1994, Ms. LJ and I reviewed records pertaining to the Air Force's atomic energy and certain mission and weapons requirements. These files were classified up to and including top secret. The period covered by these records was from 1948–1956. There was no mention of the Roswell Incident. No information pertaining to the assignment was obtained. *In several instances we noticed the classification Top Secret Restricted used on several documents. This is mentioned because in past references to this classification (Majestic 12) we were told that it was not used during this period*" (italics added). I tried to obtain copies of the materials they had seen, but was told that the materials were still classified. Clearly, absence of evidence was *not* evidence for absence. An obvious question is, why would a clever forger use a security marking that was so uncommon, rather than just a plain vanilla TOP SECRET? How did he or she know to place a slanted red-pencil line through the marking? I was informed well after discovery of the document at the National Archives that this was standard practice prior to declassification. An obscure detail indeed.

Military Rank Confusion

Kevin Randle's major complaint about the MJ-12 papers is that the military ranks are blatantly wrong. On page two of the EBD, Roscoe H. Hillenkoetter (DCI 1947–1950) is noted thusly: "BRIEFING OFFICER: ADM. ROSCOE H. HILLENKOETTER (MJ-1)," and is listed lower on the page with a beginning line of "Members of the Majestic 12 Group were designated as follows: Adm. Roscoe H. Hillenkoetter.... Gen. Nathan F. Twining. Gen. Hoyt S. Vandenberg.... Gen. Robert Montague."

The kicker here is that Hillenkoetter was not a full admiral, but only a rear admiral. However, in September 1947, Montague was only a brigadier general, and Twining and Vandenberg were only lieutenant generals. (Vandenberg got his fourth star in October 1947.) In short, the writer of the briefing was consistent in using generic ranks.

This makes perfect sense in view of three factors:

1. In a mixed groups of civilians and military people, what rank can one give the civilians?

2. The Navy has only three flag ranks—vice, rear, and full admirals—but the Army has four: brigadier, major, lieutenant, and full (four-star) generals.

3. The names were listed as they had been designated in 1947, but some ranks had changed prior to November 1952. Generic ranks avoid the problem.

Early on, Randle had asked me for other examples of Hillenkoetter signing memos as "admiral." I had to point out that there is no Hillenkoetter signature on the EBD, so the question is irrelevant. This argument may sound weak, but General Arthur Exon, Colonel Jesse Marcel, Jr., and Navy Commander Thomas Deuley had no trouble with generic ranks. Ike used them himself in his books. Fortunately, because of the work of California researcher Brian Parks, I was able to locate a relevant example of just this same approach. Andrew Goodpaster (by this time a brigadier general) had written a classified memo dated June 30, 1958, in which he listed the attendees at a meeting on June 27, 1958. Several were civilians and five were military. All of the latter, including himself, were listed as *general* or *admiral*, even though only one was a four-star. However, his signature is *brigadier general*. Goodpaster had been with Ike from the start of his presidency in 1953, so he surely knew the right protocol for the White House. During a visit to the Eisenhower Library in Abilene, Kansas, in November 2003, I found a number of these "memcons" from General Goodpaster using generic ranks for meeting attendees, including himself, but still signing as *brigadier general*.

It is difficult to find relevant evidence if one doesn't go to the archives. In case the reader is wondering, no, the material at the Truman and Eisenhower Libraries has not been scanned and is not accessible via computer from one's armchair or at the libraries. The archivists had no problem with generic ranks.

A-2

TOP SECRET / MAJIC

NATIONAL SECURITY INFORMATION

001

•••••••••••••
• TOP SECRET •
•••••••••••••

EYES ONLY

COPY ONE OF ONE.

BRIEFING DOCUMENT: OPERATION MAJESTIC 12

PREPARED FOR PRESIDENT-ELECT DWIGHT D. EISENHOWER: (EYES ONLY)

18 NOVEMBER, 1952

WARNING: This is a TOP SECRET - EYES ONLY document containing compartmentalized information essential to the national security of the United States. EYES ONLY ACCESS to the material herein is strictly limited to those possessing Majestic-12 clearance level. Reproduction in any form or the taking of written or mechanically transcribed notes is strictly forbidden.

•••••••••••••
• TOP SECRET •
•••••••••••••

TOP SECRET / MAJIC

T52-EXEMPT (E)

EYES ONLY   EYES ONLY

001

First page of the TOP SECRET *Eisenhower Briefing Document (EBD), found genuine. Courtesy of the U.S. government.*

TOP SECRET / MAJIC   002

EYES ONLY

* TOP SECRET *
****

SUBJECT: OPERATION MAJESTIC-12 PRELIMINARY BRIEFING FOR
  PRESIDENT-ELECT EISENHOWER.

DOCUMENT PREPARED 18 NOVEMBER, 1952.

BRIEFING OFFICER: ADM. ROSCOE H. HILLENKOETTER (MJ-1)

NOTE: This document has been prepared as a preliminary briefing
only. It should be regarded as introductory to a full operations
briefing intended to follow.

* * * * * *

OPERATION MAJESTIC-12 is a TOP SECRET Research and Development/
Intelligence operation responsible directly and only to the
President of the United States. Operations of the project are
carried out under control of the Majestic-12 (Majic-12) Group
which was established by special classified executive order of
President Truman on 24 September, 1947, upon recommendation by
Dr. Vannevar Bush and Secretary James Forrestal. (See Attachment
"A".) Members of the Majestic-12 Group were designated as follows:

> Adm. Roscoe H. Hillenkoetter
> Dr. Vannevar Bush
> Secy. James V. Forrestal*
> Gen. Nathan F. Twining
> Gen. Hoyt S. Vandenberg
> Dr. Detlev Bronk
> Dr. Jerome Hunsaker
> Mr. Sidney W. Souers
> Mr. Gordon Gray
> Dr. Donald Menzel
> Gen. Robert M. Montague
> Dr. Lloyd V. Berkner

The death of Secretary Forrestal on 22 May, 1949, created
a vacancy which remained unfilled until 01 August, 1950, upon
which date Gen. Walter B. Smith was designated as permanent
replacement.

****
* TOP SECRET *

TOP SECRET / MAJIC

EYES ONLY   002

*Page 2 of the EBD, listing the members of MJ-12.
Courtesy of the U.S. government.*

A-3

TOP SECRET / MAJIC

EYES ONLY

003

* TOP SECRET *
* * * * * * * * * * * * * * *

EYES ONLY   COPY ONE OF ONE.

On 24 June, 1947, a civilian pilot flying over the Cascade
Mountains in the State of Washington observed nine flying
disc-shaped aircraft traveling in formation at a high rate
of speed. Although this was not the first known sighting
of such objects, it was the first to gain widespread attention
in the public media. Hundreds of reports of sightings of
similar objects followed. Many of these came from highly
credible military and civilian sources. These reports resulted in independent efforts by several different elements
of the military to ascertain the nature and purpose of these
objects in the interests of national defense. A number of
witnesses were interviewed and there were several unsuccessful
attempts to utilize aircraft in efforts to pursue reported
discs in flight. Public reaction bordered on near hysteria
at times.

In spite of these efforts, little of substance was learned
about the objects until a local rancher reported that one
had crashed in a remote region of New Mexico located approximately seventy-five miles northwest of Roswell Army Air
Base (now Walker Field).

On 07 July, 1947, a secret operation was begun to assure
recovery of the wreckage of this object for scientific study.
During the course of this operation, aerial reconnaissance
discovered that four small human-like beings had apparently
ejected from the craft at some point before it exploded.
These had fallen to earth about two miles east of the wreckage
site. All four were dead and badly decomposed due to action
by predators and exposure to the elements during the approximately one week time period which had elapsed before their
discovery. A special scientific team took charge of removing
these bodies for study. (See Attachment "C".) The wreckage
of the craft was also removed to several different locations.
(See Attachment "B".) Civilian and military witnesses in
the area were debriefed, and news reporters were given the
effective cover story that the object had been a misguided
weather research balloon.

* * * * * * * * * * * * * *
* TOP SECRET *
* * * * * * * * * * * * * *

EYES ONLY TOP SECRET / MAJIC

EYES ONLY   T52-EXEMPT (E)

003

Page 3 of the EBD.
Courtesy of the U.S. government.

TOP SECRET / MAJIC

A-4

004

EYES ONLY
●●●●●●●●●●●●●●
* TOP SECRET *
●●●●●●●●●●●●●●

A covert analytical effort organized by Gen. Twining and Dr. Bush acting on the direct orders of the President, resulted in a preliminary concensus (19 September, 1947) that the disc was most likely a short range reconnaissance craft. This conclusion was based for the most part on the craft's size and the apparent lack of any identifiable provisioning. (See Attachment "D".) A similar analysis of the four dead occupants was arranged by Dr. Bronk. It was the tentative conclusion of this group (30 November, 1947) that although these creatures are human-like in appearance, the biological and evolutionary processes responsible for their development has apparently been quite different from those observed or postulated in homo-sapiens. Dr. Bronk's team has suggested the term "Extra-terrestrial Biological Entities", or "EBEs", be adopted as the standard term of reference for these creatures until such time as a more definitive designation can be agreed upon.

Since it is virtually certain that these craft do not originate in any country on earth, considerable speculation has centered around what their point of origin might be and how they get here. Mars was and remains a possibility, although some scientists, most notably Dr. Menzel, consider it more likely that we are dealing with beings from another solar system entirely.

Numerous examples of what appear to be a form of writing were found in the wreckage. Efforts to decipher these have remained largely unsuccessful. (See Attachment "E".) Equally unsuccessful have been efforts to determine the method of propulsion or the nature or method of transmission of the power source involved. Research along these lines has been complicated by the complete absence of identifiable wings, propellers, jets, or other conventional methods of propulsion and guidance, as well as a total lack of metallic wiring, vacuum tubes, or similar recognizable electronic components. (See Attachment "F".) It is assumed that the propulsion unit was completely destroyed by the explosion which caused the crash.

●●●●●●●●●●●●●●
* TOP SECRET *
●●●●●●●●●●●●●●

Page 4 of the EBD.
Courtesy of the U.S. government.

••••••••••••••
* TOP SECRET *
••••••••••••••

EYES ONLY   COPY ONE OF ONE.

A need for as much additional information as possible about
these craft, their performance characteristics and their
purpose led to the undertaking known as U.S. Air Force Project
SIGN in December, 1947. In order to preserve security, liason
between SIGN and Majestic-12 was limited to two individuals
within the Intelligence Division of Air Materiel Command whose
role was to pass along certain types of information through
channels. SIGN evolved into Project GRUDGE in December, 1948.
The operation is currently being conducted under the code name
BLUE BOOK, with liason maintained through the Air Force officer
who is head of the project.

On 06 December, 1950, a second object, probably of similar
origin, impacted the earth at high speed in the El Indio –
Guerrero area of the Texas – Mexican boder after following
a long trajectory through the atmosphere. By the time a
search team arrived, what remained of the object had been almost
totally incinerated. Such material as could be recovered was
transported to the A.E.C. facility at Sandia, New Mexico, for
study.

Implications for the National Security are of continuing importance in that the motives and ultimate intentions of these
visitors remain completely unknown. In addition, a significant
upsurge in the surveillance activity of these craft beginning
in May and continuing through the autumn of this year has caused
considerable concern that new developments may be imminent.
It is for these reasons, as well as the obvious international
and technological considerations and the ultimate need to
avoid a public panic at all costs, that the Majestic-12 Group
remains of the unanimous opinion that imposition of the
strictest security precautions should continue without inter-
ruption into the new administration. At the same time, con-
tingency plan MJ-1949-04P/78 (Top Secret – Eyes Only) should
be held in continued readiness should the need to make a
public announcement present itself. (See Attachment "G".)

••••••••••••••
TOP SECRET/MAJIC
EYES ONLY   T52-EXEMPT (E)
EYES ONLY

005

Page 5 of the EBD.
Courtesy of the U.S. government.

Members of MJ-12

The 12 original members of MJ-12 are listed on the second page of the EBD. Many people in ufology had serious difficulty with Dr. Donald H. Menzel being listed as a member of MJ-12. After all, he was, at the time in 1952, and for many years after that, the best-known UFO debunker. By the time of his death in 1976, he had written three negative UFO books, given a number of papers (including at the 1968 Congressional hearings, where his paper is next to mine), all attacking UFO reality. There was also the issue that all the other MJ-12 members, based on readily available information, had high-level security clearances. But surely one didn't need a clearance to teach astronomy at Harvard?

I hadn't liked Menzel, as I was not impressed with his unscientific books, and had a run-in with him at Harvard via phone after inviting him to my Harvard lecture. He claimed, "You can't be a scientist and believe in flying saucers." I laughed, which didn't please him. Of course he didn't go to the lecture. I decided that at least I would do some checking. I had viewed his UFO correspondence at the American Philosophical Library in Philadelphia, and found out that his papers were at the Harvard Archives, with some also at the University of Denver. After getting the required approval from three different people to view the Harvard holdings, I paid a visit to Harvard at the expense of the Fund for UFO Research. There I made the shocking discovery that Menzel was up to his ears in highly classified work for the CIA, NSA, and more than 30 companies. He had taught cryptography before WWII, learned a different symbolic language (Japanese), and worked on all kinds of classified problems for many years after WWII. He told Jack Kennedy he could tell him more about the NSA when they were properly cleared to each other. Menzel had been associated with the NSA and its Navy predecessor for 30 years as of 1960! None of this was noted in an eight-page appreciation in *Sky and Telescope* after his death. I published an article in the *International UFO Reporter* entitled "The Secret Life of Donald Menzel," and gave more details in my *Final Report*. Early on I had noted correspondence between Menzel's attorney and MJ-12 member Dr. Vannevar Bush thanking Bush for his support of Menzel at a terrible USAF Loyalty Hearing. The file is at the Harvard Archives, and is fascinating reading.

Many in ufology claim that Menzel couldn't have led a double life as a public debunker and a private advocate of the notion that the aliens recovered at Roswell were "beings from another solar system entirely." All admitted that they knew nothing of his clandestine post-war activities. An old associate of his with whom I had contact had no problem at all with the idea. Some, many years later, were able to obtain some government files on Menzel. None have shown that these were known prior to my discoveries in 1986. I should point out that many very bright spies led double lives for years, such as Philby, Burgess, and Maclean, who were Soviet spies working for many years in British intelligence.

Randle says little about the other MJ-12 members, but made the following comment: "Nowhere did he [Friedman] find any mention of MJ-12 [in his papers and records]. There are no marginal notes, no oblique references, no highly placed correspondence that suggests, mentions, identifies, or confirms the existence of MJ-12 or Menzel's connection to it." This is another one of those "absence of evidence" claims. Certainly I had never claimed to have found any direct evidence. But none of Menzel's files at the Harvard Archives were classified, despite all his classified activities. He had already spent 30 years (as of 1960) working for the NSA and its Navy predecessors. No rational person would expect him to have left classified materials about a TOP SECRET CODE WORD black budget activity, whose very existence was classified, in the open. The funny thing is that Randle had a long connection with the military, even having been called back in to serve as an officer in Iraq. He certainly knows the rules for storage of classified materials.

The Truman Forrestal Memo

Right from the start the TFM had been the target of the debunkers. Phil Klass, in a fast press release after Bill Moore publicized the EBD, TFM, and CTM, had claimed it was an obvious fraud because it made all kinds of mistakes, compared to real Truman letters. He used the word *letter* nine times even though it is clearly headed *Memorandum*. Many have claimed that the typewriter with which it was typed was obviously from 1960, proving it was a fraud (no forensic document analysis was provided). Most claimed that the signature was identical to that on another memo from Truman to MJ-12 member Vannevar Bush. First measurements clearly indicated it was not an exact copy, because the lengths of various segments seemed not to match. Randle, in *Case MJ-12*, provided the off-the-cuff opinion of Peter Tytell, a world-class questioned documents examiner. Moore, Shandera, and I had sent a copy of the documents to Tytell, who didn't want his name used anywhere, and prepared no report, but apparently claimed to Randle that the typewriter typeface was not in use until the 1960s. Randle quotes him thusly: "It was just perfect because the whole thing of the 12 pages or however many pages it was.... Most of the pages were just blank pages with just five words written on them like Top Secret or Appendix A or something like that." In reality, there were eight pages and only one, page 7 (not included by Randle), said "Appendix A." Fortunately, Dr. Robert M. Wood hired an expert, James A. Black, to perform a professional examination. On November 13, 1998, Black stated, "My knowledge of typewriter fonts permits me to conclude that the letter was likely to have been typed by an Underwood Standard typewriter. The portions of the type font of the letter that can be clearly visualized match those of a typewriter exemplar of an Underwood Standard typed in May 1940."

Black also added that that the disputed signature is most likely a reproduction: "I reached this opinion because the ink line is homogenous and feathering is absent at the ends of the lines." Does this prove the

A-8

008

THE WHITE HOUSE
WASHINGTON

September 24, 1947.

MEMORANDUM FOR THE SECRETARY OF DEFENSE

Dear Secretary Forrestal:

As per our recent conversation on this matter, you are hereby authorized to proceed with all due speed and caution upon your undertaking. Hereafter this matter shall be referred to only as Operation Majestic Twelve.

It continues to be my feeling that any future considerations relative to the ultimate disposition of this matter should rest solely with the Office of the President following appropriate discussions with yourself, Dr. Bush and the Director of Central Intelligence.

Harry Truman

008

Truman Forrestal memo (page 8 of the EBD). Courtesy of the U.S. government.

document is a fraud? The real question is, where would there have been an original of the memo with a signature? Forrestal's *original* would have been signed, but who else would have received a signed copy? One expects that Dr. Bush and the DCI (Hillenkoetter) noted in the memo would have had copies, most likely unsigned. Forrestal died in May 1949, three years earlier. Because we know that W.B. Smith, director of central intelligence succeeding Hillenkoetter, was (because of the 1952 presidential election) briefing Ike at this time (1952) on national security matters, presumably Hillenkoetter, then at the Brooklyn Navy Yard, may well have had the EBD typed at the CIA. Smith (who worked closely with Ike during WWII) might well have said that Ike prefers documents with signatures. Surely the CIA had the capability of lifting a signature from the memo from Truman to Bush (ironically, I had found that in the Bush papers at the LCMD). Karl Pflock, a former CIA employee, assured me that this was the case.

Of course, none of the critics of the memo note that the numerical portion of the date, "24, 1947," is offset from the September, and done with a different typewriter. Bush's office always put a period after the date; rarely did Truman's. George Elsey, who worked for Roosevelt at the White House and then for Truman during his entire term in office, told me that most of what a president signs is prepared by other people, and sometimes the documents have to have the date typed later when it is clear which date is appropriate. He could find no reason to say the EBD, TFM, or CTM were fraudulent. Truman was very busy at that time, as the new national security apparatus was being installed, the USAF was separated from the Army, the CIA was created from the Central Intelligence Group, and so on. Why would a hoaxer use two different typewriters and put a period after the date? Forgers normally do as little as possible to call attention to idiosyncrasies in their forgeries, whether of paintings or documents.

Other critics of the signature claim, based on Albert S. Osborne's book *Questioned Documents*, that no two signatures are alike. Actually, Osborne said that one *could* produce identical signatures, just not consecutively. After the 1948 election Truman commented to a family member that he was signing 500 thank-you notes an hour. Some were surely identical to others. Klass had even claimed the Osborne book was published in 1978, when it would have covered Xeroxing, when it fact it was published in 1910, and the chapter involved is entitled "Traced Forgeries." I was lucky to find a copy at the Fredericton headquarters of the RCMP. I doubt if Klass ever saw a copy.

How Did a Hoaxer Know So Much?

In my *Final Report* I provided a list of more than 37 facts not known to be true until after the EBD, TFM, and CTM had been received or found. A lot were trivial, such as the date given, August 1, 1950, for Smith having permanently replaced the deceased Forrestal as an MJ-12 member. I obtained from the Truman Library the fact that that was the only date when Truman and Smith met during a many-month period of time before Smith succeeded Hillenkoetter as DCI. They had not provided that information to anyone else.

The CTM has neither a signature nor the symbol "/s/," as do the other two memos we had from Cutler to Twining. Cutler was out of the country on that date, so could not have signed any letters. However, he left detailed instructions with James Lay, executive secretary of the NSC, to keep things moving out of his in-basket while he was gone. I published that letter and the one from Lay to Cutler while Cutler was overseas saying he was taking care of things, in my *Final Report*. It took me two years to get the latter via mandatory classification review through the Ike Library, as it was still classified when I found a withdrawal sheet noting it. I had also discovered that earlier that day (July 14, 1954) Lay had met with Ike and they had a phone conversation at around 4:30 p.m.

George Elsey told me that Lay and Cutler worked closely together, and Lay would certainly have sent a brief note for Cutler to Twining making a trivial change in schedule. How did the forger know *not* to sign the memo or use /s/ (because it was some time after the discovery of the CTM that Robert Todd found the memo from Cutler to Lay saying he would be gone)? Todd was strongly opposed to Roswell, MJ-12, Bill Moore, Jaime Shandera, Jesse Marcel, and so on. It is also interesting that the Cutler-Lay memo underlines a few words, as does the CTM. This is uncommon in documents of that era, but apparently was used by Lay and Cutler about NSC matters.

The EBD says that the detailed investigation of Roswell by Twining and Bush began on July 7, 1947. Several years *after* its receipt, in a newly declassified box of General Twining's papers, I found his flight log, which shows that he indeed flew to New Mexico from Ohio on July 7, 1947. This was confirmed by his pilot's flight log as well, also found much later. How did anybody know that date fit?

Some people have complained that anybody could have found out what I did about Menzel prior to receipt of the EBD. Yes, of course, the documents were sitting at the Harvard Archives. But it took three signatures, including his wife's, for me to gain access. No evidence has been claimed or put forth that anyone else had looked at the papers before I had. Some have even falsely suggested that I noted the letters to Kennedy and such at the readily accessible American Philosophical Society Library's Menzel UFO Correspondence file. They weren't there. No permission signatures were required for that access.

Phony Documents

Tim Cooper, of Big Bear Lake, California, had received a lot of supposed MJ-12 documents throughout a period of time. With the exception of a lengthy piece on a history of UFOs (the Bowen Document), which is on original paper but only has a magenta TOP SECRET MAJIC stamped on it, they are Xerox copies. In a number of instances the originals were very hard to read, which meant much time was spent trying to decipher the words. To some this indicates authenticity. One of the documents had bothered me because it was supposedly a memo from Admiral Hillenkoetter to President Truman (February 17, 1948), noting that President Truman wasn't receiving much of the MAJIC material. This made no sense. Truman wasn't an engineer or scientist; what would have been the purpose of so much material going to him? It sounded to me as though it should have been from General Marshall to President Roosevelt, about the MAGIC material being processed by the ton after we broke the Japanese codes during WWII. I was also concerned by its mention of "the recently discovered machines," and so much "product" being received every day. It sounded more similar to what would have been a letter from General Marshall to President Roosevelt during WWII talking about the "intelligence product" of code-breaking using a cipher machine.

My suspicions were confirmed when I discovered the original from Marshall to Roosevelt about MAGIC in the readily available book *The American MAGIC* at the University of New Brunswick Library, not far from the important book *Wedemeyer Reports* by General Albert C. Wedemeyer. On the other hand, there was one item I had thought was genuine, because some regulations that were noted in an item to C. Humelsine matched info turned up by Larry Bryant at the Pentagon. The signature was Humelsine's, according to his wife. Marshall was in New York, according to the archives, hence the need for using the referenced "secret telephone." (But then look carefully at Figure 1, clearly an emulation.) There were a number of other signatures that were questionable. A real breakthrough came when I asked for an opinion from archivist Larry Bland at the Marshall Archives about another letter supposedly from Marshall to Humelsine. He immediately recognized it as an emulation of a famous letter (see Figure 2, also from Lewin's book) from Marshall to Governor Thomas Dewey, the Republican candidate for president in the

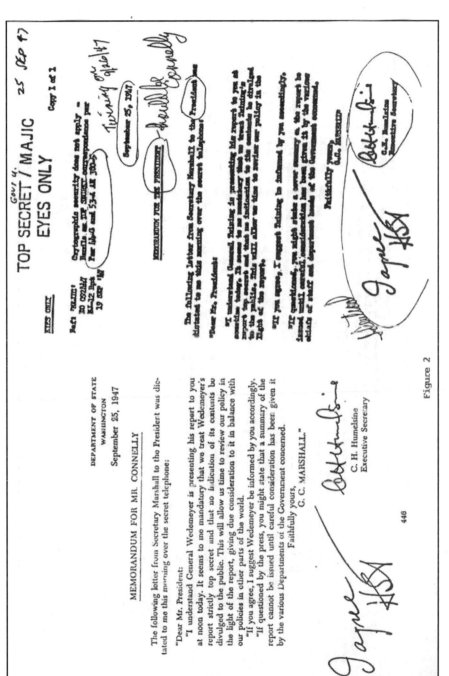

Figure 1: Genuine and emulated phony document. Courtesy of the U.S. government.

12 February 1944

MEMORANDUM FOR THE PRESIDENT:

Subject: "Magic"

I have learned that you seldom see the Army summaries of "Magic" material. For a long time, the last two months in particular, I have had our G-2 organization concentrating on a workable presentation on "Magic" for my use as well as for the other officials concerned, particularly yourself. A highly specialized organization is now engaged in the very necessary process of separating the wheat from the chaff and correlating the items with past information in order that I may be able quickly and intelligently to evaluate the importance of the product.

Recently I have had these summaries bound in a Black Book both for convenience of reading and for greater security in handling. Sometimes two or three of these booklets are gotten out in a single day. I think they contain all of the worthwhile information culled from the tremendous mass of intercepts now available and that are accumulated each twenty-four hours. The recent discovery of the Japanese Army machine code has added a tremendous amount of such material and will continue to give us a great deal from day to day. The problem is how to avoid being buried under the mass of information, and I think the present arrangement satisfactorily meets that difficulty.

I am attaching two of the current booklets which I hope you will glance through in order to familiarize yourself with the manner in which the information is presented. I should like to send these booklets each day direct to the White House and have them delivered to you by Admiral Brown.

(Sgd) *G. C. MARSHALL*

Chief of Staff.

Figure 2: Genuine letter, later emulated. Courtesy of the U.S. government.

election of 1944, trying to get Dewey not to make any public charges that the United States had broken the Japanese codes, as that would lead them to change the codes, and therefore cost many lives. Marshall noted that he, as the chief of staff to a Democratic president, couldn't be seen with Dewey—the emulation said he couldn't be seen with Humelsine! But Humelsine had been his executive secretary during WWII, and was again playing that role to Marshall as secretary of state. They saw each other almost every day. Also, it was addressed "Dear Carl," but Marshall essentially never used first names except for contemporaries, and Marshall was decades older than Humelsine. Colonel Clark was now a general, and not working with Marshall in 1947. Marshall was secretary of state, not defense (though he held that role a few years later).

This was a real break. I also asked Bland if he could see any reason why General Albert C. Wedemeyer (his signature is on one of the Cooper documents) should be connected with MJ-12, when his field was China. He had served there during WWII and was sent in 1947 to make a study about what the effects would be if the United States did or did not get heavily involved in fighting the Communists under Mao Tse Tung. Bland agreed that he couldn't see the connection either. He mentioned that there was an entire book called *Wedemeyer Reports*. I located it at the nearby University of New Brunswick Library. Almost immediately I found three documents that were the models for three phony emulations! The technique was straightforward: Retype an existing document with an old typewriter, making a few changes (dates and such) to conceal the chicanery, scan or Xerox the handwritten portions of documents, combine, and voila—a genuine-looking phony. I checked other books at the library, and, sure enough, the book *The American Magic* had both the original of the Dewey letter (Figure 2) and the original Marshall Magic letter. Bob Wood had located the original of the letter (Figure 1) supposedly from Marshall to Truman via the Humelsine letter. It was from Marshall to Truman about

Wedemeyer, not Twining. I hadn't paid enough attention to the fact that I knew from Twining's pilot log that he flew to D.C. on September 26, not September 25.

Almost all of the phony documents not only had word-for-word portions of the originals, but also the handwritten items fit right on top of them. Even though there was a Truman signature, a handwritten date (July 9, 1947), and the words "I approve," spacing matched perfectly. See the emulation (Figure 3) of a supposed July 9 directive to General Twining. Compare it to the genuine item from Wedemeyer's book (also Figure 3). A number of the non-emulation documents had direct quotes from the phony ones, establishing that they were phony as well. Also, all had mistakes in the text that made no sense, such as, "when finished in New Mexico go to Sandia." This was supposedly to Twining, but is an emulation of a real directive to Wedemeyer in which it was said, "when finished in China go to Korea." Korea is not in China, so that makes sense, but Sandia is *in* New Mexico. The handwritten date on the Wedemeyer directive is July 9. But Twining went to New Mexico on July 7. It makes sense for Wedemeyer to take along specialists from the State, the Treasury, and the Navy, because he had to look at the total Chinese picture. Not only would those people make no sense as a part of the Twining expedition, but we know who went with Twining from an article in the Alamogordo paper saying Twining had made a routine inspection of Alamogordo Army Air Field (later Holloman AFB).

The fraudulence is further noted by the supposed letter from Twining to the president dated September 19 (see Figure 1) about presenting his findings. Compare the almost identical wording to that of the real item from Wedemeyer to the president's office (Figure 1). Twining's flight log proves he was only gone from July 7 to July 11 (hardly two months). Could Twining's small group really have generated the same exact number of documents—1,200—as Wedemeyer's? I certainly doubt it.

Real

DIRECTIVE TO LIEUTENANT GENERAL WEDEMEYER

You will proceed to China without delay for the purpose of making an appraisal of the political, economic, psychological and military situations—current and projected. In the course of your survey you will maintain liaison with American diplomatic and military officials in the area. In your discussions with Chinese officials and leaders in positions of responsibility you will make it clear that you are on a fact-finding mission and that the United States Government can consider assistance in a program of rehabilitation only if the Chinese Government presents satisfactory evidence of effective measures looking towards Chinese recovery and provided further that any aid which may be made available shall be subject to the supervision of representatives of the United States Government.

In making your appraisal it is desired that you proceed with detachment from any feeling of prior obligation to support or to further official Chinese programs which do not conform to sound American policy with regard to China. In presenting the findings of your mission you should endeavor to state as concisely as possible your estimate of the character, extent, and probable consequences of assistance which you may recommend, and the probable consequences in the event that assistance is not given.

When your mission in China is completed you will proceed on a brief trip to Korea to make an appraisal of the situation there with particular reference to an economic aid program in Korea and its relation to general political and economic conditions throughout the country. Before going to Korea you will communicate with General MacArthur to ascertain whether he desires you to proceed via Tokyo.

460   APPENDIX V

You will take with you such experts, advisers and assistants as you deem necessary to the effectiveness of your mission.

Approved
Harry Truman

July 9. 1947

Figure 1

DIRECTIVE TO LIEUTENANT GENERAL TWINING   Emulation.

You will proceed to the White Sands Proving Ground Command Center without delay for the purpose of making an appraisal of the reported unidentified objects being kept there. Part of your mission there will deal with the military, political and psychological situations—current and projected. In the course of your survey you will maintain liaison with the military officials in the area.

In making your appraisal it is desired that you proceed with detachment from any opinions or designs expressed by personnel involved which do not conform to sound reasoning with regard to the possible outcome. In presenting the findings of your mission you should endeavor to state as concisely as possible your estimate of the character, extent, and probable consequences in the event that assistance is not given.

When your mission in New Mexico is completed you will proceed on a brief trip to the Sandia and facility to make an appraisal of the situation there, also of the reaction by the Los Alamos people involved. Before going to White Sands you will communicate with General Kirkland AFB.

You will take with you such experts, technicians, scientists and assistants as you deem necessary to the effectiveness of your mission.

Approved Weedemeyer
Harry Truman

July 9. 1947

this is identical to

Twining NM
flew to 1947 and

Figure 3: Original and false emulation. Courtesy of the U.S. government.

MUFON Symposium Proceeding

RECEIVED

8:22 93
Timothy Haughi

III. CONCLUSIONS

1. Current studies of other-world visitation are in three
phases:

    a.   Technology exploitation

    b.   Interplanetary travel

    c.   Cultural communication

almost identical to ACW to HST 9/19/47

2. On 19 September 1947, the IAC, JIOA, and the JIC, reviewed
a Top Secret intelligence report titled REPORT TO THE PRESIDENT, 1947, PARTS
1-V, MAJIC EYES ONLY, DTG 000190947, . the report mentions: "In compliance
with your directive . . . of 9 July 1947, the attached "REPORT ON FLYING
SAUCERS" is respectfully submitted. (In consonance with your instructions,
advisors from State, Treasury, War and Navy Departments assisted me on a
two month exploratory mission concerning the reality of other-world visitation.
The principle investigators and storage areas were visited. Successful efforts
were made to reach scientists of all levels as measured by their work in
classified defense projects. Conferences were held with national security
officials and leaders of private industry. Approximately 1,200 memoranda and
intelligence reports were considered. The report presents this situation
against a global background my estimates, current and projected, in both the
U.S., and allied countries, and recommendations deemed to be sound courses of
action for formulating plans and policies in light of recent developments.

3. All efforts have been made to identify the country or private
concern wich could have the technical and finacial resources necessary to
produce such a long-range flight. So far, no country on this earth has the
means and the security of its resources to produce such.

4. A consensus reached by members of the panel, that until
positive proof that the Russians did not attempt a series of reconnaissance
flights over our most secure installations—tho sightings and recovered
objects are interpalnatary in nature.

5. The occupants of these planform vehicles are, in most
respects, human or human-like. Autopsies, so far indicate, that these beings
share the same biological needs as humans.

-2-

T.O.P.
S.E.C.R.E.T

Figure 3A

216

*Figure 4: MUFON Symposium Proceedings. Courtesy of the U.S.
government.*

Note also the big paragraph on the first page of the supposed xxxx-Report from Twining (Figure 4). It is clearly lifted from the emulation of the Wedemeyer-to-Truman memo of September 19, 1947: "In consonance with your instructions, advisors...." Repeating a phony portion of a document in another document doesn't make it genuine.

Bob and Ryan Wood have suggested that General Marshall must have prepared both directives. Not only did General Wedemeyer (an expert on China) say he had prepared his own directive, but also he was based in Baltimore in the Army, knew many of the key figures in China, and was reporting to Secretary of State Marshall, who had spent most of 1946 in China. Twining was based in Dayton, Ohio, was head of the Air Materiel Command of the Army Air Force, had been head of the 15th and 20th Air Forces, and served on the National Advisory Committee on Acronautics, with a very strong technical background. The two situations (China in a political upheaval and an alien saucer in New Mexico) were drastically different. Wedemeyer needed presidential authority to speak for the United States in China. How could Marshall have used almost identical language, and why would he be instructing Twining? This phony-baloney stuff clearly established that almost all of the documents were fake.

Some people insist that if I can't provide the identity of the forger and the reason for forging, that the documents must be real. I can't follow that logic. My concern is whether they are genuine. One quite obvious motivation would be to cast doubts on the legitimate documents—a sort of guilt by association. Another might be to waste the time and money of researchers. Ryan Wood of *Majesticdocuments.com* claims that all the Cooper documents are genuine. However, in his paper, "Resolving the 'Emulation' in Directives Between Twining and Wedemeyer," he talks at length about the various versions of the Truman-Wedemeyer directive, but never shows the full page from Wedemeyer's book next to the Twining one, so that one can't see the identity in placement and handwriting of the three handwritten comments. This same problem holds on the Humelsine documents: He shows several slightly different versions of the directive to Wedemeyer, but never shows the other pairs of original and emulation documents as noted here. He also seems to feel that Marshall was in charge of both Wedemeyer, based in Baltimore, and Twining, though Marshall was secretary of state and not in the War (soon to be Defense) Department. Twining was head of the Air Materiel Department in Ohio, definitely in the chain of command of the Army Air Force.

It also makes perfect sense for the Wedemeyer directive to say, "In presenting the findings of your mission you should endeavor to state as concisely as possible your estimate of the character, extent, and probable consequences of assistance which you may recommend, and the probable consequences in the event that assistance is not given." China was a major foreign policy headache, with the Communists taking over, but what sense does this comment make in the Twining directive, which says, "In presenting the findings of your mission you should endeavor to state as concisely as possible your estimate of the character, extent, and probable consequences in the event that assistance is not given"? Assistance to whom, for what? It makes no sense at all. One document claims that Air Force General Carl Spaatz met with Twining in New Mexico on July 7, 1947. I was able to show, via Spaatz's flight log, his desk calendar, and a newspaper article, that he was fishing in Port Aransas, Texas, several hundred miles away. There are a whole host of false claims in other Cooper documents, including a number of technical errors such as referring to "deuterium, light hydrogen"—deuterium is *heavy* hydrogen.

The Majestic 12 documents problem is complex and extensive. On balance it appears that the EBD, TFM, and CTM are almost certainly genuine, the SOM 1.01 memo is very likely genuine (see Dr. Robert Wood's paper, "Authenticating the Special Operations Manual"), and the Tim Cooper documents are emulation, and fictional. One strange criticism of the EBD was made by Karl Pflock when he claimed, twice, that because Menzel was famous for doodling small cartoon Martians, that his comment about aliens being from Mars was just an inside joke. I am afraid the joke was on Pflock. The EBD says exactly the opposite: "considerable speculation has centered around what their point of origin might be and how they get here. Mars was and remains a possibility, although some scientists, most notably Dr. Menzel, consider it more likely that we are dealing with beings from another solar system entirely."

In a documentary called *Do You Believe in MAJIC?*, first broadcast on the Canadian Space Channel on April 28, 2004, director Paul Kimball concluded that, on the balance of probabilities (lawyers talk that way), the documents were probably genuine. Kimball, who is my nephew, later changed his mind, providing three reasons for saying the MJ-12 documents are *not* genuine. His first claim is based on the notion that because Vannevar Bush and President Truman were not on very good terms in the post-war period, Truman would not have appointed Bush, despite his outstanding background as a scientist/engineer during WWII with the Office of Scientific Research and Development, to such a position. According to the Truman Forrestal memo of September 24, 1947, Truman authorized Forrestal (not Bush) to proceed with Operation Majestic 12, but did say, "It continues to be my feeling that any future considerations relative to the ultimate disposition of this matter should rest solely with the Office of the President following appropriate discussions with yourself, Dr. Bush, and the Director of Central Intelligence."

Kimball takes care of Canadian government UFO investigator Wilbert Smith's November 21, 1950 comment about flying saucers—"(C) Their Modus Operandi is unknown, but concentrated effort is being made by a small group headed by Dr. Vannevar Bush"—by claiming that Dr. Robert Sarbacher, the source of Smith's info in a classified discussion arranged by Canada's military attaché, intentionally misled Smith with the expectation that the information, though classified, would eventually make its way up the Canadian security chain and be passed on to the Russians to convince them that the United States had access to alien technology. No evidence has been presented that this happened or was the intention of Sarbacher. Frankly, I was favorably impressed with Sarbacher when I met with him. Furthermore, Kimball attempts to discredit Smith with character assassination, bringing to light damning comments from Dr. Omond Solandt made in letters to various UFO researchers in the 1980s, long after Smith's death. Solandt was sort of the Canadian Vannevar Bush, guiding the efforts of the Defense Research Board. On September 24, 1947, Bush had been named head of the U.S. Research and Development Board, a successor to the Joint Research and Development Board that had succeeded the OSRD. This was the date of the infamous Truman-Forrestal memo establishing MJ-12, and the only date in a several-month period when Bush, Truman, and Secretary Forrestal were all together at the White House. Obviously, Truman did not appoint Bush to head MJ-12. It was to Forrestal, not Bush, that Truman said "You are hereby authorized."

Furthermore, in Bush's notes on the meeting we find this statement: "...certainly in the new post, I would be rather frequently in contact, and that if there was an impression [in the scientific community] that I did not have his confidence, he felt that that impression would soon be corrected by future relations." If Truman had no faith in Bush, why would he have named him head of R&D? His MJ-12 activities would be in total secrecy, and not a matter for public debate.

In a TOP SECRET memo of December 16, 1947, Forrestal's special assistant John Ohly noted to Bush that he had been appointed by the War Council as chairman of a special committee to deal with "preparations against a sneak attack," and many resources were available to him. (There was no indication of whether this attack would be from Russia or aliens or what.) General Hoyt Vandenberg, also an MJ-12 member and USAF chief of staff, was a member of this committee. TOP SECRET minutes of a later War Council meeting note that all members had received a copy of a TOP SECRET item from Bush, and should be prepared to discuss it. There is no clue as to what it was about. This committee and MJ-12 were not public groups wherein political considerations might have been important, but were highly classified black budget groups. It seems to me that Bush's advice and knowledge would have been sought because of his long history of contribution to the military effort via his earlier chairmanship of the NACA, and his heading of the OSRD and JRDB. Nobody knew better who had what capabilities at which installation for top-notch, highly classified research, such as trying to determine the modus operandi of flying saucers. As another indication of his high esteem by Truman, Truman appointed him chairman of a TOP SECRET committee to evaluate evidence in August 1949 that the Soviets had tested their first atomic bomb.

Truman certainly had strong views about how research grants might be distributed, and zealously guarded control. Bush had been allowed much leeway from Roosevelt. A book strongly contributing to Kimball's feelings about Bush vs. Truman is G. Pascal Zachary's 1997 *Endless Frontier: Vannevar Bush, Engineer of the American Century*. I note with dismay that Vandenberg and the War Council are not even listed in the index. I had a conversation with Zachary, a *Wall Street Journal* reporter, years ago, and at that time felt he was not familiar with Bush's classified activities.

Solandt admitted that he and Bush had indeed discussed UFOs, but weasel-worded just what was said and why, and implied that he knew of no big secret U.S. effort, though if it was accountable to the president, he probably wouldn't know about it. None of his letters were sent to people with a need-to-know, in contrast to the Sarbacher-Smith exchange.

I had located Sarbacher many years ago via a memo from Canadian Arthur Bray. I met with him on his yacht in Palm Beach, and also met later with Solandt in Ontario. My feeling was that Sarbacher was being straightforward about a small event in a busy life. I felt that Solandt was being careful in the manner I have found common with people who have classified information they cannot divulge—trying to avoid directly lying, but not giving out much information either. Solandt could denigrate Smith when no one was around to defend him. But when Smith was posthumously awarded the Canadian Engineering Award the citation noted: "The Award was made in recognition of a lifetime of dedicated and distinguished service to the advancement of technical knowledge in the Canadian broadcasting industry, the improvement of its techniques, the protection of its interests, of an example of diligence and integrity and in consideration of the universal respect and regard that Wilbert's efforts had earned throughout the broadcasting industry, in the government of Canada, and in other areas." I think all of us would greatly appreciate such praise from our professional colleagues.

Kimball also raised two other points: Why was Forrestal not replaced on Majestic 12 until August 1, 1950, even though he left office as secretary of defense in January 1949, and died on May 22, 1949? Was it MJ-11 for a while? Let us notice that the EBD states that Forrestal's "death created a vacancy which remained unfilled until 01 August, 1950, upon which date General Walter B. Smith was designated as permanent replacement." We have no way of knowing whether he may have been a temporary member and then was made permanent when Truman named him the new director of central intelligence. The first three DCIs were already MJ-12 members.

Finally, Kimball asked why I had not investigated the crash noted on page five of the EBD on December 6, 1950, in the El Indio-Guerrero area of the Texas-Mexican border. The reasons are simple: I live a long way from there and had nothing to work with—neither names of people nor a specific location. The EBD says, "What remained of the object had been almost totally incinerated. Such material as could be recovered was transported to the A.E.C. facility at Sandia, New Mexico." I have been to Sandia. The chance of getting any information from this high-security nuclear weapons lab would be nil. Furthermore, I was well aware that some investigation was being done by two Texans, Dennis Stacey and Tom Deuley, of MUFON. They had some leads that didn't pan out. I do know that there had been a National Red Alert called on that date because of something flying towards the Southwest, as noted by Dr. Bruce Maccabee in his book about The FBI and UFOs. I had my hands and budget full with my Roswell investigation, for which there was a lot to work with.

Sparks Attacks

In 2007 there was yet another attack on the MJ-12 documents. A long-time associate of mine named Brad Sparks, whom I had first known in the 1970s when he was a physics major at the University of California, Berkeley, presented a huge paper at the August Mutual UFO Network Symposium in Denver. Sparks has done a tremendous amount of fine research on UFOs. I had been warned by an associate that I wouldn't like Brad Sparks and Barry Greenwood's MUFON 2007 paper, "The Secret Pratt Tapes and the Origins of MJ-12." So I was prepared for the worst. I had also contacted the coauthor Barry Greenwood, who would not be in Denver, but indicated he was also being frozen out of the final editing.

Both Sparks and Greenwood had been active in ufology for decades. Their paper is indeed unique, being the longest (66 pages), and having the most footnotes (126) of any MUFON paper I can recall. That is, of course, far too long for an hour or so presentation, though Sparks used no visuals. He made it clear that he was opposed to the extraterrestrial hypothesis, and the reality of both Roswell and Majestic 12. He gave tantalizing hints that he may have found some undisclosed information allowing for possible Roswell reality. He didn't deal with the enormous evidence available. His main focus was on the newly released information in the papers from the late journalist Robert Pratt. These had been donated to MUFON and had been scanned as part of the Pandora Project. Of particular interest were the transcripts of tapes of U.S. Air Force Office of Special Investigations officer, Rick Doty.

Sparks's thesis seems to be that because Moore passed on everything to Doty that he and I learned from our ongoing extensive Roswell research, that Doty just fed it back as phony documents. For example, he tried to dismiss the Eisenhower Briefing Document as just an emulation of an earlier Aquarius document that is phony. No direct comparisons are given. He claims that the Cutler-Twining Memo of July 14, 1954, is just an emulation of a memo Bill Moore and I had found at the Library of Congress Manuscript Division in the papers of General Nathan Twining.

This claim frankly seems absurd. The MJ-12-related Cutler-Twining memo, on dictation onionskin made by Fox paper, is only six lines long, is not signed, and does not show the /s/. It does have the provocative line "Subject: NSC/MJ-12 Special Studies Project." The earlier July 13, 1953 memo from Cutler to Twining about an all-day meeting at the White House on July 16, 1953, is 19 lines long, has no subject line, and is signed. The only common item is "your concurrence in the above change of arrangements is assumed," the last sentence on the CTM. The last sentence in the surely genuine memo is, "In order to avoid communication on this subject, it is understood that in the absence of contrary word your concurrence in the above arrangements is assumed." (I had already pointed this out in my *Final Report on Operation Majestic 12.*)

Sparks tries to make a big deal about my comments about similarity— hardly the same as emulation. The security classifications are different, as is much else. He neglects to mention that although, yes, I had noted the similarity when Moore called the day he and Jamie Shandera discovered the

CTM, he doesn't mention that in a conversation with William McVey, Twining's pilot and aide for many years, he noted, when I asked about it, that this was standard phraseology indicating that no response was needed. The similarity of this one sentence is an indication of genuineness, not fakery.

I had noted a number of real emulations in the Tim Cooper phony MJ-12 documents in the second edition of *TOP SECRET/MAJIC* and in the Majestic 12 Update posted on my Website *www.stantonfriedman.com*— Sparks doesn't reference these two sources. The CTM is definitely not am emulation of the July 13, 1953 memo. It also has an interesting slanted red pencil mark through the unusual security marking of TOP SECRET RESTRICTED (the early one has a conventional rubber-stamped TOP SECRET). As I found out years later, the red pencil mark was standard practice when a document was to be declassified. Why add it, and how would a forger have known? It has no signature or /s/: Cutler was out of the country, so he couldn't have signed it. How did Doty know that, when it wasn't discovered until later?

It was years later that the GAO discovered a number of examples of the odd security marking. Sparks mentions a list of 10 comments expressing concerns about the CTM by Joanne Williamson at the National Archives, but seems unaware of the fact that she had to change a number of these when I pointed out errors. For example, she had noted that there was no NSC meeting scheduled for July 16, 1954, as supposedly indicated by the CTM. In fact, it only talks of an already scheduled meeting and does not say "NSC meeting." She claimed that the Ike Library had said all of Cutler's onionskin carbons were on a certain kind of onionskin. I, during a visit to the Ike Library, had noted several kinds of onionskin paper used for carbons, so that was also changed.

Sparks's dismissal of the EBD is equally shallow, besides his unsupported allegation that it is just the Aquarius document in disguise. He claims the fatal error is that the EBD says the distance to the crash site was "approximately 75 miles northwest of Roswell Army Air Base," when the driving distance on one route was 102 miles, and the GPS distance is about 62 miles. However, why would Hillenkoetter (the briefing officer) use the word *approximately* if he was trying to be precise? Obviously it didn't matter. Furthermore, there was an airplane landing strip located at a gas-line pumping station not too far from the site, and there were many small Piper Cubs at the base that would undoubtedly have been used to get people out there in a hurry. Approximately 75 miles would appear to be a good rounded number.

His second, equally questionable concern is the line: "Numerous examples of what appear to be a form of writing were found in the wreckage. Efforts to decipher these have remained largely unsuccessful." He leaves out the next item: "(See attachment E)." He then points out that, because I had later discovered from my visits to the Menzel papers at Harvard in 1986 that Menzel had taught cryptography and learned Japanese, the document, if genuine, should have said the deciphering was done under Dr. Menzel. He claims that because Doty et al hadn't been passed this info by Moore until later, this is why Menzel isn't mentioned. As in many instances in his paper, we get the strong impression that Sparks believes he is psychic and knows why people do what they do, who is telling the truth, and what is in unseen documents such as Attachment E. Careful review of the EBD finds six instances of "See Attachment B," or C, and so on. In all of these, no name is mentioned. When MJ-12 members Dr. Detlev Bronk and Menzel are mentioned by name in the text of the EBD, there is no "See Attachment." So briefer Hillenkoetter was tidy and consistent.

It seems strange that Sparks doesn't take note that the EBD says, "On 07 July, 1947, a secret operation was begun to assure recovery of the wreckage." I didn't determine that Twining had indeed gone to New Mexico on July 7 until much later, from both his and his aide's flight logs. So how did Doty know? I listed many facts not known until later. Sparks has also ignored them.

There seems to have been a battle between Sparks and Greenwood about claims that documents were faked just to make money for Moore, Doty, and Pratt. Sparks took much of this out because of fear of libel charges. He also claimed that Pratt had secretly taped his conversations with Moore, Doty, and so on. Mrs. Pratt, who was in Denver to accept a posthumous award for Bob for his outstanding UFO journalism, was upset at the use of the term *secretly*, and Sparks provided no evidence that the other party was unaware of Pratt's taping. In fact, Pratt kept copious notes and openly taped as much as he could, not surprisingly, considering his skills as a journalist and his consistent effort to be accurate.

Part of Sparks's psychic powers seem to be his belief that because there is a dearth of official documents so far relating to Roswell and/or MJ-12, they must not have been real. The old "absence of evidence is evidence for absence" ploy. I am reminded of a number of UFO sightings in which the witness can't separate observation from interpretation. In short, then, I can find no reason, in the face of these challenges, to change my mind about MJ-12—the key documents or the group.

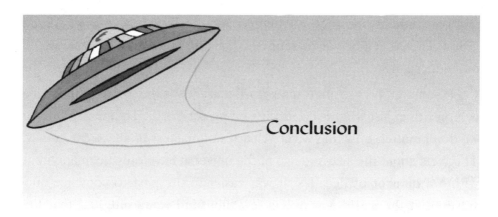

What Does It Matter?

Every so often a questioner asks me if it really makes any difference if flying saucers are real and there is a Cosmic Watergate. Aren't the great majority of the people on Earth too busy with the problems of everyday life—food, shelter, family, job, war—to really care? They can understand why it matters to me, because I have spent so much time and energy throughout the last 50 years, but what difference does it make to the larger world?

This is more of a philosophical question than a physics question. But let me see if I can outline why it should matter to most people...

Who are we? This question has bedazzled scholars for millennia. Are we the masters of all we can see? Is there a God, providing hope and perhaps fear for all of us? Or are we casting God in our image to justify our ways? These may seem to be strictly religious questions, but they are not. Many wars have been fought about interpretations of God and the Universe and governments for or by the people, and the need to fight Evil and do Good. The other guy is always the evil one, isn't he? And God is always on our side, right?

If some UFOs are alien spacecraft, that means the world of the living is larger than just what is happening on planet Earth. That doesn't mean we don't matter; only that we are clearly not masters of all we can survey. The facts about the size and age of the universe have only been apparent within a number of decades. It was easier in the past to convince ourselves that the world was only a few thousand years old, and that the Earth is the only place where there is life and beauty and truth and hate and war. Most of us don't buy that simplistic view anymore, because, with new instruments, we can not only look outward, but also backward in time. The universe is clearly very large and very old. But are all societies out there as self-destructive as those on Earth?

As far as the public knows at this time, we have not been able to visit places outside our solar system, though we have some good ideas about how that may be accomplished, if we were able to commit the huge resources to explore our local neighborhood, and then outside our solar system. But craft are coming here in fairly large numbers, apparently operated by humanoid beings who must have been building vehicles for deep-space travel for some time. Our nibbling at advanced technology has been recent compared to the age of the neighborhood. (Think of such recent topics as genetics, nuclear energy, microwaves, space travel, nanotechnology, the Internet, cell phones, and advanced computers.)

In addition to the visitors' advanced technology, it appears they must have at least some advanced sociology as well: They haven't caused wholesale destruction on our planet...yet. They don't knock down every aircraft that gets a radar lock on them and comes chasing them. As far as we know, they haven't given ultimatums to earthling governments to do certain things—or else. We haven't been told to throw out our religions, or to destroy certain groups because the aliens don't approve of them. As far as can be told, they haven't offered new and better weapons to this or that group to help them with this or that project. They haven't enslaved us. They don't seem to have intervened in any large way. That would seem to show forbearance. I must say, the fact that they are being observed all over the planet does spread the message that we are neither alone nor the big-shots in the neighborhood—a big message indeed.

When one looks at government budgets, we surely spend a lot on the tools of warfare. The defense budget of the United States is more than half a trillion dollars for 2008. The rest of the world will spend at least that much on the military. I should think it would seem strange to the visitors that 30,000 children will die every day of preventable disease and starvation, and that we apparently can't afford to spend enough money to make a dent in that tragic statistic. We know we are fouling our waterways and the skies above, but we certainly don't seem to be able to get together with others on the planet to solve what are planetary (rather than national) problems. Certainly, despite all the jokes about aliens landing and saying, "Take me to your leader," we know there is no leader of the planet to whom to be taken.

Considering that any alien star-faring civilization must be considerably older than our solar system–bound one, one must ask, what do they know about the real history of our planet? Were we originally colonized by space travelers? Are they the real "gods" from above of whom our ancestors seemed to be aware? Have there been large-scale disasters such as global warming, nuclear wars, and asteroid impacts elsewhere? Do they know more about what is in store for us, if we follow this or that sociological or technological path, than we do? Are they aware of much better means for producing electricity and transportation systems than our current technologies? Do they know better ways of diagnosing and treating diseases? What do they think, (and, more importantly, what will they do) about the population increase taking place in countries that can't provide food and health for the populations they already have?

What does it say about our supposedly democratic governments on this planet that they have been unwilling to tell the public the truth about alien visitors? Shouldn't we know the philosophy of our potential elected officials when it comes to dealing with alien visitors? Have they sold us out? Made deals about which we know nothing for personal gain or power? The press treatment in 2007 of the UFO sighting by presidential candidate Dennis Kucinich was hardly the essence of respectable journalism. How much have our leaders been told, if anything, about what happens to societies such as ours that have developed weapons of mass destruction, but without providing for practical answers to our real problems of climate change, starvation, disease, plagues, and terrorism?

I realize this sounds like a shopping list of topics for a sociology course. But one of the major terms in the Drake equation is the life span of a society. Are there societies that have lasted for millions of years as opposed to hundreds or thousands? How have they solved these problems?

I am sometimes asked if I really think our society can handle the truth about alien visitations. If the truth were told, would there be rioting in the streets? Based on the responses to my lectures, I would say most people can handle it. It may well depend on how the message was presented; I have some suggestions regarding that.

First, I think that announcements should be made by many governments at once, along with announcements that there will be international conferences on the religious, political, and economic implications of our not being alone, and not being the most advanced society in the neighborhood. If we found out an asteroid was heading toward us, would we not all need a way to avoid such a catastrophe? Surely we wouldn't say, that's not my problem, let us just continue on our way. Just as in most sporting matches there are time-outs during which the action stops, isn't there a need for a time-out for our primitive, warlike society to step back and not say, "Tell us all that scientists have learned about alien technology," but rather, "What can we do to help our own society make a better world?"

We all know, though we try to avoid thinking about it, that there is no way that the people in poor nations can possibly use as much energy and resources per person as do those in rich nations. How long will the poor continue to put up with the despoiling of the planet for the benefit of the rich?

What can we do in the absence of government leadership? We can learn from the fact that aspects of our society have been changed in response to public pressures. For example, racial segregation was a way of life for a long time, and was officially sanctified by laws. Most of those laws have been thrown out primarily because of peaceful pressures, not by guns, at least since the Civil War. There was a time when women were considered property. There was a time when many places had state religions, and woe be unto he who didn't follow it. The number is smaller now. Martin Luther King, Mahatma Gandhi, and Nelson Mandela didn't have armies behind them, but made enormous strides with peaceful protests.

We could ask for amnesty for those military people involved in close encounters with alien craft and beings to tell their stories. We could start slowly, perhaps with events of 50 years ago, then 25, then 10... Desegregation of schools worked best when it was done gradually. This year: first grade. Next year: first and second grade, and so on. We could write letters to editors of major newspapers, seeking communication from military and civilian witnesses and offering anonymity. Some of them are bound to be thinking, as General DuBose told me in his mid-80s, "What can they do to me now?" We can try to get schools of journalism to teach students about the mass of factual information available about flying saucers. We can loudly insist that budgets for black projects be reduced and discussed more in public. Who are they serving? Who profits? We who have a serious interest in and knowledge of flying saucers could get together to respond to foolish TV programs and stupid articles. The debunking community has been successful in putting anti-flying-saucer-reality junk in Wikipedia and in major magazines. I don't doubt that government disinformation specialists have greatly helped in erecting the laughter curtain. What if major publications were deluged with sensible letters correcting false information published about flying saucers? Being an optimist, I see some helpful glimmers from the media about the sightings in Stephenville, Texas, in January 2008, and the sudden Air Force lies about 10 F-16s being responsible, after denying there were any flying at the time. The *Washington Post* was successful with considerable effort in blowing the lid off the political Watergate more than 30 years ago. Is it time for the Cosmic Watergate?

If our governments (definitely not just the U.S.) are withholding the facts about flying saucers—which they are—what else are they withholding? Is there truly a secret government? Have other items of great importance been withheld? How much has NASA learned about our visitors that we haven't been told? After all, they have observers circling the planet.

I, for one, would like to see my great-grandson grow up in a world that has a much truer picture of our planet's place in the scheme of things. I would like to see everyone on the planet recognize that, regardless of all other allegiances, we are all earthlings. Can we not step back and see ourselves as our visitors must see us? I don't think we have to continue to be a primitive society whose major activity is tribal warfare. As a scientist, it seems to me that we should be looking at the evidence, not reacting in a knee-jerk fashion with ridicule and fear. The time for action is now.

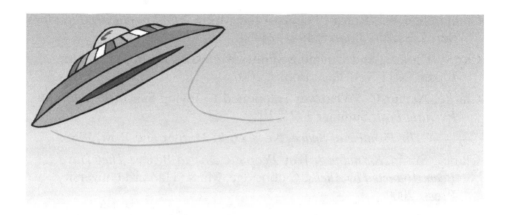

Bibliography

AIAA UFO Subcommittee. "UFO: An Appraisal of the Problem." *Astronautics and Aeronautics* 8:11, 1970, 49.

Asimov, Isaac. *Is Anyone There?* New York: Ace Books, 1967.

———. "The Rocketing Dutchman." *Fantasy and Science Fiction*, February 1975.

———. "UFOs: Are They Visitors From Outer Space—Or Unreliable False Observations?" Background, *TV Guide*, December 14, 1974, 41.

Berlitz, Charles, and William Moore. *The Roswell Incident*. New York: Grossett and Dunlap, 1980.

Bloecher, Ted. *Report on the UFO Wave of 1947*. Washington, D.C.: NICAP, 1967.

Bova, Ben. "Brass Tacks." *ANALOG*. December 1975, 172.

Broad, William. "Wreckage in the Desert was Odd But Not Alien." *New York Times*, Sunday, September 18, 1994, 1.

Burrows, William E. *By Any Means Necessary*. New York: Farrar, Strauss, Giroux, 2001.

Campbell, J.W. "Rocket Flight to the Moon." *Philosophical Magazine* Ser. 7, 31:204, January 1941, 24–34.

Carey, Thomas, and Donald Schmitt. *Witness to Roswell*. Franklin Lakes, N.J.: New Page Books, 2007.

Clarke, Arthur C. "Whatever Happened to Flying Saucers?" *Saturday Evening Post*, Summer 1971, 10.

———. *The Promise of Space*. New York: Harper and Row, 1968.

Clancy, Susan. *Kidnapped: Why People Come to Believe They Have Been Abducted by Aliens*. Cambridge, Mass.: Harvard University Press, 2000.

Condon, Edward U. *Scientific Study of Unidentified Flying Objects*. New York: Bantam Press, 1969.

Deardorff, James, Bernard Haisch, Bruce Maccabee, and Hal Puthoff "Inflation Theory Implications for Extraterrestrial Visitation." *Journal of the British Interplanetary Society* 58 (2005): 43–50.

Drake, Frank, and Dava Sobel. *Is Anyone Out There?* New York: Delta Books, 1994.

Druffel, Ann. *Firestorm: Dr. James E. McDonald's Fight for UFO Science*. Albuquerque, N.M.: Wildflower Press, 2003.

Edwards, Frank. *Flying Saucers: Serious Business*. Fort Lee, N.J.: Lyle Stuart, Inc., 1966.

Eisenhower, Dwight D. *Mandate for Change 1953-1956*. Garden City, N.Y.: Doubleday& Co., 1963.

Faughn, Jerry S., and Karl F. Kuhn. *Physics for People Who Think They Don't Like Physics*. Philadelphia: Saunders, 1976.

Feschino, Frank Jr. *Shoot Them Down*. Flatwoods, W.V.: Frank Feschino, Jr., 2007.

Flying Saucers Are Real. DVD. UFO-TV, 2005.

Friedman, Stanton T. *Final Report on Operation Majestic 12*, 1990 from UFORI.

———. "Science Fiction, Science, and UFOs" *MUFON Symposium Proceedings* 1977.

———. "The Secret Life of Donald Menzel." *International UFO Reporter*, Jan./Feb. 1988, 20–24.

———. *TOP SECRET/MAJIC 2nd Edition*. New York: Marlowe & Co., 2005.

————. "Ufology and the Search for ET Intelligent Life" *MUFON Symposium Proceedings* 1973.

Friedman, Stanton T., and Donald Berliner. *Crash at Corona*. New York: Marlowe & Co, 1997.

Friedman, Stanton T., and Kathleen Marden. *Captured! The Betty and Barney Hill UFO Experience*. Franklin Lakes, N.J.: New Page Books, 2007.

Friedman, Stanton T., and William D. Rankin. "Indirect Measurement of Nuclear Heating in Poison Control Vanes." *Transactions of the American Nuclear Society*. June 1968.

Fuller, John G. *Incident at Exeter*. New York: G.P. Putnam's Sons, 1966.

————. *The Interrupted Journey: Two Lost Hours Aboard a Flying Saucer*. New York: Dial Press, 1966.

————. *Aliens in the Skies: The New UFO Battle of the Scientist*. New York: G.P. Putnam's Sons, 1969.

Gallup, George. "Only A Third Deny Existence of UFOS." *Palm Beach Post*. March 14, 1987. (Covers Polls for 1966, 1973, 1978, 1987.)

Goldberg, Leo. "An Appreciation of Donald Howard Menzel." *Sky and Telescope*. April 1977.

Goldberg, Robert Allan. *Enemies Within: The Culture of Conspiracy in Modern America*. New Haven, Conn.: Yale University Press, 2001.

Greenewald, John. *Beyond UFO Secrecy 2nd Edition*. Minneapolis, Minn.: Galde Press, 2008.

Grinspoon, David. *Lonely Planets: The Natural Philosophy of Alien Life*. New York: Ecco, 2003.

Hall, Richard. *The UFO Evidence*. NICAP, 1964.

————. *The UFO Evidence Vol. 2: A Thirty-Year Report*. Lanham, Md.: Scarecrow Press, 2003.

House Committee on Science and Astronautics. "Symposium on UFOs." July 29, 1968.

Hynek, J. Allen. *The UFO Experience: A Scientific Enquiry*. Chicago: Henry Regnery, 1972.

Klass, Philip J. *UFOs Explained*. New York: Random House, 1974.

Krauss, Lawrence M. *The Physics of Star Trek*. New York: Basic Books, 1995.

Lewin, Ronald. *The American MAGIC*. New York: Farrar, Strauss, and Giroux, 1982.

Maccabee, Bruce. *Abduction is My Life*. Thurmont, Md.: Granite Publishing, 2001.

Marcel, Jesse A., Jr., MD. *The Roswell Legacy*. Helena, Mont.: BigSky Press, 2007.

McDonald, James E. "Statement on UFOs to Congress." New York: UFORI, July 29, 1968.

Menzel, Donald Howard. *Flying Saucers*. Cambridge, Mass.: Harvard University Press, 1953.

———. "Those Flying Saucers." *TIME Magazine,* June l8, 1952.

MJ-12: Do You Believe in Majic? DVD. UFO-TV, 2006.

Newcomb, Simon. "The Outlook for the Flying Machine." *The Independent, A Weekly*. October 22, 1903, 2508–2512.

Park, Robert L. *Voodoo Science: The Road from Foolishness to Fraud*. New York: Oxford University Press, 2001.

———. "Welcome to Planet Earth." *The Sciences*. New York Academy of Sciences, May/June 2000, 20–24.

Pflock, Karl T. *Roswell: Inconvenient Facts and the Will to Believe*. Amherst, N.Y.: Prometheus Press, 2001.

Phillips, Ted. *Physical Traces Associated With UFO Sightings*. Evanston, Ill.: Center for UFO Studies, 1975.

———. *Landing Traces: Physical Evidence for the UFO*. MUFON Symposium Proceedings, 1973.

Project Blue Book Special Report Number 14. New York: Battelle Memorial Institute for Project Blue Book (UFORI), 1955.

Randle, Kevin. *Case MJ-12: The True Story Behind the Government's UFO Conspiracies*. New York: Harper Torch, 2002.

Recollections of Roswell. DVD. Fund for UFO Research, 1992.

Ruppelt, Edward J. *The Report on Unidentified Flying Objects*. New York: Doubleday, 1956.

Sagan, Carl. *Contact*. New York: Pocket Books, 1997.

———. *COSMOS*. New York: Ballantine Books, 1985.

Sagan, Carl, and Ann Druyan. *The Demon Haunted World: Science as a Candle in the Dark*. New York: Ballantine Books, 1997.

Saunders, David R., and Roger Harkin. *UFOs? YES! Where The Condon Committee Went Wrong*. New York: World Publishing, 1969.

Shermer, Michael. *Why People Believe Weird Things: Pseudo Science, Superstition, and Other Confusions of Our Time*. New York: Henry Holt and Company, 1997.

Vallee, Jacques, and Claude Poher. "Basic Patterns in UFO Observations." AIAA paper 75–42, presented in January 1975.

Verne, Jules. *Journey to the Center of the Earth*. Hertfordshire, England: Wordsworth Edition Limited, 1996.

Wedemeyer, Albert C. *Wedemeyer Reports*. New York: Henry Holt and Company, 1958.

Wells, H.G. *War of the Worlds*. New York: New York Review of Books Edition, 1960.

Wood, Robert M. "Authenticating the Special Operations Manual." *UFO Crash Retrieval Conference Proceedings*. Broomfield, Colo.: Ryan Wood Enterprises, 2003, 165–184.

Wood, Ryan. "Resolving the 'Emulation' in Directives Between Twining and Wedemeyer." *UFO Crash Retrieval Converence Proceedings*. Broomfield, Colo.: Ryan Wood Enterprises, 2003, 199–240.

Zachary, G. Pascal. *Vannevar Bush: Engineer of the American Century*. Florence, Mass.: Free Press, 1997.

Index

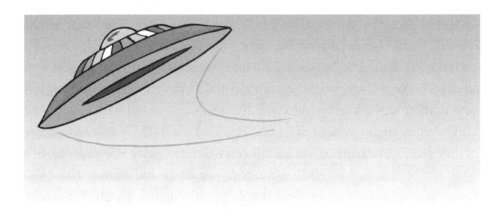

About the Author

Nuclear physicist/lecturer Stanton T. Friedman grew up in Linden, New Jersey, spent two years at Rutgers University, and then received his BSc and MSc degrees in physics from the University of Chicago in 1955 and 1956. He was employed for 14 years as a nuclear physicist by such companies as GE, GM, Westinghouse, TRW Systems, Acrojet General Nucleonics, and McDonnell-Douglas, working in such highly advanced, classified, eventually cancelled programs as nuclear aircraft, fission and fusion rockets, and various compact nuclear power plants for space and terrestrial applications.

He became interested in UFOs in 1958, and since 1967 has lectured about them at more than 600 colleges and 100 professional groups in 50 U.S. states, nine Canadian provinces, and 16 other countries, in addition to various consulting efforts. He has published more than 80 UFO papers and has appeared on hundreds of radio and TV programs, including *Larry King* in 2007 and 2008. He is the original civilian investigator of the Roswell

Incident, and coauthored *Crash at Corona: The Definitive Study of the Roswell Incident* with Donald Berliner. *TOP SECRET/MAJIC*, his controversial book about the Majestic 12 group (established in 1947 to deal with alien technology), was published in 1996 and went through six printings. A new edition was published in 2005. Stan was presented with a Lifetime UFO Achievement Award in Leeds, England, in 2002, by *UFO Magazine* of the UK. He is coauthor, with Kathleen Marden (Betty Hill's niece), of a book in the summer of 2007, *Captured! The Betty and Barney Hill UFO Experience*. The City of Fredericton declared August 27, 2007, Stanton Friedman Day.

He has provided written testimony to Congressional hearings, appeared twice at the UN, and has been a pioneer in many aspects of ufology, including Roswell; Majestic 12; the Betty Hill–Marjorie Fish star map work; analysis of the Delphos, Kansas, physical trace case; crashed saucers; flying saucer technology; and challenges to the SETI (Silly Effort To Investigate) cultists. He has spoken at more MUFON symposia than anyone else.

Stanton T. Friedman is a dual citizen of the United States and Canada, and lives at:

> 79 Pembroke Crescent
>
> Fredericton, NB, Canada E3B 2V1
>
> (506) 457-0232

He can be contacted at:

> fsphys@rogers.com
>
> and
>
> *www.stantonfriedman.com*.

Expect Something Different from New Page Books

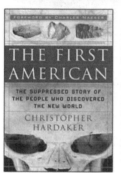

Expect the Latest Developments from New Page Books

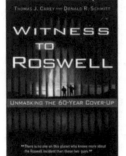
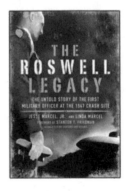